Modern Tragedies and Aristotle's Theory

K. S. MISRA

M.A., LL.B., Ph.D.,
P.D.T.E., P.D.E.S. (Leeds)

Chairman
Department of English
Sana'a University
Sana'a Y.A.R.

HUMANITIES PRESS
Atlantic Highlands, N.J.

First published in 1983 in the
United States of America by Humanities
Press Inc., Atlantic Highlands, NJ 07716

PR
633
M5 | 35,963

Printed in India

Preface

The present study aims at a critical examination of the principal types of the twentieth-century tragic drama in the light of the criteria provided by the Aristotelian concept of tragedy as embodied in the *Poetics,* explicitly as well as implicitly, in order to demonstrate the validity and utility of those ancient principles in our complex age when literature is supposed to have liberated itself from the clutches of the set conventional rules and fixed groves of old genres. At the very outset, however, we hasten to disclaim any the least intention of reviving the old heresy of Aristotle's infallibility or his dictatorship which was not universally accepted even in the age of classical revival. We do believe in the dynamic nature of literature which must constantly reflect the changing spectacle of a nation's life, external as well as (and even more importantly still) internal. At the same time we cannot afford to forget or ignore the oft repeated truth that the essence of human nature does not change and, in consequence, the basic aim of art which has its root there, survives intact through all the changes and 'transvaluation of values'. When Aristotle states that the aim of poetic 'imitation' is to provide delight, and, tragedy, a major form of it, must yield the pleasure peculiar to it, he is emphasizing an artistic truth which time has not been able to render stale or outmoded. In the same way much that was purely 'local' in his theorizing has dated' fast, but a good deal in it is still valuable and valid whether we acknowledge it or not.

The approach, however, is open to two pit-falls which every care has been taken in the present work to steer clear of. In the first place, it may tend to make a Procrustean bed of Aristotle's *Poetics* and fit the modern tragedies to its dimensions, at the cost of a good deal of wrenching, distortion, even mutilation and disfigurement of the living works of art. Secondly, the principles themselves may be stretched and transformed so much as to lose their contextual moorings and 'native hue' and spirit. We have pleaded for a liberal interpretation of some of these rules in order to bring out their potential significance and implication, but the process has never been suffered to cross that limit of 'moderation' which Aristotle regarded as a golden rule of life and in art.

The book is divided into two parts, the first comprising Chapters I—IV and the second occupying the seven chapters which follow. The first part deals with the theoretical aspect of the problem such as the statement of Aristotle's theory of Tragedy and the modifications which it underwent from the Middle Ages downwards to the end of the neo-classical period in the eighteenth century. This is followed by a brief account of the philosophical speculation in nineteenth-century Germany and the psychological and sociological approaches to it in our own age. The section ends with a final assessment of the Aristotelian theory in the light of these later attempts of thinkers, critics and interpreters of the *Poetics*.

The second section is in the nature of practical criticism in which an attempt has been made to apply the basic principles of Aristotle's *Poetics* to seven modern tragic plays which, taken together, constitute the principal varieties relevant to our study. The selection of the plays has been guided by one tacit assumption that the empirical method of Aristotle is inherently exclusive involving elimination of certain types which were extant even in his own age. It is, for example, profitless to apply the standard of Aristotle to the modern 'surrealistic' plays dealing, as they do, with the irrational impulses of the 'sub-conscious,' patently at variance with the rational norm which is the essence of that standard. Our guiding principle of selection is based on Aristotle's postulate that tragedy is the imitation of a serious action, pertaining to a protagonist of a peculiar nature and calculated, 'through pity and fear to effect a catharsis of these emotions,' thus yielding the delight peculiar to this kind of poetry.

This method of examining a set of plays by one definite standard, however, involves a certain amount of repetition and reiteration of the crucial statements on many occasions which may verge on monotony. I have been on my guard against this risk, yet its complete avoidance has not always been possible.

I wish to express my gratitude to Dr. V. Rai, formerly Professor and Head of the Department of English, Banaras Hindu University, for his guidance and criticism of the present work. I am indebted to the late Professor R. A. Dwivedi who initiated me into the present line of thinking on Aristotle and tragic plays. Thanks are also due to the Librarians, Banaras Hindu University Library, Delhi University Library and the British Council Library, India, for their valuable help in the preparation of the present work which was originally presented as my doctoral dissertation to the Banaras Hindu University, Varanasi (India).

K. S. MISRA

CONTENTS

CHAPTER I

The Aristotelian Statement

It was Aristotle who for the first time gave serious thoughts to the problem of tragedy and enunciated a theory which remains important even today on account of its inherent elasticity and comprehensiveness. As it is well known, Aristotle's method was empirical. He had at his disposal the works of the great tragic poets of the 5th century B.C. He studied this material and tried to arrive at general principles with the aid of his philosophical thoughts. Thus what impresses us is the simultaneous presentation of conclusions arrived at by a pragmatic process and abstract thoughts of a philosophical nature.

The Aristotelian theory of tragedy has elements of abiding value but in the past few centuries there have been endless discussions about its scope and applicability. Some have tried to assess the correctness or otherwise of the concept in a wider perspective, while others have contented themselves with a literal interpretation of it. The first task of an investigator of this subject is, of course, to give an interpretation and elucidation of the concept of tragedy conforming to Aristotle's own view as outlined in the *Poetics*. Our purpose in this chapter, therefore, is to understand Aristotle and not to judge him.

He defines tragedy as an "imitation of an action that is serious, complete, and of a certain magnitude ; in language embellished, with each kind of artistic ornament, the several kinds being found in separate parts of the play ; in the form of action not of narrative ; through pity and fear effecting the proper purgation of these emotions "[1]. The definition says that "tragedy is an imitation not of men but an imitation of an action by men. That is, what they imitate in the first instance is not themselves but the thing they do, and the end toward which their action moves, is happiness or unhappiness. "[2] So tragedy imitates action. Now, 'action' does not mean mere outward physical movements, but also the inward working of mind and soul.

The 'action' which tragedy imitates is to be ·serious'. Here it differentiates tragedy from comedy. The term, says F.L. Lucas, means (from its Greek translation) 'that matters;" "that is worth troubling about."[3] The action is concerned with a serious end, namely, the representation of life. "It is a picture of human destiny in all the significance. The word 'serious' contains, according to Butcher, the ideas conveyed by the words 'grave' and 'great'.[4]

Next, the action should be 'complete and of a certain magnitude,' which implies the length and the compactness of the plot which the poet should achieve in constructing the structure of events keeping in view the suggestions given by Aristotle (*Poetics* XVII and XVIII). The 'several kinds of embellishments,' as explained further by Aristotle, are the 'verse' and 'song'. Then unlike epic, it has to be in action, that is, to be acted and not narrated. All these have to achieve a dramatic end, which is the purgation of the emotions of pity and fear.

After having described tragedy, Aristotle proceeds to analyse its different parts. "Every tragedy," he says, "must have six parts, which determine its quality, namely, Plot, Character, Diction, Thought, Spectacle, Song." The parts are arranged in order of their importance in the economy of the tragic drama.

Aristotle is quite explicit in his conception of the plot. "By plot," he says, "I mean the arrangement of incidents."[5] But this does not mean merely a planned sequence of events and episodes, but, "a sequence that develops a single course of action from its origin to its conclusion."[6] "Plot is the imitation of action,"[7] not merely external action, events, incidents, situations, etc., but also mental processes and motives which are the sources of external action. Tragedy is the imitation of action and of life, and life consists of both the external and internal aspects. A man is happy or unhappy by the deeds he does and the deeds are sponsored by his motives and are directly connected with the working of his inner self. Again, such an action is not an abrupt happening or a series of such or other events, but a growth, an organism. Hence plot "is not any series of events connected with a hero or a theme, but a course of action that shows a purpose from its rise in an individual's will, through a struggle against obstacles to a decisive conclusion."[8]

Out of the six elements of tragedy, Aristotle rates plot as the most important, and places it above character. He goes so far as to say that "without action there cannot be a tragedy; there may be without a character."[9] Here one should not press the interpretation too literally.[10] This only implies that action takes first and foremost place and character comes only after it. Butcher suggests that Aristotle probably meant that ". . .there may be a tragedy in which the moral character of the individual agents is so weakly-portrayed as to be of no account in the evolution of the action. Persons may be mere types, or marked only by class characteristics or lacking in those distinctive qualities out of which dramatic action grows."[11]

There is no arguing the point that "there cannot be a tragedy without action" (internal or external), for "action is the differentia of drama and must ever remain the primary and controlling principle."[12] Aristotle explains the point further by an illustration from painting: "The most beautiful colours, laid on confusedly, will not give as much pleasure as the chalk outline of a portrait."[13] Beautiful colours divorced from the outlined framework of the picture cannot yield pleasure or sense. Character without plot cannot develop into a lifelike personality. "Plot is the groundwork, the design, through the medium of which ethos derives its meaning and dramatic value."[14]

Aristotle is not satisfied with the remark that plot is superior to ethos. "It is the first principle and as it were, the soul of tragedy," he says. Here the equation of plot with soul is not merely for the sake of analogy but carries a deeper significance. His meaning is that the relation between plot and tragedy is similar to that of soul and body in his philosophical system. A play is a living organism and plot is its animating principle. The development of the play proceeds from the plot, which is the nucleus and the very basis of the play. It gives inner meaning to the play as soul does to the body. "The plot is the structure of the play, around which the material parts are laid, just as the soul is the structure of man."[15] It is well known that in Aristotle's biology the soul, i.e., the form, is prior to body.[16] For him the plot precedes the poem, but it too is essentially made by the poet, even if he is using traditional materials.

Again, "plot is the end of tragedy." The purpose of a tragedy is to arouse the tragic emotions. The emotions of pity and fear are produced not by other elements in the tragedy, but by the 'structure of events.' because it contains the 'Reversal of Situation,' 'Recognition' and 'Pathos' as its parts. The intended effect of tragedy is inherent in the plot, the structure itself, not in the stage representation because Aristotle in his advice for the construction of the best plot insists that it should convey the tragic effect even when read. The tragic pleasure is the result of the plot, hence it is the end of tragedy.

After having discussed the supremacy of plot among the elements of tragedy, Aristotle proceeds to enumerate the essentials of a plot. He says that it should be "complete and whole and of a certain magnitude." A whole' is that which has a beginning, a middle and an end. Poetry represents a fragment of life and in order to make the representation pleasurable and beautiful it has to be 'whole'. Our pleasure in this representation is due to our instinct of imitation and an instinctive desire for form and design and order. Events in life are in succession related to the principle of cause and effect. "The dramatist like any other story teller must draw out of this chain of events a particular limited sequence which for one reason or the other may be thought of as significant in itself and as relatively complete in itself. That is, this sequence may be understood without the necessity of too great a reference to what has gone before and it comes to rest without leaving too many threads of action incomplete. It is a segment of life which can stand by itself. . . . There must be a moment or series of moments in the succession of circumstances which rises sharply above the level of ordinary experience; that is there must be a middle, a point to which action leads up and from which it fades away in a climax or turning point."[17] A certain series of situations is complete in itself in the sense that out of it there emerges a unified symbolical significance which in a work of art has always the unity of impression upon the mind of the audience. This will give the plot a completeness and a comely shape. The idea of the 'wholeness' of plot implies a development of the story depending upon the concept of conflict, because where "action is the end we require a conflict of purpose,"[18] though Aristotle does not refer to it directly.

The plot should have "a certain magnitude." By 'magnitude' Aristotle means size, length of the story. In order to make the plot beautiful, the poet should not only try to arrange the incidents properly but give it a proper length. The size should neither be too short to make the parts of tragedy appear 'blurred to the viewer,' nor too long to obstruct the view of the play as a whole. The story should be such as to be embraced by the memory of the reader or spectator as a single action. Again, a proper length is required for the purpose of allowing the action to develop on the principle of cause and effect, 'probability' or 'necessity,' so that it may "admit of a change from bad fortune to good, or from good fortune to bad."[19] Though Aristotle does not prescribe any strict scale for the length of action, yet his preference is for "the greater the length, the more beautiful will the piece be by reason of its size, provided that the whole be perspicuous."[20]

The 'magnitude,' however, is subordinated to the unity of action. "The unity of plot," says Aristotle, "does not, as some think, consist in the unity of the hero. For infinitely various are the incidents in one man's life which cannot be reduced to unity; and so, too, there are many actions of one man out of which we cannot make one action."[21] Aristotle is quite explicit on the point of the unity of plot. It is not merely the determination of the length of the plot or the arrangement of incidents in a particular way, but an inner principle which brings harmony in the organic construction of the action and "reveals itself in the form of an outward whole."[22] It is not merely mechanical piecing together of the several parts of the play, but a vital union of these parts. The plot, as already discussed in connection with the wholeness, should have an organic growth on the principle of cause and effect, keeping in close view the law of 'probability' or 'necessity'. There is, thus, an inward connection, a harmonious unity, because the principle of cause and effect is strictly followed and the chain of action is not stretched beyond the point where the artistic beauty of the work may be endangered. The episodic plot is dismissed by Aristotle as the worst because of its lack of an inward causal connection among the incidents.[23] By the same token epic structure is discouraged as it may bring "the multiplicity af plots,"[24] detrimental to the unity of action.

The conception of the unity of action is defined by

Aristotle as "the structural union of the parts being such that, if any one of them is displaced or removed, the whole will be disjointed and disturbed. For, a thing, whose presence or absence makes no visible difference, is not an organic part of the whole."[25] Butcher has summed up the idea of this unity and its manifestations in a wider sense: "Unity is manifested in two ways. First, in the causal connexion that binds together the several parts of a play,— the thoughts, the emotions, the decisions of the will, the external events being inextricably interwoven. Secondly, in the fact that the whole series of events, with all the moral forces that are brought into collision, are directed to a single end. The action as it advances converges on a definite point. The thread of purpose running through it becomes more marked. All minor effects are subordinated to the sense of an evergrowing unity. The end is linked to the beginning with inevitable certainty, and in the end we discern the meaning of the whole. In this powerful and concentrated impression lies the supreme test of unity."[26]

The plot movement has two major stages—'complication' and 'unravelling'. "By complication," says Aristotle "I mean all that extends from the beginning of the action to the part which marks the turning point to good or bad fortune. The 'unravelling' is that which extends from the beginning of the change to the end."[27] Gustav Freitag in his *Technique of Drama* has divided a play into two parts on the basis of the Aristotelian concept: the rising and the falling movement with the crisis in the middle. Aristotle disapproves of the employment of *deux ex machina* in the course of the complication and the denouement.[28] They should arise out of the plot itself. However, this external device can be permitted "only for events external to the drama,—for antecedent or subsequent events, which lie beyond the range of human knowledge, and which require to be reported or foretold "[29]

Aristotle emphasizes the point further not from the structural point of view but from the emotional point of view also, the function of plot is to arouse tragic effect in the highest possible degree. This is why Aristotle prefers the change in the hero's action not from bad to good but from good to bad, though the former satisfies our sense of justice. It is on this score that he disfavours double plot, i.e., two issues in the action being resolved in the end—one ending happily and the other ending unhappily. "A well-constructed plot should, therefore, be single in its issue rather than double as some maintain."[30]

Aristotle, then, divides plot into two kinds—'simple' and 'complex'. Plot is the imitation of action and "actions in real life...obviously show a similar distinction"[31] between the simple and the complex. There is no basic distinction between the two kinds of plot regarding the structural harmony, single-ness of issue and organic development. The only distinguish-ing elements are the 'Reversal of Situation' and 'Recognition' which are essential to a 'complex' plot, while a 'simple' plot generally dispenses with them.

So 'Reversal of Situation' and 'Recognition' are the elements which make a plot 'complex'. "Reversal of Situation is a change by which the action veers round to its opposite, subject always to our rule of probability or necessity."[32] It is an unexpected change in the events of the play which is logical and based on the principle of necessity or probability. This should be inherent in the plot itself and should come in the course of the natural development of the action. It produces a result opposite to that intended by the course of the action.[33] It is an unexpected change. The expectation is not of the hero, but of the audience. "The test of the paradox is that we are affected, surprised, moved to pity etc., not that the hero is. It lies in the nature of the case that the hero will be surprised and emotionally affected also."[34] The two elements of the plot—'Reversal of Situation' and 'Recogni-tion,' says Aristotle, turn upon surprise.[35] And surprise comes when things happen contrary to our expectation. But what about those plays the stories of which are already known to the audience, like that of Oedipus ? How can the element of surprise be achieved in a case like this ? Though Aristotle does not seem to give any explicit reply to it yet the natural answer may be that in the advance knowledge of the story the expectation is not based "on the facts as they are given in the course of the play."[36] In a good play the 'Reversal' is not immediately obvious. It appears to be the natural outcome of the logical development of the plot based on the principle of probability. Really speaking, the factual materials of the story already known to the audience are not of much consequence in regard to the aesthetic response by the spectator, for what matters is not the facts themselves but the artistic presentation of them involving emotional response to "reversal and recognition turning upon surprise." It is the facts charged with emotions that make the difference when presented artistically in a work of art based on the facts already known to us.

"Recognition....is a change from ignorance to knowledge. It is the realization of the truth, the opening of the eyes, the sudden lightning flash in the darkness."[37] This knowledge may come either before it is too late or after. In the former case the fatal act is averted and in the latter it occurs. 'Recognition' produces "love or hate between the persons destined by the poet for good or bad fortune," and the one most conducive to the production of the tragic emotions is the 'recognition' of persons, which may be either of one person or on both sides (persons). This 'recognition' between persons presupposes a bond of blood kinship. Upon this natural state of relationship between the 'dear ones' contrary factors supervene, so that he who had taken one to be an enemy or a stranger recognizes the blood relationship between them of which he was ignorant. Or he might have been taken to be a 'dear one' and now the true state of relationship is revealed, i.e., he is disclosed to be an enemy. Mr. Else sums up the definition of 'recognition' thus: "the tragic recognition is the discovery by a person who has been in a clearly defined status of 'happiness' or 'unhappiness,' of the identity of a naturally dear person with whom he has been involved or is in danger of being involved in a fatal act."[38] He assigns the general effect of recognition to the uncovering of a "horrible discrepancy between two sets of relationships; on the one hand, the deep ties of blood on the other, a casual or real relation of hostility that has supervened or threatened to supervene upon it."[39] Although Aristotle does not say so explicitly, the tragic effect depends mainly upon the tension inherent in this discrepancy, "ultimately therefore, upon the deep-seated, immemorial power of the taboo against the shedding of kindred blood."[40] In Oedipus the tragic effect does not depend on the fact that the hero has killed a man but upon the 'recognition' that he has killed his father. It is, therefore, the 'recognition' of person that matters not of deeds.

TRAGIC HERO :

No true assessment of plot from the point of veiw of its emotional 'charge' is possible unless we consider the nature and character of the tragic hero whose action is being 'imitated'. Since the 'imitation of action' should be such as to excite pity and fear which are the "distinctive mark of tragedy," the change of fortune should be that of a man especially suited for this purpose. Aristotle recommends a particular type of person as the ideal hero for tragedy. First of all, he should not be a perfectly good or virtuous man, brought down to adversity from prosperity, because the sight of such a man will produce neither pity nor fear. Besides, it is shocking.[41] Secondly, he should not be a "bad man passing from adversity to prosperity, because it is foreign to the spirit of tragedy and can arouse neither pity nor fear but moral indignation. Thirdly, the change of fortune should not be the "downfall of the utter villain," which may gratify our sense of justice without stirring up the true tragic sentiments, because we feel pity for a man undergoing unmerited suffering and fear for the misfortunes of a man who is 'like us'. 'Like us' means 'average,' neither very far above nor very far below the usual moral level of the race, whereas 'good' is a long jump above the average. Tragedy presents 'men of higher type. . .better than in real life.''[42] But if the hero is too distinctively so, his fall will not arouse pity or fear, rather it will be morally revolting, and if he is merely an average man he will not be significant. Hence the hero must fall somewhere not between good and bad but between good and average,—high enough to awaken our pity but not so perfect as to arouse indignation at his fall, and near enough to us to elicit our fellow-feeling, but not too near to forfeit all stature and importance; hence generally good, but not perfect, and average.

But Aristotle's ideal hero should not be confused with a morally ideal hero. He is not a perfect man. He is subject to some flaw of character. "He is not eminently good and just," says Aristotle, and there is no moral depravity or vice in his character.[43] His misfortune is due to 'some error or frailty,' and he comes from some highly reputed and illustrious family.

Here is a Serbonian bog of controversy over the plain-looking term, 'error or frailty,' known as the principle of *hamartia*. The word connotes different shades of meaning. It has to be a part of the structure of the plot because it denotes a single act of error due to the ignorance of the circumstances or an inadequate knowledge thereof. The act is unintentional in regard to its moral connotation. Such acts, bringing misfortunes, arouse pity and fear. Then it may be an act of error done intentionally but in the heat of the moment, not a deliberated act, because the man is motivated from within to act on the spur of the moment and probably there is no time for deliberation.[44] Again, the term may be interpreted to denote a defect of character, i.e., some human frailty ingrained in the very nature of the race, not a purely personal moral defect. It is a weakness to which the human beings in general are subject. "It describes not an isolated act, but a more permanent state."[45] Alan Reynolds Thompson suggests that the requirement of *hamartia* in an otherwise good man is based on sound reason. "The tragic flaw," he says, "is a weakness in an otherwise noble hero. Aristotle's idea regarding it seems to have been that it was a means of making the hero 'human,' not a justification for his downfall."[46] As suggested earlier, this and such other statements are partially true. One should not insist upon restricting the meaning of the principle to the defect of character only.

This brings us to the second constituent of tragedy, i.e., character. Aristotle mentions four points as essential to character: 'goodness,' 'appropriateness,' 'consistency,' and 'truth to life'. 'Goodness' is measured in terms of moral purpose which may be found even in a woman or a slave. 'Appropriateness' means 'appropriateness to station'. A woman may have the virtue of courage, for example. But if she has "manly valour," or is "unscrupulously clever," she will be 'inappropriate' to her status as a woman. 'Goodness' goes by class or 'category,' and 'appropriateness' is a test of faithfulness to the class within the play. This should not be confused with the idea of characters as types. It does not mean Aristotle's dislike for 'individual' character, although his predilection for 'types' cannot be gainsaid.

Again, "character must be true to life." G.F. Else here apprehends two meanings—i.e., that they are "mythical prototypes," and that "they are like men in general or like us;" hence true to life. But the first meaning is not intended by Aristotle. He does not recommend the limitation of the scope of dramatis personae. It is clear from his unreserved concession to poets for inventing stories and characters.[47] That the characters are true to life, means that they have feelings and emotions as all human beings have and that they are acting under the circumstances as any of us would have done.

The fourth point in connection with character, says Aristotle, is 'consistency'. He does not permit the change of class or category of the character during the development of the action. A character may be inconsistent with the object it imitates, its original source, yet it should observe 'consistency' with the class or the category assigned to it in the play.[48] This is with the view of making the character rationally understandable and is in keeping with Aristotle's much emphasized law of 'probability' or 'necessity'.

Besides presenting characters as 'true to life,' the poet, like a portrait painter should make them beautiful. The function of tragedy is to present life through an ennobled image. In Chapter II of the *Poetics* Aristotle makes it clear that tragedy imitates men better than what they are. There is some vagueness about the Aristotelian distinction between the 'goodness' of character and its 'truth to life'. This vagueness and its probable cause have been summed up by Langbaum in his *Poetry of Experience* :

The interesting thing is that Aristotle recognizes the reality of character as something other than the categories by which character is understood. It is not clear whether he recognizes that the reality may be in direct opposition to the categories. For he states the third point in the one vague sentence. . .and never alludes to it again, possibly because he could not fit it into his system.

What then is his system and how does his conception of character fit into it ? His conception fixes all the qualities of character as norms, except for moral purpose which is the single variable. The result is to reduce character to a quantity, a weight on the moral scales and to exclude from judgement (except judgement of their aesthetic rightness) all those personal idiosyncrasies which do not lend themselves to moral measurement. Such a conception makes admirable sense once we remember that 'tragedy is essentially an imitation not of persons but of actions. . . ,' In a play accordingly they do not act in order to portray the characters; they include the characters for the sake of the action. Where action is the end we require a conflict of purposes; and for the action to have meaning the purposes must have relative values—we must be able to evaluate one as better than another. It follows that the action will be clearer and less interrupted to the extent that we eliminate qualities which confuse the lines of force and over-evaluation of the forces. Personal idiosyncrasies which endow a man with charms or defects, having nothing to do with moral purpose or value, are just such superfluous qualities.[49]

To sum up, the ideal tragic hero is a person superior to the average human beings with a morally exalted status,[50] who is good but not perfect and, owing to some weakness in character or some error committed in ignorance he meets with unmerited misfortune. He like us in feelings, emotions and sentiments. We pity him while we admire him because he has been presented as one struggling with some insurmountable force. Though made 'human' by his frailty, he is, nevertheless, an illustrious man, elevated in character and rank. In connection with other *dramatis personae* including the protagonist, Aristotle says that the poet should present them as 'good,' 'appropriate' to their class, 'true to life' and 'consistent'. Their presentation should ennoble and not demean human nature.

THOUGHT OR DIANOIA :

Tragedy has been defined as an "imitation of an action, and an action implies personal agents, who necessarily possess certain distinctive qualities both of 'character' and 'thoughts'; for it is by these that we qualify actions themselves, and these—'thought' and 'character'—are the two natural causes from which actions spring."[51] Dramatic persons have 'character' and 'thought'. These two terms express the intellectual and ethical sides of a character. "Character in its most comprehensive sense depends upon these two elements,"[52] because a dramatic person in order to be presented as a living character must possess these qualities. It is pertinent to recall here the remark of Mr. Lajos Egri that we should not limit the conception of character, and following Aristotle, think that the moral and intellectual elements alone constitute a living and life-like character. For 'every human being consists of three dimensions : physiological, sociological and psychological. If we make a further break-up of these dimensions, we shall perceive that the physical, social and mental make-up contains the minute 'genes'—the builder, the mover in all our actions which will motivate everything we do.''[53] Mental make-up or intellectual side is only one of the elements requisite for the presentation of a life-like and vital character.

'Thought' is not only one of the distinctive qualities of the dramatic persons, but it qualifies the action also. 'Character' and 'thought' are the source from which action springs. 'Personal agents' 'act' or do something because they have some 'character' and 'thought'. Antigone must explain her mind which made her act in a particular way as Ismene has to do for not acting. All that the character does must be accounted for by him or her. Every rational behaviour of the dramatic person is known by 'thought'. "It is the intellectual element," says Butcher, "which is implied in all rational conduct."[54]

Since 'thought' is conveyed by the deliberate use of speech, characters converse and argue in their dialogue. While doing so they prove or disprove certain convictions; they reflect upon certain problems and thus bring their personalities into the limelight. At the same time they throw light upon the character of other persons also. In this way the general maxims of life and human conduct are expressed. These are not metaphysical maxims, but the truths elicited by their actions and the mode of their reasoning. Besides the production of this effect of "proof and refutation," Aristotle says that it has its subdivisions: "the excitation of the feelings, such as pity, fear, anger and the like ; the suggestion of importance or its opposite...or probability."[55] We pity Antigone, and we pity her because she has certain convictions, which are in conflict with the opposite element. The incompatibility between the two loyalties—one in which she has her deep-rooted conviction and the other which is directly opposed to it—are responsible for Antigone's tragedy and hence our pity for her. While the two conflicting loyalties are argued by her, the importance or otherwise of these duties which she owes becomes clear. Our feelings in connection with any character are aroused mainly because of the views or convictions which a character adheres to and when these convictions bring about his or her tragedy. An unthoughtful act which cannot be attributed to any cause or conviction as is the act of a mad man, does not evoke such tragic feelings. 'Thought' has to do with 'probability' also, because "in drama it is not enough that the characters act or be known to have acted ; they must tell us or show us why they do so."[56] 'Thought' is "the faculty of saying what is possible and pertinent in given circumstances."[57] This brings the idea of 'probability' so essential for poetry. The elements of plausibility and logic are required in the case of 'thought,' as in the case of incidents. "The dramatic incidents must be treated from the same points of view as the dramatic speeches, when the object is to evoke the sense of pity, fear, importance or probability."[58] The difference between 'action' and 'thought' is that the former is expressed without any verbal exposition while the latter depends for its effects upon the speaker, and the result of the speech.

Thus 'thought' is the intellectual element in the dramatic persons as 'character' is the 'ethical', and it can only be expressed though speech. Characters through their conversations make their intentions, convictions, views—the intellectual aspect—known. They argue, meditate and draw conclusions from their reasoning. The element of 'thought,' therefore, has to do with such generalities, maxims of life and truths as come out of their convictions. Butcher suggests that here Aristotle probably was conscious of the influences of the time. 'The emphasis laid by Aristotle on this dialectical 'dianoia' is, doubtless, connected with the decisive influence exercised by political debate and forensic pleading on the Greek theatre."[59]

There is a close relationship between 'thought' and 'character,' although the highly analytical system of Aristotle has made the understanding of it difficult. By his sharp logic Aristotle dissects the organic parts of tragedy and discusses them in isolation from each other which blurs the obvious relationship. 'Character' and 'thought' are the qualities of the personal agents of the tragedy; the first reveals the moral purpose of the agents and the other expresses their intellectual qualities. They are only the opposite sides of the same thing. Both are conveyed through speech, though 'character' has the privilege of being expressed through action also. They together make a character living and vital. 'Thought' may have some bearing upon the moral choice of the person. The dramatic person may make or alter his moral choice by self reflection, or argument with himself, or being influenced by others. Sometimes the moral choice of the character may affect the mental make-up or the thought of the character. If we interpret 'character' in its widest sense, it includes inner, moral and intellectual qualities. But Aristotle discusses them separately. Butcher says, "dianoia is the thought, the intellectual element, which is implied in all rational conduct, through which alone ethos can find outward expression and which is separable from ethos only by a process of abstraction."[60]

DICTION :

After having discussed 'thought' and 'character,' Aristotle goes on to tell us of the medium of their expression in tragedy. 'Character' is revealed through action and speech, and 'thought' exclusively through speech, dialogue, through self-reflection or argument. The effect of such expressions depends upon the diction that the dramatic persons use. Aristotle says clearly, "by diction I mean the expression of the meaning in words ; and its essence is the same both in verse and prose."[61] There is no difference, according to Aristotle, in the use of words in tragedy where either verse or prose is chosen as the medium of expression. What types of words are to be used and what to be avoided is discussed by Aristotle in Chapter XXI of the *Poetics*.

The terms used by a poet may be divided into six kinds : "Every word is either current or strange, or metaphorical or ornamental, or newly coined or lengthened, (or contracted or altered)."[62] By a "current or proper word" Aristotle means that "which is in general use among a people." This does not mean the current words in a language but such words in the language of "a people," the type or class of persons represented in the tragedy. Hence it may differ from people to people. 'Strange' words mean words imported from other languages. Thus the same word may be strange as well as current in regard to different people with different languages or dialects. The third one is metaphor, "which is the application of an alien name by transference either from genus to species, or from species to genus, or from species to species, or by analogy, that is, proportion." 'Ornamental' words are not a separate class of words, foreign or current. It is their use which makes those words ornamental; for example, the use of periphrasis as in the expression, "the son of Thetis," "the tame villatic fowl." "A newly coined" word is that "which has never been in local use but is adopted by the poet himself." These words may be current or strange. They already exist but in other shapes, and pass through the mintage of the poet's mind and are infused with new or more emphatic expressions, such as ' jabber-wock" or "the fairy mimbling—mimbling in the garden." Lastly, there are words used by poets which are not entirely new or invented. Lucas says that they are "modified" words by means of either "lengthening like fairy, or by shortening like 'sovran' or by simple variation, as 'corse' for corpse."[63]

Now, none of these words can effectively be used separately from other words. Out of these sometimes three or four kinds of diction may be evolved. Aristotle's prescription for a perfect style is that it should be clear but not mean. Clarity can be brought about only by the use of current words. But if the style consists of too many current words, it is bound to be mean and trite, while the use of 'strange' words raises the diction above the commonplace. Unusual words—strange, metaphorical or 'modified,' i.e., words different from "normal idiom"—make the style lofty. At the same time it is to be borne in mind that if only such words—unusual words—are used, the style will either be a riddle, the meaning of which will not be obvious, because it might consist of metaphors "which express true facts under impossible combinations," or a jargon if only strange words are employed. In order to achieve a "lofty style" a certain infusion of these elements is necessary, for the strange words, the metaphorical, the ornamental and other kinds of words mentioned above, will raise it above the commonplace and the mean. But 'perspicuity' can be achieved only by the use of 'proper' or current words. Words which are not current but are conducive to clarity are 'modified' words which result from "the lengthening, contraction and alteration of words." Aristotle recommends deviation from "normal idiom" in exceptional cases only, but not always, lest language should result in a riddle or a jargon, as such deviations will bring distinction in the diction and make it 'marked'. But at the same time to retain clarity of diction, "partial conformity with usage" is prescribed.

The use of such 'modified' words should not be made at will by the poet lest it should degenerate into licence, and the language will become obstrusive and 'appear grotesque'. In the employment of any kind of diction, 'moderation' should be observed. Even metaphors or strange words, if used inappropriately, will be ludicrous. Any kind of diction will damage the style if the sense of appropriateness is not there, because one kind of word may make a style beautiful in one place and context, while the same kind of diction instead of increasing the beauty of the style may make it trivial in another place. Hence appropriateness of the kinds of diction is desirable.

But the most important thing, remarks Aristotle, is "the command of metaphor." "It is the mark of genius, for to make good metaphors implies an eye for resemblances." The metaphorical diction is most suited for iambic verse of drama, as compounded words[64] are for dithyramb and rare words for heroic poetry for this metre being closest to the prose of ordinary life, is most befitting the imitation of life.[65] Hence metaphorical diction, which is most suitable for this metre, is closest to the language of ordinary life. But all poets, says Aristotle, cannot use metaphors because it implies an inborn eye for likenesses. The metaphorical is the best diction as it is closest to the language of ordinary life and can even be used in prose. But metaphors should not introduce riddle in the language ; similarly, strange words should not be allowed to degenerate into jargon. A judicious combination of these words is necessary for the perfection of style.

SONG OR THE LYRICAL ELEMENT :

Song is one of the six elements of tragedy discussed by Aristotle in the *Poetics*. Song, as we understand, means rhythm and melody. "Speech is the basic food, rhythm and melody are the frosting on the cake."[66] In dialogue, the lyrical element is always desirable as it eases the tragic tension by its sweetenings. But Aristotle considers song as a different part of tragedy from speech. He regards the play as falling into just two alternating parts, the verse (dialogue) and the songs. In tragedy, he says, "some parts are rendered through the medium of verse alone, others again, with the aid of song."[67] Song introduces beauty in the play. After having discussed plot, character, thought and diction, Aristotle remarks, "of the remaining elements, song holds the chief place among the embellishments."[68]

Songs are sung by choruses. Aristotle does not approve of imported songs. The chorus also should be regarded as part of the tragedy, "as one of the actors." And these chorus actors should "share in the action." They should help the development of the plot or give an impression that they are not redundant and a dead weight upon the play. The songs, therefore, must be relevant. By this Aristotle does not mean any artistic or technical relevance, but suggests that relevant songs will ensure a better success from practical or theoretical point of view. Music, according to Aristotle, is one of the most potent elements of appeal to the audience. Hence if the poet aims at theatrical success, that is, if he is anxious that there should be the desired appeal of the action to the audience, he should use song, which is connected with the dramatic element in a relevant way. If it is a disconnected and 'imported' one, it may have the function of an interlude, no doubt, as is the case with the songs of Agathon but it cannot have the potential appeal, which it ought to.

The rule of making the chorus one of the actors and at the same time the confidant of the audience as in *The Suppliant* of Aeschylus may not be acceptable to many, because it depends upon the technique that a playwright follows, i.e., he may keep the audience in close touch with the actual drift in the hero's fortune or may keep him totally in the dark to spring on him a surprise. In the former case the chorus has a definite function to perform "It can expound the past, comment on the present and predict the future course of the event. It provides the poet with a mouthpiece and the spectator with a counterpart of himself. It forms a 'iving foreground of common humanity above which the heroes tower, a living background of pure poetry which turns lamentation into music and horror into peace."[69] While it establishes a relationship between the legendary heroes and the common humanity of the audience, it severes the drama from the real world also, its lyrical element being the most potent and significant part.

In the latter case, the dramatist may not like that the audience be in the know or guess of the actual turn of events. Moreover, there are certain sentiments which can best be expressed in privacy, such as, love. This idea is best expressed by Gray in his correspondence to Masson (1751) : "A greater liberty in the choice of the fable and the conduct of it, was the necessary consequence of retrenching the chorus. Love, and tenderness delight in privacy. The soft effusions of the soul, says Mr. Masson, will not bear the presence of a gaping, singing, dancings, moralizing, uninteresting crowd. And not love alone, but every passion is checked and cooled by this fiddling crew."[70]

Whatsoever be the point of view and desirability or otherwise of the chorus, this much can be ascertained here that the element of song, "the chief of the embellishments," has an important role in the total impression that we get from the drama. Songs may be sung by other characters also, because there is no such restriction prescribed by Aristotle, but for the chorus it is the main function. The only important suggestion of Aristotle is that if these songs are integrated organically with the play, a better theatrical success may be ensured.

SPECTACLE OR THE VISUAL ELEMENT :

Speech and song are, no doubt, important media of dramatic presentation. But when the play has to be staged, certain other visual elements are deemed necessary. Costume, stage-scenery and painting may be included under the term 'Spectacle'. Aristotle assesses the importance or otherwise of an element in tragedy from the point of view of its power of producing the tragic effect. "The spectacle," he says, "has, indeed, an emotional attraction, but of all the parts it is the least artistic, and connected least with the art of poetry,"[71] The emotions of pity and fear are aroused by the inner structure of the play and not by the acting and the stage scenery and other such extraneous elements. A good playwright does not depend upon spectacular elements for the tragic effect of his play. This is why Aristotle recommends that the "plot ought to be so constructed that, even without the aid of the eye, he, who hears the tale told, will thrill with horror and melt to pity at what takes place."[72]

The production of spectacular effects depends more on the art of the stage machinist than on that of the poet. The stage producer may detract from the effect of the play because he may introduce spectacular elements unchecked (and sometimes foolishly also) and thus shatter the unity of impression of the tragedy. "The drama has suffered," says Lucas, "from three enemies above all—the puritan, the pedant, and the theatre-manager, and of these the last has sometimes been the worst."[73]

In the interest of unity and a harmonious structure of the play Aristotle strongly disfavours the introduction of extraneous elements in the play, including *deus ex machina* for the unravelling of action, which is so potent a weapon in the hands of the dramatist, and disapproves of anything irrelevant. On this very score he does not seem to recommend spectacle to produce the tragic effect, which is a "less artistic method, and dependent on extraneous aids." Pity and fear through imitation give a pleasure peculiar to tragedy and this is possible through the structure of events. If spectacle, instead of creating a sense of the terrible, creates a sense of the monstrous, it will spoil the tragic effect of even the incidents. F.L. Lucas suggests that Aristotle "may perhaps have been thinking of things like that famous first performance of the *Eumenides* of Aeschylus when the audience, says a tradition, was frozen with horror, and women miscarried in the theatre at the terrible appearance of the Erinys."[74]

Here it can be remarked that Aristotle's theory of tragedy and his analysis of its elements have to do with the dramatic and not the theatrical elements. Because upon the latter, the the dramatist does not wield much control and therefore an unwise introduction of extraneous elements will detract from the dramatic effect. A play should be effective not only on the stage but also in the closet. But, at the same time, it is well known that plays are primarily meant for the stage, so spectacle cannot altogether be dispensed with. It does arouse the tragic sense, but it should not exceed the limit and thus threaten to spoil the tragic effect inherent in the plot, speech, song, etc.

From this discussion it is clear that Aristotle regarded drama primarily as a form of poetry depending for its effect on inner harmony and imaginative appeal, The stage paraphernalia was, thus, only of secondary importance to him. This Aristotelian position is different from that taken by many important critics of drama who maintain that drama is dependent on the theatre and more than half of its charm is lost if it is only read in the closet. Critics like Archer, Granville-Barker, Allardyce Nicoll, and some prominent theatre-critics on the Continent have lent support to this modern view. Aristotle, however, has rightly emphasized the primacy of the artistic over the theatrical elements in tragedy and his view is supported by our actual experience of great tragedies old and new alike.

CATHARSIS :

Aristotle is practically silent on the meaning of 'catharsis' and this silence has naturally evoked a vast volume of critical literature. It has been the cock-pit of controversy, and unanimity is no where within sight. John Morley in his *Diderot*[75] says that the undecisiveness of the catharsis-controversy is an indication of "one of the disgraces of the human intelligence, a grotesque monument of sterility." Every critic tries to read something new in the concept which finds a bare mention in one sentence in Chapter VI of the *Poetics*. But discussion "with so little determinate result" has continued "that one sometimes wonders whether it should not be declared officially closed or debarred."[76]

Tragedy has been defined by Aristotle as "an imitation of action...through pity and fear effecting the proper catharsis of these emotions." The true test of tragic action is that it arouses the emotions of pity and fear. The theory of catharsis has to do with these emotions. But at the outset controversies raise their heads, and translations differ. Whether Aristotle meant strictly the emotions of pity and fear, or implied other emotions also, is a matter of controversy. F.L. Lucas opines that Aristotle does not say that tragedy purges "these emotions" of pity and fear, but talks of "the relief of such emotions"—"emotions of that sort." "A tragic audience," he says, "has also such feelings as sympathy and repugnance, delight and indignation, admiration and contempt."[77] The audience reacts to a situation in a play and this reaction is the reaction of some emotion or sentiment. We feel delighted or indignant, we admire or feel contemptuous, when situations or the motives of the characters so necessitate. But why has Aristotle not mentioned these emotions? It is probably because they seemed less important or less intense. Pity and fear are certainly very powerful and intense emotions. But Lucas' view is untenable when we consider his statement that the emotions are 'purged' after they are excited. The feelings included under "emotions of that sort" are, no doubt, aroused by tragedy. But they do not need to be purged, as they are not 'painful' or 'disturbing' emotions,—the purgation of which, according to Aristotle, is the essential function of tragedy. But if 'catharsis' means 'purgation' or 'purification,' it is the 'purgation' of the 'painful emotions,' to bring normalcy in the emotional life of the audience. Hence the statement "these emotions" seems appropriate in regard to the theory of 'catharsis'. But it is true that other feelings and sentiments and emotions are also aroused by tragedy.

Some critics have thought of 'catharsis' on a completely different line. G.F. Else,[78] for example, substitutes 'pathetic and fearful' events in place of the emotions of pity and fear. His thesis is that the purification is the purification of 'pathos,' the pathetic and painful act done by the hero. 'Catharsis' purifies the act of the hero which appears as consciously done with a guilty motive. Otherwise, if the hero remains throughout the play a detestable criminal whose act can be attributed to some guilty motive, we will not sympathize with his fall. According to him, 'catharsis' is integrally connected with the structural idea of 'hamartia' and 'recognition'. It is a concept of structure. The tragic hero by some frailty or mistake of character commits some fatal acts, either innocently or unaware of the fatal consequences. This motive is not tainted. But how is this to be proved that his motive was pure? G.F. Else says that it is the function of 'catharsis'.

It purifies the apparently guilty act of the hero, of its criminal motive,[79] and thus, it is a part of the story and at the same time makes the hero a fit object of our sympathy. Hence the "pathetic and fearful" act is the "fulcrum upon which the emotional system balances."[80] It is the basis of the story, of the structure of action.

Again, Else proves his point in another way. Plato, he says, objected to poetry because it feeds our emotions, the irrational part of our being. Aristotle in his concept of 'catharsis,' as it were, gives implicitly a reply to Plato. It is like this : 'catharsis' purifies the apparently tainted motive of the hero in the fatal act. Unless this 'catharsis' is effected, the tragedy is not able to elicit our sympathy. We sympathize with the hero not involuntarily, reacting sentimentally on the spur of the moment, but after we have realized that the hero is worthy of such emotions. Thus it is not the irrational part of the drama which means sentimentalism, and a weak emotional excitement. It is quite rational and is expressed only when the pure motive of the hero's act is certified. And this is done by the whole structure of the play, particularly by recognition, which testifies to the purity of the hero's intention.

He further says that 'catharsis' is a process and not an end-result which is operated by the poet through his "structure of events." The medium through which 'catharsis' works is the structure of the events and hence it cannot be a standard result, automatically attained by any play, called tragedy. Some plays may do it in a better way while others may do it in a bad way.

It is difficult to accept Else's view in all its implications. In the expression "the purification or purgation of these emotions," the last two words should not be read as "pathetic and fearful" events. Because here Aristotle is telling us something about the function of tragedy and this function cannot be only the structural element or the composition of drama as such. The play is to be staged or read. Its success or failure will be judged by the audience or the reader in accordance with its impression created upon them. Since true literature has more to do with emotions than morality, it is in the fitness of things, that the function of tragedy should be considered in terms of emotional effect and not as a part of the structure like 'recognition' or 'hamartia'.[81] The function of a tragedy is something different from its technical perfection. The function is always assessed in terms of its effect upon the reader or spectator, which is emotional.

The most serious flaw in the interpretation under review is that Mr. Else professes to interpret Aristotle's theory of tragedy exclusively out of the *Poetics* itself, which is practically silent on the nature of 'catharsis'. It will naturally be misleading to base one's ideas on the *Poetics* alone. Moreover, an important idea of a particular thinker can be comprehended only when the composite mental output of such a man is well in the mind of the reader. Aristotle fortunately is not an inconsistent writer, and, for a better elucidation of his views his statements in the *Poetics* and *Rhetoric* may fruitfully be taken into account.

As regards the theory of 'catarsis,' we depend upon the *Politics* as our primary source of this conception. In the *Politics* Aristotle declares, "what we mean by 'catharsis' we will now state in general terms, hereafter we will explain it more clearly in our treatise on poetry."[82] But in the *Poetics* the much desired explanation does not occur and we have to base our interpretation on the materials supplied mainly by the *Politics*. In the *Politics* (Chapter VIII) Aristotle talks of musical 'catharsis,' the effect of music upon the morbid state of persons where the cure of the internal trouble of mind is effected by wild and tumultuous music. All music does not have this effect, because some music may bring only relaxation while other types may bring higher aesthetic pleasure. This musical reference is a key to the nature of 'catharsis' in the *Poetics*. All emotions, though many of them quite important in their own ways and even for the total tragic feeling, are not concerned with 'catharsis'. Butcher says that the terms "these emotions" do not mean "all such emotions," or "these and such like emotions," but by a frequent and idiomatic use he means "the aforesaid emotions," namely, pity and fear. It is with these and these emotions only that tragedy is concerned throughout the *Poetics*.

In *Rhetoric*[83] Aristotle has defined pity and fear, each as a form of pain. In every human being we have passions, and a tendency to pity and fear. But when these passions and emotions do not get a periodic vent, they affect the normal emotional life of the spectator. In tragic 'catharsis' this 'excess' of emotions is moderated so that the spectator may fall on the normal emotional life. The stage provides a harmless and pleasurable outlet for instincts which demand satisfaction, and which can be indulged here more fearlessly than in real life."[84]

Butcher approves of Bernay's explanation of the theory of catharsis. It is, according to him (Bernay), a medical metaphor and means 'purgation'. As medicine has a purgatory effect on body so tragedy has on soul. The difficulty with us moderns lies in our conception of medical purgation. We tend to mean by it total evacuation of these emotions on the basis of the medical analogy. It is 'purgation' in the older sense "which included the partial removal of excess 'humours'."[85] It moderates the excess of accumulated emotions. Here Aristotle probably has in mind Plato's charge of emotionalism against drama. He says that "it is not necessary to starve emotions and that a regulated indulgence brings balance of nature."[86] Tragedy excites the emotions of pity and fear and by excitation offers a pleasurable relief. It brings a tranquillizing effect rather than evacuation of tragic feelings. "First, tragedy excites the emotions to allay them. Pity and fear, artificially stirred, modify the excess of the latent pity and fear which we bring with us from real life, or at least such elements which are disquieting.[87]" As in the medical 'purgation' relief comes after excitation, similarly, in tragedy, "the pleasurable calm" follows the emotional excitement. "Through pity and fear effecting the proper purgation of these emotions" is akin to the homeopathic treatment. In tragedy the emotions of pity and fear are first excited in regard to the situations in the play (outside the spectator) and then are purged of their excess and disturbing elements, thus allaying, or tranquillizing these 'disquieting' emotions in the soul of the spectator himself. This is the 'cure' of emotions by emotions which are like in kind, but not identical.

Butcher follows Bernay's medical metaphor and the idea of the removal of excess 'humours'. But he further suggests that when the element of 'pain' is removed from these emotions, the emotions are also 'purified'. There is morbidity in the feelings of pity and fear as they are found in real life. These feelings are purified as they are excited, and the disturbing and morbid elements in the emotions are removed. As there is the tranquillizing process of the emotions already aroused, the lower elements being removed, we find the emotions, purified, ennobled and, as Lucas says, our selfish emotions 'sublimated'.[88]

It is bad to be selfishly narrow in our emotional response. What happens in tragedy? We sympathize with the hero and make him the object of our pity because he is like us and is meted out unmerited suffering. There is an inner affinity of moral character between the audience and the tragic hero which elicits the former's sympathy for the latter, because the hero is not a faultless person, but like us liable to error. Fear comes where under similar circumstances we put ourselves. "Pity, however, turns into fear where the object is so nearly related to us that the suffering seems to be our own."[89] Thus pity and fear in Aristotle are correlated emotions. In 'catharsis' pity does not undergo any change because whenever we see a hero who is not completely faultless but meets with undeserved sufferings, we pity him. But fear does change. The emotion of fear is profoundly altered when it is transferred from the real to the imaginative world";[90] because there is no fear of any danger to the spectator, but only a shudder that he feels in his blood. The hero has certain human frailty so that we can identify ourselves with his personality. But in certain respects he is raised above the common humanity in his stature, courage and resolute grappling with some great issue of life. Thus he is distanced from us, and the reader or the spectator, while merging himself with the hero's personality, forgets his petty concerns of real life and finds himself for the time being absorbed in the great issue which has significance for the whole humanity.

Thus the spectator or reader is raised above his petty level through the medium of the imaginative merger of his personality with that of the hero and thus he may have the feel of a different personality in himself.[91] This refining process of the emotions. as interpreted by Butcher, through 'catharsis' leads him to the idea of the universalizing of these emotions. These emotions are excited by the situations and characters which are typical, representative and probable under the given circumstances according to the law of cause and effect. Even the unexpected has to appear as 'inevitable'.[92]

One thing is clear here that Aristotle is thinking in terms of the removal of certain elements from these emotions so that the spectator may be restored to the normal emotional life. As mentioned earlier, in our real life the element of pain attaches to the emotions of pity and fear. This element of pain is bound more or less with our selfish concerns in regard to these emotions. In order to bring the man out of his selfish emotional cell, the removal of this narrow element of 'pain' is to be effected. Thus the idea of 'catharsis' as the refining process through impersonalization of these emotions through art is quite consonant with Aristotle's demand for pleasure peculiar to tragedy.

To conclude, 'catharsis' is a principle of Art. It relates to the spectator's or the reader's emotional response to tragedy. It reduces the emotional tension in the real life of the spectator to a healthy balance. It has been objected that the medical approach to 'catharsis' implies a presupposition of an abnormal spectator who is suffering from the excess of emotional accumulation. He comes to the theatre to let out these excess 'humours,' as it were. It may sound paradoxical, yet it is true that in our real life many painful elements attach to our emotions and these emotions get a free vent in the theatre so that the painful elements are removed while the spectator merges his being with that of the character in the play. The reader is lifted out of himself as he forgets his selfish concern in the larger concern of the hero through identification. 'Catharsis' does not remedy any defect, it only reduces the unhealthy excess of feelings.

It is pertinent here to touch upon another aspect of the problem by way of concluding this discussion. Aristotle obviously emphasizes the aesthetic blending of pity and fear as the primary function of tragedy, yet his remarks shrewdly hint at some other sentiments also which have been commended by critics from time to time as elements more appropriate to tragic drama. These sentiments may be described as a 'note of reconciliation,' a 'sense of waste' and a 'feeling of admiration' aroused by the dignity of the suffering hero. In Aristotle the 'note of reconciliation' is implied by the exclusion of the 'eminently good or virtuous' hero whose suffering will shock and crush us and undermine our sense of 'justice'; the 'sense of waste' is implicit in the 'unmerited suffering' which is productive of pity, and 'admiration' is embedded in the remark that the hero should be high and illustrious, not merely in his social standing but also in his moral and spiritual stature, quite capable of attaining to a degree of exaltation through his struggle and suffering.

We have explained and elaborated the Aristotelian concept of tragedy only to show that though his theory is mainly based on the Greek drama, his generalizing power has made the *Poetics* a repository of some universally valid principles of poetry. In certain cases he has made clear and explicit statements which may pass muster even today, but some of his statements have raised a great dust of adverse criticism through ages and may still be regarded as moot points, e.g., his assertion of the superiority of plot over character. Then he has been silent on some crucial points which has simply unleashed a veritable strife of tongues among his critics. The theory of 'catharsis' is a fit case in point here. In absence of a clear guidance from Aristotle the reader has to wade through a quagmire of conflicting criticism in order to find out for himself some solid ground of certainty.

But whatever Aristotle has explicitly stated is not all that his literary theory stands upon. Not less important are his implied statements which have been subsequently elaborated by literary thinkers in different ages and countries. For example, Aristotle does not explicitly mention anywhere dramatic conflict and dramatic irony as essential to tragedy through the plays which formed the basis of his theory contained these elements markedly. Without conflict the plot will not move. Aristotle only says that "the action capable of this effect (tragic effect) must happen between persons who are either friends or enemies or indifferent to one another."[93] This indicates the outward conflict where there is a clash between two physical forces, or characters, or between two minds or between a person and a force beyond his control as we have in ancient Greek tragedies. Thus the idea of dramatic conflict is implied here because it is implicit in the very nature of action.[94]

Similarly, the idea of dramatic irony is present by implication. The principle of 'hamartia' is closely connected with it. The hero does something in ignorance, or if consciously, without any anticipation of the fatal consequences. This brings about an adverse turn in his life and the catastrophe is out of all proportion to his error. This process is quite fruitful of tragic irony. Aristotle further states that the misfortune or suffering resulting from 'hamartia' is unmerited, i.e., of a magnitude surprisingly far in excess of the human error. In this statement the idea of 'fate' is implicit, though Aristotle does not take note of this factor, because his approach is rigorously rational.

Thus, we have many stated and unstated rules of tragedy in the *Poetics*. Many of these rules have stood the test of time and others have proved only of ephemeral value, more suited to the tragedies of ancient Greece than to the later developments of this form. Aristotle himself is free from the least touch of dogmatism and if his interpreters codified his rules into a rigid system, the blame does not lie at his door. We may, however, conclude with a reference to certain cogent principles of the art of Tragedy which emerge from the Aristotelian discussion in the *Poetics*. They may be summarized as follows :

(a) Tragic action should be great, serious, painful, leading to death generally though not invariably. This should spring from some conflict and pass logically through 'complication' to denouement.

(b) The hero should be larger than the average man and should pass from prosperity to adversity. But he should be near enough to us to excite fear and pity.

(c) The tragic hero should have some human frailty which releases sufferings out of all proportion to his mistake.

(d) High tragedy always brings emotional relief and leaves us reconciled to our fate and the dual position of man, his littleness as well as his greatness.

(e) In the development of the action of tragedy there is

an element of suprise, and unexpected turns of situations which may upset all calculations and underline
the futility of human wisdom,

(f) Tragedy should have an appropriate atmosphere
sustained throughout and also a suitable style, varying
according to the change in situations.

(g) The element of change is not ruled out but it should
be brought under the law of 'probability' and
'necessity'.

(h) Tragedy should depend for its peculiar effect on the
artistic elements integral to it and quite independent
of the theatrical, histrionic and scenic resources. It
should be effective in the closet as much as on the
stage.

(i) Aristotle mentions four types of tragedy, which are the
'simple,' the 'complex,' the 'pathetic' and the 'ethical'.[95]

FOOTNOTES

1 *Poetics* VI-2 Butcher's translation of the *Poetics in his Aristotle's Theory of Poetry and Fine Art* (Dover Publications, Inc., 1951) has been followed throughout.

2 Else, Gerald F., *Aristotle's Poetics: The Argument* (Harvard University Press, Cambridge, Massachusetts, 1957), p. 256.

3 Lucas, F. L., *Tragedy: Serious Drama in Relation to Aristotle's Poetics* (The Hograth Press, London, 1957), p. 31.

4 Cleanth Brooks explains the word 'serious' with reference to the object tragedy deals with. "Tragedy deals with ultimates...it treats seriously a life and death problem...deals with the meaning of suffering." See Brooks, C., ed. *Tragic Themes in Western Literature: Seven Essays of B. Knox and Others* (Yale University Press, New Haven, 1960), p. 4.

5 *Poetics* VI-6.

6 Thomson, Alan Reynolds, *The Anatomy of Drama* (University of California Press, 1946), p. 5.

7 *Poetics* VI-6.

8 *The Anatomy of Drama*, p. 120.

36

9 *Poetics* VI-11.

10 John A.M. Rillie finds in this supremacy of Plot over Character—an argument for melodrama.

See *The Review of English Studies,* Vol. XIII, 1962, "Melodramatic Device in T.S. Eliot," pp. 267-81.

11 Butcher, S.H., *Aristotle's Theory of Poetry and Fine Art,* p. 345.

12 *Ibid.*

13 *Poetics* VI-15.

14 *Aristotle's Theory of Poetry and Fine Art,* p. 346.

15 *Aristotle's Poetics: The Argument,* p. 242.

16 Ross, W.D. *Aristotle* (London, 1949), pp. 74-75.

17 Asthon, John W., *Types of English Drama* (Macmillan, 1940), p. 3.

18 Langbaum, R., *Poetry of Experience* (Chatto and Windus, 1957), pp. 210-11.

19 *Poetics* VII-7.

20 *Ibid.*

21 *Ibid* VIII-1.

22 *Aristotle's Theory of Poetry and Fine Art,* p. 275.

23 *Poetics* IX-10. "I call a plot 'episodic' in which the episodes or acts succeed one another without probable or necessary sequence."

24 *Ibid* XVIII-4.

25 *Ibid.* VIII-4.

26 *Aristotle's Theory of Poetry and Fine Art,* pp. 284-85.

27 *Poetics* XVIII-1.

28 See *Philological Quarterly,* Vol. XIV, Oct., 1935, Duncan, Thomas. Shearer, "The Deux ex Machina in Greek Tragedy," pp. 126-41.

29 *Poetics* XV-7.

30 *Ibid.* XIII-4.

31 *Ibid.* X-1.

32 *Ibid.* XI-1.

33 *Tragedy: Serious Drama in Relation to Aristotle's Poetics,* p. 111.

34 *Aristotle's Poetics: The Argument,* p. 345.

35 *Poetics* XI-6.

36 *Aristotle's Poetics: The Argument,* p. 346.

37 *Tragedy : Serious Drama in Relation to Aristotle's Poetics,* p. 114.

38 *Aristotle's Poetics : The Argument,* p. 352.

39 *Ibid.*

40 *Ibid.* p. 352.

41 See *Philological Quarterly*, Vol. XXIV, Jan., 1945, Pitcher, Seymour M., Aristotle's Good and Just Heroes," pp. 1-11.

42 *Poetics* II-4.

43 *Ibid.* XIII-3.

44 Oedipus kills Laius intentionally, knowingly, but there is no deliberation and probably he did so, like an average man, in self defence.

45 *Aristotle's Theory of Poetry and Fine Art*, p. 319.

46 *The Atanomy of Drama*, p. 281.

47 *Poetics* IX-7.

48 *Ibid.* XV-4.

49 *Poetry of Experience*, p. 210.

50 *Aristotle's Theory of Poetry and Fine Art*, p. 261.

There is a gain in the hero being placed in an exalted position and thus at an ideal distance from the spectator. "We are not confronted with outward conditions of life, too like our own. The pressure of immediate reality is removed; we are not painfully reminded of the cases of our own material existence. We have here part of the refining process which the tragic emotions undergo within the region of art. They are disengaged from the petty interest of self, and are on the way to being universalized."

51 *Poetics* VI-5.

52 *Aristotle's Theory of Poetry and Fine Art*, p. 340

53 Egri, Lajos, *The Writer's Notebook* : 'Plot or Character—Which ?' (Barnes and Noble, 1960), p. 166

54 *Aristotle's Theory of Poetry and Fine art*, p. 340

55 *Poetics* XIX-2

56 *Aristotle's Poetics : The Argument*, p. 244

57 *Poetics* VI-16

58 *Ibid.* XIX-4

59 *Aristotle's Theory of Poetry and Fine Art*, p. 343

60 *Ibid.* p. 340

61 *Poetics* VI-18

62 *Ibid.* XXI-2

63 *Tragedy : Serious Drama in Relation to Aristotle's Poetics*, p. 147

64 Compounded words are those which are "composed either of a significant and non-significant element or of elements that are both significant." (*Poetics* XXI-1)

65 "In iambic verse which reproduces as far as may be, familiar speech, the most appropriate words are those which are found even in prose." (*Poetics* XXII-10)

66 *Aristotle's Poetics : The Argument*, p. 223

38

67 *Poetics* VI-3

68 *Ibid.* VI-18

69 Lucas, F.L., *Tragedy : Serious Drama in Relation to Aristotle's Poetics*, p. 83

70 *Correspondence,* ed., Toynbee and Whibley, quoted in *Tragedy : Serious Drama in Relation to Aristotle's Poetics*, p. 85

71 *Poetics* VI-19

72 *Ibid.* XIV-1

73 *Tragedy : Serious Drama in Relation to Aristotle's Poetics*, p. 163

74 *Ibid.* p. 162

75 John Morley, *Diderot*, quoted in *Tragedy : Serious Drama in Relation to Aristotle's Poetics* : "The immense controversy, carried on in books, pamphlets, sheets and flying articles, mostly German, as to what it was that Aristotle really meant by the famous words in the VI chapter of the *Poetics* about tragedy accomplishing the purification of our moods of pity and sympathetic fear, is one of the disgraces of the human intelligence, a grotesque monument of sterility," p. 35.

76 *Aristotle's Poetics : The Argument*, p. 225

77 *Tragedy : Serious Drama in Relation to Aristotle's Poetics*, p. 43

78 *Aristotle's Poetics : The Argument*, p. 423

79 Because in tragedy we witness the kindred bloodshed by the act of the hero, which may be inadvertent, or if consciously done, then the hero did not foresee the fatal consequences. But the motive is not criminally wicked, and this proof is furnished by 'catharsis'.

80 *Aristotle's Poetics : The Argument*, p. 424

81 Mr. Else has interpreted 'hamartia' as a part of the plot and links it directly with the tragic 'recognition'.

82 *Politics* V-viii-7, H. Rackam's translation of the *Politics* in his *Aristotle : Politics* (William Heinmann Ltd., London, 1950), has been followed.

83 *Rhetoric* II-5, John Henry Freese's translation of the *Rhetoric* in his *Aristotle : The "Art" of Rhetoric* (William Heinmann Ltd., London, 1947), has been followed.

84 *Aristotle's Theory of Poetry and Fine Art*, p. 243

85 *Tragedy : Serious Drama in Relation to Aristotle's Poetics*, p. 37.

86 *Aristotle's Theory of Poetry and Fine Art*, p. 246

87 *Ibid.*

88 *Tragedy : Serious Drama in Relation to Aristotle's Poetics*, p. 37.

89 *Aristotle's Theory of Poetry and Fine Art*, p. 256.

90 *Ibid.* p. 258.

91 One of Plato's objections to drama was that there the reader or the spectator loses his personality and becomes many personalities. This objection Aristotle accepts and seems to say, 'Yes, man loses himself by merging his personality with the responsibilities of the characters and by proving false to himself, proves true to his real self. Because forgetting his selfish concerns, he is raised above himself, his selfish, petty emotions are purged and emotionally he is a different man.

92 *Poetics* IX. 2-4.

93 *Ibid.* XIV-4.

94 *Poetry of Experience* : "Where action is the end, we require a conflict of purposes and for the action to have meaning the purposes must have relative values, we must be able to evaluate one as better than another," p. 212.

95 *Poetics* XVIII-2.

CHAPTER II

Variations on the Aristotelian Concept of Tragedy

(Mediaeval, Renaissance and Neoclassical)

In order to place the Aristotelian concept of tragedy in a proper perspective conducive to a clear understanding of its relevance to the theory and practice of the tragic drama in the present age, it is necessary to glance at the various interpretations it evoked through the subsequent ages and the mutations which the concept itself underwent in response to the changing demands of those epochs. The vastness of the subject combined with the paucity of the space and the limited degree of the bearing of this retrospective survey on the principal argument of the present study necessitates and justifies a treatment which is, on the face of it, rather superficial.

I

MEDIAEVAL CONCEPTION OF TRAGEDY :

"The influence of Aristotle's *Poetics* in classical antiquity, so far as it is possible to judge, was very slight. There is no apparent reference to the *Poetics* in Horace, Cicero or Quintillian, and it was entirely lost sight of during the Middle Ages... *Poetics* in any form was probably unknown to Dante, to Boccaccio and beyond a single obscure reference, to Petrarch."[1] Though the Renaissance is the period when literary criticism actually began and when critics gave thought over Aristotle's views on tragedy, we find some discussion of the concept of tragedy in the mediaeval age also. Regarding literary criticism, it was "less dark than was once supposed,"[2] The mediaeval concept of tragedy was didactic with a marked emphasis on the 'wheel of fortune,' which, as we shall see, is echoed by many a Renaissance critic in Italy and England.

We shall concentrate here only on Chaucer for a representative Mediaeval statement on Tragedy. To Chaucer tragedy was essentially a story of the fall of an exalted personage from prosperity to misery, and such disaster was due mainly to the machinations of Fortune,[3] though moral considerations involving human responsibility are not altogether negligible :

I wol bywaile in maner of tragedye
The harm of hem that stode in high degre
And fallen so ther has no remedye
To bring hem out of his adversite,
For certeynly whan the cours of hir whiel holde.
Let no man truste on blynde prosperite.
Beth war these ensamples trewe and olde.

(Chaucer's *Monk's Tale*)

The existence of a righteous God and ordered universe compelled belief in the working of a moral law. The 'reversals' in the plays were attributed to the breach of moral law. Both these ideas, the fickleness of Fortune and the operation of Nemesis for the change in the fortune of the exalted tragic heroes are exemplified by Chaucer.

Thus, though Chaucer's conception of tragedy was derived from the ideas prevalent in the Middle Ages, he introduces some significant modifications. The attitude to story and tragic 'fall' of the hero due solely to the caprice of the heartless and irrational Fortune[4] was modified. Wrong deeds,[5] pride, and misgovernment of the hero[6] were also responsible for his tragic fall. At the end of *Troilus and Criesyde*, Troilus himself says that his downfall had been due to his "a-guilt and doon amis." In the Monk's Tale also the various disasters are ascribed to sins of pride and misgovernment. Before Chaucer the tragic catastrophe was not accounted for : it is he who "ascribed to the influence of Fortune or else to moral forces the tragic change in the life of the hero."[7]

The general features of tragedy in the Middle Ages may be briefly summarized as follows :

(a) Tragedy was not necessarily a dramatic form, being more generally a narrative. Even Chaucer conceives of tragedy as a species of narrative poetry, distinct from the dramatic one. This shows the absence of any real conception of ancient dramatic art.[8]

(b) Tragedy dealt with great and terrible actions.

(c) The characters in tragedy were kings, princes and great leaders.

(d) Tragedy began happily and ended terribly.

(e) Fortune played an important role in bringing about the downfall of the hero who deviated from the moral path.

(f) The style of tragedy was to be elevated and sublimed.

(g) The aim of tragedy was ethical. The tragic story dealt with the deeds of human beings of exalted status but the intervention of the invisible power to bring about the 'reversal of fortune' enforced the truth of *Vanitas Vanitatum*.

(h) The sense of the probable was utterly lacking in the mediaeval conception of tragedy in glaring contrast to the repeated insistence of the 'law of necessity or probability' in the *Poetics*.

II

RENAISSANCE CONCEPTION OF TRAGEDY :

Many of the mediaeval ideas concerning the nature of tragedy persisted through the Renaissance. Tragedy was still the fall of a prince and it was more a dialogue in high style than a sequence of action on the stage.[9] "Renaissance tragedy was classicised, indeed, in style; but in composition it remained as immune to the example of the Greek tragedies as the *Poetics* to the theory of Aristotle. It still imitated Seneca. Often it was not even intended for the stage."[10]

Aristotle was "practically unknown in Italy at the beginning of the Renaissance."[11] But at a later stage many critics claimed Aristotle's *Poetics* as the fountainhead of their dramatic and other literary ideas. But more often than not Aristotle was read by these critics and later by their followers in France through the spectacles of Horace, author of *Ars Poetica*. Bernard Weinburg has pointed out[14] that the insistence in *Ars Poetica* on instruction was "oriented so to speak towards the audience." After Horace, Robertelli too considered the audience as a determining factor in dramatic composition. This tendency culminates in Castelvetro where "audience is not only the chief consideration but the character of the audience itself is carefully restricted and described." We should be clear about the fact that this was not the Aristotelian approach. The mostly textual and isolated-from context interpretation of the Aristotelian text by the Renaissance Italian critics combined with their insistence on the audience as a determining factor in tragic composition establishes a pseudo-Aristotelian concept that persists through the centuries to come. "Aristotle's conception of the poem as a totality producing a total artistic impression has already been lost."[13] As a consequence of this, the principles of internal organization of the poem, Aristotle's 'necessity' and 'probability' are translated into principles for relating the poem to nature and to the beliefs of the audience. In this way the requirement of "credibility becomes a dominating consideration for Robertello."[14] The question how the artistic structure of tragedy is attained, does not bother the critics much. The important consideration now is whether an action or a character is true and the audience can believe in them. Weinburg concludes that "this shift is entirely consistent with the general movement away from the poem towards the demands or the expectations of the audience."[15]

The subject-matter of tragedy concerned kings and their empires only : "tragic poets treat of deaths of high kings and the ruins of great empires," says Daniello.[16] Almost all the critics agreed that the action of tragedy should be serious, grave and magnificent, to distinguish it from that of comedy. Historical realism was emphasized by critics like Castelvetro whose concern was oriented towards the 'credibility' of the play. "The arguments in support of tragedy as history," says G. Giovannini, "were developed by Italian critics of the later sixteenth century, particularly by Castelvetro....The arguments were repeated into the eighteenth century when they began to lose their force with the rise of humble and unhistorical characters as tragic heroes."[17] There were, however, critics like Scaliger who said that playwrights were not obliged to stick to the historical truth of their materials. They were required to treat the subject-matter of tragedy according to the principle of 'probability'. The 'poet' was taken by them to mean, it its ancient Greek sense, 'the maker' and hence 'imitation' was interpreted by these critics[18] as the imaginative re-creation of the subject-matter drawn from history. Even Castelvetro, while favouring historical realism, says that the poet's world is not necessarily the actual world that he sees. He allows the "invention of the things or the subject : which invention or subject comprises the invention of the things and the invention of the invisible things."[19] But despite this liberal approach to the problem, it became almost a common-place in the Renaissance to say, in the words of William Alexander, that "it is more agreeable with the Gravity of tragedy that it be grounded upon true History, where the greatness of known Person, urging Regard, doth work the more powerfully upon the Affection."[20] This historical verisimility was required for credibility and also for the production of the tragic effect. Giovannini says that as tragedy "involves grave and painful matters of public moment," these critics argued that the audience did not like to be told lies about such things. "He hates a lie about serious matters, and so a fiction in tragedy will not move him or barely move him to pity and fear."[21] Thus it was the historical verisimilitude upon which depended the tragic effect of the play.

'Action' was variously interpreted. Some of the critics took it to mean only external happenings while others inter-preted it more liberally and correctly and said that it included passions, emotions, etc.[22] "Tragedy," for example, says Minturno, "is concerned with the imitation of serious and weighty happenings..."[23] Scaliger adds that tragedy deals with horrifying events, and may end even happily. Such a conception of 'action' limits tragedy to specific events which have been enumerated by Spingarn in his *History of Literary Criticism in the Renaissance*.[24]

As pointed out earlier, it was accepted by all the Renais-sance critics that the tragic hero was a person of high stature, the affairs of whose life affected the life of the public. The play shows him in high position of prosperity in the beginning and in the end plunges him into adversity, leading sometimes even to his death. This obviously is a continuation of the Mediaeval conception of the tragic hero. Aristotle's four points in regard to character[25] gave rise to a curious concep-tion in the Renaissance, namely, "decorum." According to this, fixed characteristics were assigned to people according to their social categories : "it was insisted that every old man should have such and such characteristics, every young man certain others, and so on for the soldier, the merchant, the Florentine or Parisian and the like. This fixed and formal mode of regarding character was connected with the distinction of rank as the fundamental difference between the characters of tragedy and comedy"[26] and was more consonant with the Horatian than Aristotelian idea of tragedy.

The function of tragedy in the Renaissance was less emotional and more ethical, though critics like Minturno interpreted 'catharsis' in terms of homeopathic treatment i.e., effecting the cure of one emotion by means of another of similar nature. But moral edification by tragedy remains paramount in the minds of all the critics. Minturno says that tragedy aims at "arousing the feelings of pity and terror and tending to purge the mind of the beholder of similar passions, to his delight and profit."[27] All the critics interpreted the function of tragedy as the production of the emotions of pity and fear. But the arousal of such emotions was readily connected with moral edification. Scaliger even went so far as to say that Aristotle's idea of 'catharsis' was not necessary, because "it is too restrictive...(and) not every subject produces it."[28]

This ethical purpose of tragedy was based on the idea of moral education of the audience,[29] and the preoccupation with the audience prompted the specification of the types of events suitable for the purpose of the peculiar tragic effect. Similarly, the observance of the three unities was emphasized for making the 'action' credible to the audience. Castelvetro says, "Tragedy ought to have for subject an action which happened in a very limited extent of time, that is, in that place and in that time in which and for which the actors representing the action remain occupied in action ; and in no other place, and in no other time...The time of action ought not to exceed the limit of twelve hours. . . . There is no possibility of making the spectators believe that many days and nights have passed, when they themselves obviously know that only a few hours have actually elapsed ; they refuse to be so deceived."[30]

The unities of time and place are necessitated by stage-representation—its physical considerations and the audience. It is because of the paramount importance attached to the stage-consideration that a tragedy was required to be in verse.[31] Besides its being in verse, tragedy was to be written in a serious and grand style. All the critics in the Italian Renaissance have stated that tragedy is considered primarily in terms of its stage representation. "Tragedy," says Castelvetro, "cannot effect its proper function with a reading, without staging and acting."[32] Here we see that the Mediaeval conception of tragedy as a narrative has been replaced by its being primarily meant for the stage.

It is clear from the brief analysis of the main principles of tragedy in the Renaissance that the Mediaeval conception of tragedy so far as it related to the fall of a man of high rank was freely mixed with Aristotle's principles which the critics professed to follow. A representative definition of tragedy, such as that by Castelvetro, has clear echoes of Aristotle's *Poetics* : "Tragedy is an imitation of an action, magnificent, complete, which has magnitude, and comprises each of those species which represent with speech made delightful separately into parts and not by narration and, moreover, induces through pity and fear the purgation of such passion."[33] But the elaboration of the elements of tragedy by these critics betrays only a superficial acquaintance with or a deliberate modification of Aristotle. Their conception of tragedy as primarily concerned with the stage (though Aristotle accepts it equally for the closet), the production of pity and fear, the unity of action and the gravity of the subject-matter and style are Aristotelian. But the conception of 'imitation' as historical verisimilitude, boiling everything down to the credibility of the audience, the tragic hero as king or prince (though Aristotelian examples show such heroes), the emphasis on the unities of time and place, the ethical nature of tragic effect and the necessity of verse in tragedy are not strictly Aristotelian. The major shift from the Aristotelian position is the emphasis on individual elements of tragedy separately as conducive to the production of the tragic effect[34] and focus on the audience as the main factor in shaping tragedy.

Yet the Italian Renaissance on the whole, though un-Aristotelian on many points, testifies to a revival of Aristotle's theory, though it was apt to take its necessary cue from Horace as well as the Mediaeval interpretation of tragedy, with an eclecticism quite characteristic of its essential temper.

English criticism in the Renaissance betrays a profound influence of the Italian critics, an influence which is self-evident in Sir Philip Sidney,[35] the most representative figure of the period. The definition of tragedy that Sidney gives "agrees substantially with what might be designated Renaissance Aristotelianism."[36] Tragedy, he says, is that which "openeth the greatest wounds and showeth for the ulcers that are covered with Tissues, which maketh kings feare to be tyrants and Tyrants manifest their tyrannical humours... teacheth the uncertainty of this world and upon how weak foundations guilden roofes are builded."[37] Here Sidney's idea is obviously reminiscent of the mediaeval tradition combined with the Aristotelian conception as interpreted by the Renaissance Italian critics. Tragedy, as conceived in the Middle Ages, dealt with high personages, and serious and grave actions to illustrate the transistoriness of human pride, pomp and glory.

So far as the function of tragedy is concerned, Sidney follows the Italian Renaissance critics quite closely. Following Minturno, he uses 'admiration and commiseration'[38] instead of the Aristotelian 'pity and fear'. That poetry instructs delightfully, is a continuation of the Renaissance Italian conception of the function of tragedy. In stressing the need of moral teaching and stately speeches, Sidney shows his indebtedness to Scaliger.[39] Following Castelvetro, he strongly favours the unities of time and place : "the stage should alwaies represent but one place and the uttermost time pre-supposed in it should be both by Aristotle's precept and common reason but one day."[40] He disapproves of the forced mingling of the comic and the tragic in tragedy. He demands the unity of action by insisting upon the removal of all that is irrelevant, and the narration of what is necessary but likely to affect the unity of plot, if included in the main body of the 'action'.

Like Sidney, Jonson[41] and Milton also follow the Italian Renaissance conception of the Aristotelian theory of tragedy with varying emphasis on different aspects of tragedy. The subject-matter of tragedy remains the concern of princely affairs, and "the dignity of persons, gravity and height of elocution (i.e., lofty style),"[42] are emphasized again and again under the influence of the Senecan model of tragedy. 'Verisimilitude' is stressed by Jonson in his demand for the "truth of argument,"[43] though Sidney says that the poet can "feign an entirely new story keeping in view the law of 'probability' or 'necessity'. Jonson prescribes that the details of the story should be constructed "to the most tragical conveniency" of the plot.[44] The three unities are demanded by all the critics. Even Milton, who shows a better under-standing of Aristotle, says : "The circumscription of time wherein the whole drama begins and ends, is according to ancient rule and best example, within the twenty-four hours."[45] Then the importance of a careful and artistic handling of the plot was recognized by all the critics,[46] and the elements of plot were elaborately discussed by the critics like Ben Jonson.[47] The most notable feature of the Renaissance English criticism is the interpretation of 'catharsis' at the hands of Milton, who "gives for the first time in English a clear and correct idea of 'catharsis' which later on was to be subjected to various interpretations." Milton observes : "Therefore said by Aristotle (tragedy has) to be of power of raising pity and fear, to purge the mind of those and such like passions, that is to temper and reduce them to just measure with a kind of delight, stirred up by reading or seeing those passions well imitated. Nor is Nature wanting in her own effects to make good his assertion : for so in physic, things of melancholic hue and quality are used against melancholy, sour against sour, salt to remove salt humours."[48]

In connection with Milton's statement of the tragic theory, Atkins remarks that "with this belated reference to the Greek dramatic standards, Renaissance influence on English criticism may be said to have practically ceased."[49]

By way of concluding this discussion of the Renaissance interpretation of Aristotle's principles of tragedy which, in fact, meant a tentative attempt to codify and re-mould the tenets of the Greek critic in the light of the later and stricter formulations of Horace, we may glance at the new type of tragedy, e.g., the Romantic English tragedy of which Shakespeare became the most outstanding exponent. It was evolved in flagrant disregard of the classical unities, even though in style, subject-matter and the essential dignity of the protagonist and the final tragic effect, it was not, in essence, far removed from the requirements of Aristotle. It is the example of Shakespeare which militated against the unreserved acceptance of the neo-classical code on the part of major English critics like Dryden and Johnson, who were otherwise profoundly influenced by the French law-givers of the day.

III

FRENCH NEO-CLASSICAL CRITICISM :

In France, however, the situation was different. Here we find a progressive bridging of the gulf between theory and practice under the influence of the French Academy. France did not have any obstacle in the form of a great romantic model as England had in Shakespeare, and the role of Richelieu and the French Academy was decisive in shaping the critical thoughts as well as the creative efforts in that country. We may briefly glance at the efforts of the French critics to define and systematize the principles governing Tragedy in the light ostensibly of the *Poetics* as it was understood in that period.

The French neo-classical critics borrowed freely from the commentaries on the text of Aristotle and its interpretations by the Renaissance Italian critics.[50] But France, with the new set-up under Louis XIV and Richelieu and the Academy, attempted to achieve a system and discipline in criticism and creative literature alike. The famous 'Cid' controversy illustrates the ideal of tragedy that was officially approved and enforced. This play was criticized for lack of moral consideration, truth and probability, decorum and the unities.[51]

The subject-matter of tragedy according to the neo-classical critics was some serious action, which was to be "founded upon...either noble passions or upon an intricate and pleasing plot, or upon some extraordinary spectacle and show."[52] Further, the subject-matter proper to "the dignity of tragedy needs some great state interest of passion nobler and more virile than love."[53] This action, which involves the death of the hero and shedding of kindred blood, should have historical basis and truth for the credibility of the audience, because actions against blood relations, says Corneille, are always "so criminal and so contrary to Nature that they are not credible unless supported by one or the other, and they never have the probability without which invented actions cannot be played."[54]

The tragic hero was to be one of exalted rank whose sufferings taught others that even such eminent people were not exempted from "the strange accidents" of life.[55] The principle of 'decorum' was to be observed. The three unities were to be strictly adhered to, to make the representation credible to the audience. Boileau in his *Ars Poetique,* says :

The unity of action, time and place,
Keep the stage full, and all our labors grace.[56]

Rapin argues that "unless there be the unity of Place, Time and Action in the great poem there can be no verisimility."[57] For Voltaire the unities safeguard the emotional effect against improbability and lead to beauty.[58]

So far as the function of tragedy is concerned, we notice that a variety of interpretations are given to 'catharsis' with an overwhelming emphasis on the moral edification of the audience. Boileau says:

Thus to delight us, Tragedy, in tears
.. provokes our hopes and fears ;
If in a labored act, the pleasing rage
Cannot in our mind a feeling pity raise,
In vain with learned scenes you fill your plays.[59]

(*Ars Poetique*)

Rapin, whose interpretation of 'catharsis' "became with some modification the standard interpretation among the sentimentalists of the eighteenth century,"[60] says in a general way : "For no other end is poetry delightful than that it may be profitable."[61] "Tragedy," he says, "rectifies the use of passions by moderating our fear and our pity which are obstacles of our virtue....It rectifies the passions by the passions themselves calming by their emotion the troubles they excite in the heart." [62] Rapin goes on to say that the production of pity and fear may be harmful "because man is naturally timorous and compassionate, he may fall into another extreme, to be either too fearful or too full of pity ; the too much fear may shake the constancy of mind and the too great compassion may enfeeble the equity."[63] Tragedy regulates these weaknesses by showing the 'disgraces' meted out even to persons of eminence, and uncertain accidents which they encounter. The pleasure of tragedy, adds Rapin, "consists in the agitation of the soul moved by the passions."[64] Pleasure from tragedy comes when the spectator feels "interested in the adventures, fear and hope" of the protagonist and "afflicts himself and rejoices" with the protagonist,[65] and all this is done for 'profit'. Dacier defines 'catharsis' thus : Tragedy "by means of compassion and terror perfectly refines in us all sorts of passions and whatever else is like them."[66] He says that man becomes inured to the tragic import of life by seeing the tragic events happening in the life of even great people. This helps him in real life. He can make light of his real miseries when he compares it with what he saw on the stage.[67] He further says that "tragedy is a true medicine which purges the passions, since it teaches the ambitious to moderate his ambition, the wicked to fear God, the passionate to restrain his anger, etc., but it is a very agreeable medicine and works by pleasure."[68]

The neoclassical principles of tragedy as formulated by the critics of this period may be summarized in the words of A.W.H. Atkins :

In general its appropriate themes were held to be historical in character, the dignity of tragedy requiring subjects that involved great interest of state. Verisimilitude, decorum and the three unities were, moreover, to be observed throughout ; the treatment was to be illuminated by great thoughts and noble expressions and the tragic hero was to be of exalted rank. Then too its structure was also defined. There was to be 'protatis' in which the characters reveal themselves ; and this was to be followed by the main intrigue, the reconnaissance and denouement. The play was to consist of five acts; three or four actors alone were to appear simultaneously on the stage; and the tragic effects for the most part were described as those of pity and fear.[69]

As we move from France to England, we find two strong but conflicting forces determining the shape that the theoretical criticism of tragedy eventually took in the latter country : the one was the effective influence of the French neo classical doctrine of tragedy and the other was the native literature of England, especially the practice of Shakespeare in tragedy. This conflict colours the criticism of Dryden, the most distinguished figure in the Restoration era. Dryden's principle of tragedy is largely neo classical but with a strong liberal and patriotic leaven. Drama is defined by him as "a just and lively image of human nature, representing its passions and humours, and the changes of fortune to which it is subject, for the delight and instruction of mankind."[70] Tragedy, to him, is "an imitation of one, entire, great and probable action, not told but represented which by moving in us fear and pity is conducive to the purging of those emotions in our minds."[71] The function of tragedy is ethical besides being aesthetic. Tragedy shows us that "no condition is privileged from the turns of fortune."[72]

For the production of proper tragic effect, the hero should of necessity be a virtuous man so that his sufferings may arouse pity, which means not absolute virtue in him but "virtuous inclinations and degrees of moral goodness."[73] There should be some "alloy of frailty" in the hero for the production of tragic effect.[74] The three unities were mentioned but no rigidity was attached to them.[75] Dr. Johnson frowned upon the demand of the unities of time and place and accepted only the unity of action which has been followed even by Shakespeare who rejected the other two unities. He says "it is ununderstandable to decide where the limits of this illusion are to be fixed. It is rarely observed that minds not prepossessed by mechanical criticism feel offense from the extension of the intervals between the acts ; nor can I conceive it absurd or impossible that he who can multiply three hours into twelve or twenty-four might imagine with equal ease, a greater number."[76] By the same token Johnson rejects the unity of place saying that the audience who accepts the initial falsehood of taking the stage to represent some other place, near or distant, can imagine many more such things. "The playgoer, in a state of elevation above the reach of reason or of truth, and from the height of empyrean poetry" disregards all details of time and place.

Dryden defends the Shakespearean inclusion of sub-plots in tragedies and the mixture of tones. About the latter he observes that the mixture of the tragic and the comic in tragedy is good because it brings variety and the comic in the play provides tragic relief.[77] Dr. Johnson evers that the neoclassical objection to the mixing of the tragic and the comic in tragedy is inconsistent with the actual experiences of playgoers. "All pleasures," he says, "consist in variety," and a true picture of life consists in both the serious and the frivolous. As the aim of all poetry, adds Johnson, is "to instruct by pleasing," it will be found that 'mingled dramas' do it more effecitvely.

Despite Dryden's and Dr. Johnson's liberal interpretations of the principles of tragedy on the points of the unities and the purity of *genre*, the prevalent notion of tragedy was neoclassical. Tragedy dealt with serious subject-matters and elevated characters. Its function was delight and instruction. 'Decorum' was to be observed[78] and the poetic justice was implicit in the conception of double plot, though it was expressly demanded by Dennis and Rymer.[79]

The presence of the two conflicting ideals, the classical and the romantic or the Shakespearean, naturally resulted in a good deal of confusion so that even the great critics of the age' Dryden and Johnson, could not maintain a single consistent attitude free from wavering and contradiction.

But by this time we find that the neoclassical creed has begun to dissolve in England as well as in France. In England, says B.H. Clark, with Johnson's emphatic statement that no "literary dictator has authority to enact for others," "all the ruling doctrines of the 16th, 17th and 18th century criticism receive notice to quit."[80]

The neoclassical period, however, shifted the emphasis from the tragic heroes of royal rank to the common middle class protagonists. In France, we have the pronouncements of critics like Diderot and Beaumarchais. "Diderot," says B.H. Clark, "sounded the call against what was false in the neoclassical ideal. The age was ready for him."[81] Diderot recommends domestic affairs to form the subject-matter of tragedy, as opposed to the French neoclassical conception of the subject-matter as serious and dignified in the sense of some state concern centering round a king or prince. He also rejected the French neoclassical demand for the unities of time and place and intricate fables. He discarded "the whole social milieu of remote antiquity and remoter orient."[82] What he recommends is not simply realism but rather "sensationalism in which realistic devices are valued only as contributing to an intense emotional effect."[83] Diderot demands that the play should be moving and 'pathetic'.[84] This requires the tragedy of common man his demestic affair which would bring a sentimental emotional effect on the audience. Beaumarchais says that tragedy can appeal to us only if it "resembles serious drama" dealing with "real objects" around us and portraying men and not kings, because only the former type of characters can arouse in us sympathetic feelings for them.

Here it is pertinent to mention Lessing, who is regarded as the liberator of tragedy from the dominance of French neoclassicism which he described as the "circumvention" of Aristotle's rules.[85] He rejected the unities of time and place and 'verisimility' saying that these unities instead of conducing to 'vraisemblance' bring "improbabilities and absurdities."[86] The neoclassical 'vraisemblance' was rejected and great emphasis was laid on the inner logic of the plot and 'probability' and 'necessity'.[87] Then the characters of tragedy should be human beings like us—"of the same wheat and chaff" as any of us is[88]—not too low or too above the average humanity to affect our identification with them which is necessary for the tragic effect.[89] The tragic effect of 'catharsis' does not mean to Lessing the inuring or hardening of the minds of the audience against the feelings of pity and fear, nor is it a tempering, purification or cleansing of pity and fear. 'Purgation' to him is a balancing of the emotions. He equates 'catharsis' with the right mean of the passions as taught in the *Nichomachean Ethics*. 'Purification' consists in nothing else than this transfiguration of passions into virtuous habits. This conception betrays Lessing's neoclassical leanings in considering tragedy as a "school of the moral world."[90]

In England, Johnson, the last bulwark of neoclassicism, was definitely in favour of the domestic themes and common characters as factors more effective in producing sentiments peculiar to tragedy and softening the hardness of heart and the wildness of passions through the chastening effect of fear and pity. Dr. Johnson admitted that tragedy produced pity and terror and that these two emotions purged other harmful passions in the audience. "The passions," he says, "are the great movers of human actions; but they are mixed with such impurities that it is necessary they should be purged or refined by means of pity and terror. For instance, ambition is a noble passion but by seeing upon the stage a man, who is so excessively ambitious as to raise himself by injustice, punished, we are terrified at the fatal consequences of such a passion. In the same manner a certain degree of resentment is necessary; but if we see that a man carries it too far, we pity the object of it, and are taught to moderate the passions."[91]

In conclusion, we may say that the neoclassicism of the seventeenth and eighteenth centuries was the extreme logical culmination of the idolatry of the ancients, notably of Aristotle, which was a strong strain in the classical revival of the early sixteenth century. This blind enthusiasm for the classics, combined with a passionate desire for guiding the native literatures along proper lines to the height of the excellence achieved by the ancients, was partly responsible for the modification of the ideas of Aristotle in the light of the prescriptions of Horace and the practice of Seneca and the changed social and moral contexts of the new ages. The trend towards codification, however, was opposed from the very beginning and voices were continually raised against this absurd and ominous attempt to fetter the dynamic soul of poetry by the iron rigours of fixed rule. Practice never submitted wholly to the theoretical demands even in the neoclassical France as is evidenced by Corneille's protest against the three unities which Dryden was quick to capitalize in his *Essay of Dramatic Poesy*. Yet till the end of the eighteenth century, criticism followed the pattern, however modified or misunderstood, prescribed by Aristotle in the *Poetics* and all departures from that norm were invariably measured in terms of that old pattern. With the beginning of the nineteenth century, however, we witness the emergence of new approaches to the nature of tragedy, which have continued, in different guises, of course, in the present century as well. This new orientation in the discussion of the nature of Tragedy is the subject of the chapter which follows.

FOOTNOTES

1 Spingarn, J.E., *A History of Literary Criticism in the Renaissance* (Columbia University Press, 1925), p. 16.

2 Atkins, A.W.H., *Literary Criticism : The Mediaeval Phase* (Methuen 9143), p. 16.

3 *Ibid.* "Already in the decadent Rome," says Atkins "the goddess Fortuna had been regarded as a capricious and ruthless deity, gifted with occult power over the lives of men," p. 160.

See Haweis, H.R., *Chaucer for Schools,* "Notes on the Monk's Tale" (Chatto and Windus, London, 1916), p. 125.

4 In *Troilus and Cresyde* the deity is described as the mistress of destiny, "executrice of wierdes" who "under God" was the controller, 'hierdes' of events and their mysterious causes.

5 As Troilus says at the end of the play.

6 As the Monk says in his story.

7 *English Literary Criticism : The Mediaeval Phase,* p. 186.

8 *Ibid.,* p. 160.

9 Baldwin, C.S., *Renaissance Literary Theory and Practice* (Columbia University Press, 1939) : "The great persons of Greek tragedy, Oedipus, Medea or the House of Atreus are revived not to interact towards their doom but to make speeches," p. 137.

See also Vaughan, C.E., *Types of Tragic Drama* (Macmillan, London, 1908), p. 100.

10 *Renaissance Literary Theory and Practice,* p. 133.

11 Clark, B.H., *European Theories of Drama* (D. Appleton & Co., London, 1929), p. 54.

12 *Comparative Literature,* Vol. V, No. 2, 1953, "From Aristotle to Psuedo-Aristotle," p. 100.

13 *Ibid.* p. 101.

14 *Ibid.*

15 *Ibid.*

16 'La Poetica' quoted in *European Theories of Drama,* p. 54.

17 *Philological Quarterly,* Vol. XXXII, 1953, "Historical Realism and Tragic Emotions in Renaissance Criticism," p. 306.

18 See *History of Literary Criticism in Renaissance,* for a discussion of the conception of 'imitation' in Renaissance as held by Daniello, Robertelli, Fracrastero, Varchi, Scaliger, Castelvetro and Minturno, pp. 28, 30, 31, 35, 36, 70 and 84.

19 *European Theories of Drama,* p. 64.

20 Spingarn, J.E., *Critical Essays of the Seventeenth Century* (Oxford University Press, London, 1909), p. 186.

21 *Philological Quarterly,* Vol. XXXII, 1953, p. 307.

22 See *History of Literary Criticism in Renaissance,* pp. 39-42.

23 *European Theories of Drama,* p. 56.

24 "...the mandates of kings, slaughters despairs, executions, exiles, loss of parents, parricides, incests, conflagrations, battles, loss of sight,

tears, shrieks, lamentations, burials, epitaphs and funeral songs." p. 69.

25 *Poetics* XV. 1-4. : "In respect of character there are four things to be aimed at. First...it must be good. The second...is propriety. Thirdly, character must be true to life. The fourth point is consistency."

26 *History of Literary Criticism in Renaissance,* p. 85.

27 *European Theories of Drama,* p. 56.

See *European Theories of Drama,* p. 64, for Castelvetro's text on 'catharsis'.

28 *Ibid.,* p. 61.

29 *Ibid.,* p. 58.

Tragedy teaches the audience that even "those of high rank...(for the) favours of fortune, have fallen into extreme misery through human error," which implies that "nothing here below is so durable and stable that it may not fall and perish, no happiness but may change to misery."

30 *Ibid.,* p. 64.

31 As the audience may be great in number, the platform will be large and the audience must hear the actors' verse is necessary. Then as the audience consists of all types of people, the play should deal with the elemental passions and interests of man and for the credibility of the action, historical verisimilitude is necessary. And as the platform is narrow, dreadful violence, such as death should not be shown on the stage.

32 *European Theories of Drama,* p. 64.

33 *Ibid.*

34 *Philological Quarterly,* Vol. XXXII, 1953., G. Giovannini shows that historical verisimilitude was taken to be conducive to the tragic emotions, pp. 306-318, in his "Historical Realism and the Tragic Emotions in Renaissance Criticism."

35 See *The Review of English Studies,* Vol. XX, 1944, Dowlin, Cornell March, "Sidney and other Men's Thought," p. 257.

36 *History of Literary Criticism in Renaissance,* p. 269.

37 Collins, J. Churton, ed., *Apologie for Poesie* (Oxford at the Clarendon Press, 1934), p. 31.

38 *Ibid.,* "Stirring admiration and commiseration teacheth the uncertainty of life..., etc., p. 31.

39 Ben Jonson has said about the function of tragedy :

"The ends of all who for the scene do write
Are, or should be to profit and delight."

(*The Silent Woman,* 2nd Prologue)

40 *Apologie for Poesie,* pp. 51-52.

41 See *English Studies,* 1949, Potts, L.J., "Ben Jonson and the Seventeenth Century," pp. 16-17.

42 *History of Literary Criticism in Renaissance,* p. 287.

43 *Works,* p. 272.

44 *Apologie for Poesie,* p. 52.

45 Preface to *Samson Agonistes.*

46 *English Literary Criticism : 17th and 18th Centuries,* p. 342.

47 Adams and Hathaway, ed., *Dramatic Essays of the Neoclassical Age* (Columbia University Press, 1950) "The fable is called the imitation of one entire and perfect action, whose parts are so joined and knit together as nothing in the structure can be changed or taken away without impairing or troubling the whole of, which there is a proportionable magnitude in the numbers.... By perfect, we understand that to which nothing is wanting.... Whole we call that, and perfect, which hath a beginning, a midst and an end. So in a fable if the action be too great, we can never comprehend the whole together in our imagination. Again, if it [be too little, there ariseth no pleasure out of the object, it affords the view no stay, it is beheld and vanisheth at once...., etc., p. 131.

48 Preface to *Samson Agonistes.*

49 *English Literary Criticism : 17th and 18th Centuries,* p. 342.

50 Rene Wellek, *A History of Modern Criticism* (New Haven, Yale University Press, 1955), pp. 5-6.

We have a "view of literature which is substantially the same in 1750 as it was in 1550."

51 Questions like, "Is it proper for Chimene to consent to a marriage with her father's murderer ? Would a Spanish noble-man like Don Diegue have so many men at his command ? Would the port of Seville be left unguarded in the time of war ? Is it acceptable for a king to play a joke ? Can all these events really have happened within twenty-four hours ? were raised and discussed by outraged critics.

52 Abbe D'Aubignac quoted in *European Theories of Drama,* p. 131.

53 Corneille quoted in *European Theories of Drama,* p. 142.

54 *Ibid.*

55 Rapin quoted in *Dramatic Essays of the Neoclassical Age,* p. 124.

Saint-Evremond demands "for our hero's principal traits which we consider human and which evoke admiration, as being rare and elevated.... In the human the mediocre must be avoided, in the great the fabulous." Greatness or mediocrity has to be taken not as a social but a moral or intellectual factor because his emphasis is on "purely natural but extraordinary things...(on the) hero's principal traits being "rare and elevated." p. 112.

56 *European Theories of Drama,* p. 158.

See *European Theories of Drama,* pp. 124-127 and 131 for Jean Chapelain's and Abbe D'Aubignac's statements on the three unities.

57 *Dramatic Essays of the Neoclassical Age,* p. 123.

See *Dramatic Essays of the Neoclassical Age,* p. 24, where Corneille says that sometimes the unities of Time and Place "may exempt us from probability, even though it does not permit us the impossible."

58 *European Theories of Drama,* Voltaire's "Letter to Father Jesuit," p. 281.

59 *Ibid.* p. 158.

60 *Dramatic Essays of the Neoclassical Age,* Introduction to Rapin, p. 121.

61 *Ibid.,* p. 124.

62 *Ibid.*

63 *Ibid.*

64 *Ibid.*

65 *Dramatic Essays of the Neoclassical Age,* p. 124. Saint-Evremond says, "it can only with difficulty be persuaded that a mind accustomed to being frightened at what concerns the woes of another can be entirely easy in the presence of the woes that concern itself.... Is there anything so ridiculous as to found a science which surely brings on sickness in order to establish another which uncertainly effects its cure—that of putting a perturbation in a mind in order to try afterwards to calm it by the reflections that it can make to itself on the shameful state in which it finds itself," pp. 113-14.

66 *Ibid.,* p. 168.

67 *Ibid.,* p. 170.

68 *Ibid.*

69 *English Literary Criticism : 17th and 18th Centuries* p. 14-15.

70 Ker, W.P., ed., *Collected Essays,* Vol. I (Macmillan, London, 1925), p. 36.

71 *Ibid.,* p. 187.

72 *Ibid.,* "Preface to *Troilus and Cressida,*" p. 210.

See Critical *Essays of the 17th and 18th Centuries,* Dennis interpreted it as "softening the most obdurate heart" by representing the punishment of evil and reward for virtue, p. 194.

Also See *European Theories of Drama,* "The Spectator, No. 29," Addison says that tragedy produces pity and fear to "soften insolence, soothe affliction and subdue the mind to the dispensation of Providence."

73 *European Theories of Drama,* "Preface to *Troilus and Cressida,*" p. 210.

74 It can be remarked here that Dryden's conception of the tragic hero is essentially congruent with that of Aristotle.

75 See Verrall, Margaret De G., ed. *A.W. Verrall : Lectures on Dryden* (Cambridge at the Clarendon Press, 1914), p. 132.

76 *European Theories of Drama,* "Rambler, No. 156," p. 234.

77 *Collected Essays*, Vol. I.

The objection that it is not possible for us to turn from the tragic to the comic is answered by Dryden thus : why should we "imagine the soul of man more heavy than his sense ? Does not the eye pass from an unpleasant object to a pleasant one in a much shorter time, and does not the unpleasantness of the first commend the beauty of the other," p. 69.

78 *European Theories of Drama,* Rymer says that this "decorum" should conform to what he calls "humanity." "Humanity (for example) cannot bear that an old gentleman in his misfortune should be insulted with such a rabble of scoundrel language.... A woman never loses tongue, even though after she is stifled." (p. 150) "In the days of yore soldiers did not swear in this fashion." etc., pp. 149-52.

79 See *Literary Criticism : A Short History,* p. 206, for a discussion of this principle in the English Neoclassical Criticism.

80 *European Theories of Drama,* p. 229.

81 *Ibid.,* "Introduction to Diderot," p. 285.

82 *A History of Modern Literary Criticism,* p. 48.

83 *Ibid.*

It is for this purpose that Diderot favours melodramatic plots and recourse to dramatic pantomime. Rene Wellek remarks, "This naturalistic emotionalism in Diderot was perfectly compatible with the traits which have been hailed as anticipations of symbolism or modern impressionism because he was not satisfied with the ordinary device of achieving this emotional effect by language, however ornate and flowery it might be," p. 49.

84 *Ibid.,* p. 47.

85 *European Theories of Drama,* p. 226.

86 Ibid., *"Hamburgische Dramaturgie,* No. 19," p. 258.

87 *European Theories of Drama,* p. 259.

88 See *Modern Language Review,* Vol. LXV, 1950, Heitner, Robert, "Concerning Lessing's Indebtedness to Diderot."

89 *European Theories of Drama,* p. 226.

90 See *The Modern Language Review,* Vol. XII, 1917. Robertson, J.F., "Lessing's Interpretation of Aristotle," pp. 326-7.

91 *Literary Criticism : A Short History,* p. 293.

CHAPTER III

Later Speculations on the Nature of Tragedy

(Philosophical and Psychological Approaches)

PHILOSOPHICAL APPROACHES :

So far we have considered the interpretations of tragedy in relation to the stage, as an important genre of poetry. In the nineteenth century Germany a set of philosophers, Schopenhauer, Nitzche and Hegel, attempted a methaphysical exposition of tragedy in the light of their respective philosophical systems. These discussions of tragedy are neither literary or aesthetic nor are they very exhaustive. They tell us in a very general way something about the subject-matter of tragedy and of the nature and source of its effect upon the mind of the spectator. Nevertheless, the views of tragedy of these philosophers, particularly those of Hegel, have exerted a great influence on the minds of some of the critics of tragedy, such as A.C. Bradley and Professor Frye and we cannot afford to ignore them in the present survey.

SCHOPENHAUER :

Schopenhauer regards tragedy as "the summit of poetical art." Tragedy, he says, "is the representation of the terrible side of life. The unspeakable pain, the wail of humanity, the triumph of evil, the scornful mastery of chance, and the irretrievable fall of the just and innocent are presented to us."[1] In depicting thus the suffering and pain of mankind, tragedy gives us a "significant hint of the nature of the world and of existence."[2] He calls the ultimate reality 'will'. This 'will' which is the "thing-in-itself' is an irrational, blind and self-conflicting impulse to existence. It is incessantly striving without attaining final satisfaction. Hence there is a continuous conflict between the desire to find satisfaction and the ultimate failure to do so. The 'Will' objectifies itself in the world of phenomena. Multiplicity, individuality, particularity which are conditioned by space and time—the "principium individuationis"—are all only empirically real and the manifestations of the 'Will'.[3] The 'Will' mainfests itself in all grades of life and supremely in man. Conflict, which is the essence of the 'Will', is, therefore, present in man, and this is a source of his suffering, besides life itself being essentially painful; temporary satisfaction, the quieting of desire only incites this striving further.[4]

In tragedy, the 'Will' is "at the highest grade of its objectivity (and) comes into fearful prominence.[5] This fearful objectivity of the 'Will'—the suffering and pain of human life —"becomes visible in the suffering of men, which is now introduced, partly through chance and error, which appear as the rulers of the world, personified as fate, on account of their insidiousness, which even reaches the appearance of design; partly it proceeds from man himself, through the self-mortifying efforts of a few, through the wickedness and perversity of most."[6]

In tragedy we behold the 'Will's' strife with itself objectified. which affords some characters a knowledge of the true nature of the world, knowledge purified by personal suffering, a momentary penetration through the veil of Maya and the principle of individuation, productive, in the long run, of an attitude of resignation and the surrender of the very will to live.[7]

Tragedy does not represent the reward for the virtuous and the punishment for the wicked.[3] "The true sense of tragedy is the deeper insight, that it is not his own individual sins that the hero atones for, but the original sin, i.e., the crime of existence itself. For the greatest crime of man is that he was born."[9] Schopenhauer, therefore, disapproves of *dues ex machine* employed by tragedies to bring in a poetical justice which is contrary to the truth of life.

"The representation of a great misfortune is alone essential to tragedy." This can be done in more than one way—by portraying wickedness, as in Iago, Shylock, Creon or by depicting the cruel strokes of Destiny as in *Odeipus Rex*, or by presenting the dramatis personae at cross purposes, harming each other wittingly but under the compulsion of circumstances. Schopenhauer looked on this last form of tragedy as the best, in as much as the very ordinariness of the characters and circumstances bring the meaning and effect of tragedy very close to us and sharply remind us of our own liability to be involved in their fate.

Now the aesthetic effect of tragedy, the tragic 'catharsis,' says Schopenhauer, does not belong to the sense of the beautiful but to that of the sublime.[10] "Sublimity involves the Will only to this extent that something which is recognized as hostile to the Will is made into an object of disinterested contemplation, so that the feeling of the sublime arises precisely when the relationship of the object to the particular Will of the subject is transcended and disregarded. (While) the charming or attractive (which is the opposite of the sublime) draws the beholder away from pure contemplation by directly exciting the Will."[11] Thus, "what gives to all tragedy, in whatever form it may appear, the peculiar tendency towards the sublime is the awakening of the knowledge that the world, life, can afford us no true pleasure, and consequently is not worthy of our attachment."[12] In the third and fourth Acts of tragedy, says Schopenhauer, perhaps the spectator is distressed and disturbed by the even more clouded and threatened happiness of the hero. In the fifth Act he finds that the happiness is entirely wrecked and shattered. This brings in him the sense of a certain elevation of the soul, a pleasure, which the happiness of the hero, however great, would have never brought. This drives him into the "haven of entire resignation." The tragic effect of the catastrophe induces a spirit of resignation, and brings the exaltation of mind in both the tragic hero and the spectator.

NIETZCHE

Nietzche followed Schopenhauer in the conception of human life on this earth. Like Schopenhauer he found human life full of pain and torture. But he differed from Schopenhauer radically in his estimate of tragedy and its effect on the mind of the audience. Schopenhauer thought that tragedy by presenting before us the suffering and pain in human life taught us resignation to fate and a denial of the will to live. But Nietzche found in tragedy the most powerful stimulants of the will to live made possible through the artistic representation of human suffering and pain With Schopenhauer, he admits that the cruel reality of human life, brought home to us by tragedy, may produce a pessimistic, nihilistic attitude in our mind towards life. But art saves us from any such impression and presents life before us as something worth living and pleasurable.[13]

Such a pleasurable effect of tragedy, says Nietzche is brought about by a "duplexity" of the two art impulses—the Apollonian and the Dionysian, embodied in the two Greek deities. Apollo is the god of the poised, harmonious, plastic art. He is the god of light and of dream. This dream world which Apollo creates is pleasurable and "we take delight in the immediate apprehension of form,"[14] and "experience our dreams with deep joy and cheerful acquiescence."[15] But this world of ideal representation which the Apollonian dreaming art produces, may degenerate into "a flaccid and sterile academicism."[16] For this reason the Dionysian counterbalancing is needed.

Again the Apollonian demands moderation and due proportion. 'Know thyself' but not too much to avert the fate of Oedipus. It also demands "that measured limitation, that freedom from the wilder emotions, that philosophical calmness of the sculptor-god."[17] But this moderation and 'absence of undueness' may tend toward coldness and rigidity. This also needs to be counterbalanced by the Dionysian exuberance and wildness. Then the Apollonian dream-world gives the "sublimest expression" to the "principium individuationis," when man sits wrapt in the veil of Maya, surrounded by the atmosphere of painful reality. But man believes in his 'individuality' thinking it to be real, unmindful of the larger reality in which it itself exists. Apollo is thus "the glorious divine image of the "principium individuationis," from out of the gestures and looks of which all the joy and wisdom of "appearance" together with its beauty, speak to us."[18] This "principium individuationis" also is destroyed by the Dionysian drive to give us a knowledge of the universal reality.

Now Dionysus is the god of wild flute music, of wine and intoxication, of the dancing throng and of the orgy in which men as satyrs were connected with their darker, subterranean selves and with the primordial unity of nature.[19] The Dionysian represents undueness, rejection of moderation and proportion and abolishes the 'principium individuationis, and the "covenant between man and man is again established.... Now is the slave a free man, now all the stubborn, hostile barriers, which necessity, caprice, or shameless fashion has set up between man and man are broken down,"[20] and "at the evangel of cosmic harmony," each one feels himself one with the Primordial Unity.

These two art impulses which are in conflict create

tragedy with the mediation of the will of the artist. The Dionysian cancels the individuality of the artist and he, becoming one with the universal soul of things, visualises completely the supreme truth of life. The truth of life which the artist beholds is of suffering, pain and loss inherent in the earthly existence of man. But this view of the 'Silenus's' wisdom of life would, if presented to us as such, be unbearable and there would be a danger of its producing a Buddhistic negation of life—a pessimistic, nihilistic attitude towards life.[21] Here the Apollonian comes to the rescue. Apollo represents the Dionysian in a symbolic embodiment of dream figures. Through this artistic representation of life, we become primordial beings for the moment and feel its indomitable desire for being and joy in existence.

Nietzche states that the Apollonian wrests us from Dionysian universality and "fills us with rapture for individuals.... To these it rivets our sympathetic emotions, through these it satisfies the sense of beauty which longs for great and sublime forms ; it brings before us biographical portraits and invites us to a thoughtful apprehension of the essence of life contained therein."[22] Thus, the Apollonian influence "uplifts man from his orgiastic self-annihilation and beguiles him concerning the universality of the Dionysian process into the belief that he is seeing a detached picture of the world."[23] Here one may get the illusion that the Dionysian is at the service of Apollo.

But "in the collective effect of tragedy, the Dionysian gets the upper hand, (and) tragedy ends with a sound which could never emanate from the realm of Apollonian art. And the Apollonian illusion is thereby found to be what it is,—the assiduous veiling during the performance of tragedy of the intrinsically Dionysian effect, which, however, is so powerful, that it finally forces the Apollonian drama itself into a sphere where it begins to talk with Dionysian wisdom and even denies itself and its Apollonian conspicuousness."[24] Neitzche explains this intricate relation between the Apollonian and the Dionysian in tragedy as a symbolized fraternal union of the two deities : "Dionysus speaks the language of Apollo; Apollo, however, finally speaks the language of Dionysus; and so the highest goal of tragedy and of art in general is attained."[25]

Tragedy has a peculiar pleasurable effect upon the spectator. But this effect should not be looked for in the "struggle of the hero with fate, the triumph of the moral order of the world, or the disburdenment of the emotions through tragedy."[26] Tragedy does not bring a cathartic effect as Aristotle believed. It yields a metaphysical comfort—a purely aesthetic pleasure. It is not cathartic and it should not be restricted to the "domain of pity, fear or the morally sublime."[27] It is tonic and healing and has the "enormous power of exciting, purifying and disburdening the entire life of people."[28] It goes beyond "terror and pity to realize, in fact, the eternal delight of becoming, that delight which even involves in itself the joy of annihilating."[29]

To sum up, tragedy, according to Nietzche, is "not merely an imitation of the reality of nature, but in truth a mataphysical supplement to the reality of nature."[30] It is the artistic representation of life—life which is essentially painful and miserable. The pleasure we derive from tragedy is a metaphysical comfort, a healing and tonic effect. This effect, which is the effect of joy, comes at the annihilation of the protagonist. Nietzche disapproves of the tragedy in which the hero "after he had been sufficiently tortured by fate, reaped a well-deserved reward through a superb marriage or divine tokens of favour."[31]

HEGEL

Hegel thinks that in tragedy there is some kind of conflict between ethically justified forces—conflict of feelings, modes

of thoughts, desires, wills, purposes, etc. The essential point
in tragedy, according to him, is not suffering but its cause
which is conflict. The spectacle of conflict and its attendant
suffering produce true tragic pity and fear.

The tragic conflict is the collision of two incompatible
ethical demands on the hero, who embodies in himself only
one of the ethical forces. This force is in itself right and
proper but it is one-sided. The hero sticks to this force and
denies the other which is otherwise valid and justifiable. But
as these forces, though right in themselves, are incompatible
in the situation, they come in conflict with each other.
Tragedy occurs because the hero refuses to accept the other
equally justified claim over him.

This conflict results in tragedy because of the nature of
the hero. The hero has a consistency of adherence to and a
firmness in espousing an ethical force exclusively. He does
not do so half-heartedly. His tenacity to an ideal and un-
flinching courage are at the same time his greatness and his
doom. He identifies himself completely with the ethical
force in him and would not accept even the existence of any
other which interferes with this.

Professor A.C. Bradley sums up Hegel's view of the cause
of this conflict : "The essentially tragic fact is the self-division
and intestinal warfare of the ethical substance, not so much
the war of good with evil as the war of good with good.
Two of these isolated powers face each other, making incompatible demands. The family claims what the state refuses,
love requires what honour forbids. The competing forces are
both in themselves rightful and so far the claim of each is
equally justified; but the right of each is pushed into a wrong,
because it ignores the right of the other, and demands that
absolute sway which belongs to neither alone, but to the
whole of which each is but a part."[32]

The end of tragedy is the denial of both the exclusive
claims. The catastrophe in a tragedy which closes this con-

flict of competing ethical forces is not because of any freak of chance or blind fate. "It is the act of the ethical substance itself, asserting its sbsoluteness against the excessive pretensions of its particular powers."[33] It is the inevitable reassertion of outraged ethical justice. The ethical force with which the hero has identified himself, is not rightful as it is one-sided, and not absolute as considered by the hero. In the catastrophe, therefore, the eternal justice is vindicated and we feel a sense of reconciliation—the hero reconciles himself with the eternal justice, the ultimate power, which he has disturbed by denying it and which is re-established by his destruction. In the death of the tragic hero, Hegel says, there is an aspect of reconciliation. It is because that, which has been denied, is not the rightful power with which the combatants have identified themselves. On the contrary these powers, and with them the only thing for which the combatants cared, are affirmed. What is denied is the exclusive and therefore wrongful assertion of their right."[34]

Whatever justification Professor Bradley might advance for Hegel's conception of the reaffirmation of the eternal justice in tragedy, it would be hard to deny that Hegel's conception comes very close to the principle of poetical justice. "Although Hegel's theory," remarks John S. Smart, "proceeds from a philosophic basis, yet, when it is applied to certain tales or dramas, it ends by being little more than the old doctrine of poetical justice expressed in a new way. Indeed, it almost begins to resemble the familiar morality of the Sunday School : be good and you will be happy ; be wicked and you will be punished."[35] Besides this, a tragedy representing life in this light of Hegelian concept cannot be true to life. Smart says that Hegel has not so much explained tragedy as he has explained it away because of his approach being too much rational and moralistic. We don't fail to find in tragedy an element of mystery. A genuine tragedy seems to point to the existence of something wrong in the world and to an inexplicable failure in the general justice of things. It does not only say that the universe is entirely rightful and the tragic hero is exclusively responsible for his destruction.

Then again, Hegel says that conflict or action is the chief cause of tragedy. But we understand that the conflict is more the effect than the cause in tragedy. It is because conflict is the result of the peculiar situation in which the hero is caught. The most important objection to Hegel's theory of tragedy would be that the very occurrence of situations which bring about a conflict between two forces, upon both of which we set a high spiritual value, is a painful fact, and a sense of the assertion of a supreme ethical power at the close of the play is not capable of reconciling us to the situation, and removing the pain of the great spiritual loss which we have witnessed all through the play. Again, that this conflict is resolved in a reconciliation, is not always true. In his *Philosophy of Religion*, says Bradley, "he (Hegel) himself plainly states that in the solution even of tragedies like the *Antigone* something remained unresolved."[36]

Robert Langbaum, in his *Poetry of Experience*, remarks that "in spite of Hegel's idea that tragedy deals with the conflict between good and good, between incompatible moral obligations, the obligations are never quite equal. If they were, the action would come to a standstill ; there could be no movement toward a right conclusion."[37] Although Hegel's moralistic concept of tragedy does not stand the scrutiny of the literary critic, yet his conception of the element of conflict in tragedy—not necessarily the conflict between good and good—the tenacity and the whole-hearted adherence of the hero to his conviction which results in his destruction are important points which every genuine tragedy has in some form or the other.

As we saw above, these philosophers looked at tragedy not strictly as a literary form but as a part of their philosophical systems. "The trouble with all of them is that they approached their data with a ready-made metaphysics to which tragedy had to be fitted willy nilly."[38] It would not be very fruitful to try to find in these philosophers any elucidation of Aristotle's concept of tragedy as their approach to the problem was quite different. But the conception of the universal truth of life as constituting the subject-matter of tragedy, of conflict as essentially desirable for tragedy and the peculiar effect of tragedy on the mind of the audience are points which are common to both Aristotle and these philosophers.

PSYCHOLOGICAL APPROACHES :

From Nietzche's concept of tragedy as an artistic demonstration of the primitive Dionysian energy hidden behind the Apollonian placidity it would be a convenient transition to the psychological view of our being as a complex of conflicting forces working within us, as has been emphasized by Freud and his followers.

Freud and the psychoanalysts have revolutionized our way of looking at ourselves.[39] Freud showed that the apparently irrational symptoms which had puzzled physicians for centuries were meaningful when seen in terms of painful memories which had been repressed into the unconscious but not stifled altogether. Freud pictured the unconscious "as a dynamic force rather than as a mere waste-paper basket of ideas and memories which had fallen below the threshold of awareness because they were relatively unimportant and lacked the mental energy to force their way into consciousness. He was able to show . . . that the unconscious plays a predominant part in mental life, since it takes its energy from the instinctual drives, and its contents are kept out of awareness not because they lack significance but because they may be so significant as to constitute what is felt as a threat to the ego."[40] There is a conflict between primitive drives seeking an outlet and learned ego and super ego behaviour-patterns which must inhibit them as unrealistic, contrary to the individual's own values or what he regards as the expectations of others.[41] Thus man is not what he appears to be. To this conception of the unconscious, Freud adds the hereditary limitations of man, his original sin and predestination. Freud's biological approach did not stress social and environmental factors as determining human behaviour which, he says, is determined by hereditary constitution and the psychic predeterminism of man. Yet social factors do play an important role as a source of inhibition which is productive of neurotic conditions.

Freud found man enchained in heredity and controlled by his unconscious. Adler found environment confronting man's free sway of his will to power. Jung found something larger than these as affecting man's conscious life. His conception of personality is inherently unitary, drawing together culture, religion and history within the single context of the human psyche.[42] Jung says that the complexity of human life is not only what Freud thinks, i.e., something determined by the 'Personal Unconscious,' but it has a larger and more important determining unconscious which embraces the religion, culture and social tendencies of the past which have been recurring again and again in human life. These primordial recurrences, the "pre-established instinctual substrata" are inherited by man which determine and guide his conscious life. Man's conscious life is not what he really is but only a "persona," a mask to his real inner self. Jung says that the conception of the 'Collective Unconscious' affecting man's present life is what is known as the 'Karmic' factor in Indian Philosophy.[43]

Thus psychology has exposed to us a larger and new vista of human life and has discovered for us the dark recesses of man's unconscious, thereby providing a new mode of looking at man's behaviour in society. Ira Progoff says that such knowledge and analysis of man's inner self has become more important in the modern cultural context which is characterized by spiritual crisis. Man has accumulated around him such a huge lot of sophisticated and hypocritical social and spiritual factors that he has turned in a sense neurotic because of his too much suppressing his real self.[44]

Now because of these repressive social forces, impulsive expression becomes distorted and inadequate. For this reason it is necessary, and more so in cases of maladjustment, that the patient be simply given opportunity to accept himself emotionally and thus release his repressed emotions. This is possible if he does this in an atmosphere where his expression has not to face any social restriction and is not socially rejected and there is no danger of any punishment.[45] This release of the emotions repressed in the past needs the process of re-living the 'conflict situation' and re-experiencing the attendant anxiety and the emotional tension. This psychoanalytic process which effects emotional release is called 'abreaction' or catharsis'.

In 'catharsis' confession is the most important thing. But the confession, should be "genuine and straightforward" Confession, says Jung, is the bringing of the unconscious to the daylight and of the "patient in correspondence to the hinterland."[46] "The goal of the cathartic method is full confession, not merely the intellectual recognition of the fact with the head, but their confirmation by the heart and the actual release of the suppressed emotion.[47] Jung says : This was the "extraordinary significance of genuine, straightforward confession—a truth that was probably known to all the initiation rites and mystery cults of the ancient world. There is a saying from the Greek mysteries : 'Give up what thou hast, and then thou wilt receive....' The beginnings of psychoanalysis are in fact nothing else than the scientific re-discovery of an ancient truth ; even the name that was given to the earliest method—catharsis or cleansing—is a familiar term in the classical rites of initiation. The early cathartic method consisted in putting the patient, with or without the paraphernalia of hypnosis, in touch with the hinterland of his mind, hence into that state which Yoga systems of the East describe as meditation or contemplation.[48] The patient is "called upon to abandon all his cherished illusions in order that something deeper, fairer and more embracing may arise within himself anew. It is a genuine old wisdom that comes to light again in psychoanalytical treatment."[49]

Apropos this release of emotion, Freud says that 'libido' cannot be repressed for a long time. If it is "dammed up and not allowed free expression, then it will find oblique channels by which to escape and so form art, literature, religion and everyone of the manifestations which are, called sublimations."[50] Dramatic performances are such opportunities of sublimations for the release of repressed emotions. By empathy, by identifying itself with the characters of the play, the audience gives an expression imaginatively to the urges without any social or parental fear, which it would have repressed in its normal social life. Plays have been used for psycho-therapeutic treatment in the ancient times and have the same effect now, though this truth may be disputed[51] because "in our modern industrial civilization there seems less danger or emotional excess than of emotional atrophy."[52]

The above discussion shows that man has something in him which is not known to him or to others. His real self— his unconscious—contains the Nietzchean Dionysian impulses and Freudian repressed sexual urges and can be extended to Jung's 'archetypes,' the images of the social, religious and cultural past of the human race whose recurrence determines man's real existence. Man is not the master of his passions but the slave of his heredity, and his 'biological past,' as O'Neill says. He is in conflict with his environment which always thwarts the free sway of his 'animal impulses' which

Darwin has discovered to have always existed in man. With his best attempts overtly he cannot circumvent heredity, his biological past and his racial unconscious which are there at the back of his real self as Fate was in the ancient time. Thus because of psychoanalysis with its great emphasis on man's unconscious, modern thinking about man is mostly concentrated on the working of his inner self. Naturally enough, tragedy written with this concept of man has also been internalized. As environment and society play a great part in the unconscious self, there is naturally a conflict between man and his society. Now, therefore, there seem to be two types of conflict, one between man and his inner self—the "terra Incognita" in him which is so largely inhibited by savage,"[53] and the other between man and his environment, society.

Lucas remarks that psychology has discovered that man has aggressiveness which, he postulates, "can turn against himself. Indeed, there is reason to believe that many suicides are self-retribution for previous death-wishes against others."[54] Applying this truth to literature he adds : "Long ago Aristotle pointed out that the tragedy where a man blindly destroys himself is more poignant than the tragedy of ruin brought by outside enemies. It required a tragic irony. But tragic irony of self-destruction is not a mere stage-device; it would be far less dramatic if it were ; it is based, often, on a deep psychological reality. We are betrayed by what is false within."[55] This is why, he says, critics have misunderstood the principle of 'peripeteia' in the *Poetics* by interpreting it as 'the reversal of fortune.' "A 'peripeteia' occurs when human blindness produces exactly the opposite of what it hoped and planned."[56] There is always something in the hero's personality ununderstood by him which brings his ruin.

Aristotle's principle of 'catharsis,' remarks Lucas, is psychologically sound upto a point, because "in this way the sufferer may live out his emotions in the realm of fantasy" without feeling overwhelmed by the guilt or the fault of the hero in the play. This is because in the universality of art he gains, as goethe advised, "his distance from the thing."[57] The essential function of tragedy is the "complicating and strengthening of the psyche by means of shocks from outside, not, of course, violent and disorganizing shocks, but mild, preventive, reorganizing ones. Participating in tragic conflict may be a part of such reorganizing."[58] But if the tragedy is horrible, this may result in a real shock, like shell-shock-from which the patient would have to be cured. "In practice, however, we can usually protect ourselves by recalling, if we are forced, that what is happening on the stage is not real. There is probably a level of tragedy, involving not too drastic a reorganization of the psyche, at which tragedy is most effective."[59]

The audience follows the hero's aspirations and explorations in new realms of feeling where even his defeat brings in the audience an experience of a reorganizing from the old to a new fuller experience of his psyche.[60] Morrell remarks that the effect of tragedy is "simply calmness and readiness, the discovery that even in the harshest experiences there is, to quote Richards, 'no difficulty' ; the difficulty arises from the illusion and subterfuges by which we seek to dodge reality, and which, we unconsciously fear, are going betray us."[61]

Now the effect of tragedy depends upon its end, the death of the hero, or the end of what he stands for or the end of his life of hope and not the ordeal he suffers. It is the end of tragedy which releases the spectator's emotions and enables him to adjust himself to reality. The tragic purgation does not depend only upon empathy or transference—but also indispensably upon the way it is broken. If the tragic hero does not fail tragically and is allowed to live "happily ever afterwards," a pathological state of dependence akin to the condition of Breuer's patient, develops. It is because the tragic effect lies not in the wishfulfilment of the ego but in the frustration of the wish.

Here it is necessary to remark that social and religious attitudes of man affecting the conception of tragedy have been changing through ages, but we shall see that the basic concept of tragedy has not materially changed and the modern psychological interpretation of it confirms some of the ancient truths about it. Since ancient time it has been accepted that tragedy represents a struggle between man and fate, the controlling force of the universe and the laws of nature. The conception of tragedy of the Greeks originated in their religious rituals. They had their gods who used to foil their attempts in their life. There was a conflict between man and fate, his gods, the divine order. "Man because of a lack of comprehension of the divine order or of an inherent tragic flaw must achieve his salvation through suffering. He preserves his worth and dignity by maintaining his courage within. And he re-establishes harmony with a moral order."[62] But with the breaking of the authority of the Church which had persisted throughout the Middle Ages, God could be questioned in the Elizabethan times. Coffman remarks that "from the philosophical and ethical point of view, the inrush of secular literature caused the thoughtful person to consider his worth as an individual. Both of these tended to fix authority and responsibility within man himself. The individual is the master of his own destiny, but through the law of causality he has to suffer the consequences of his own acts. The belief in an ordered universe, however, still prevailed. The one who violates a moral law expiates the sin through his suffering or death and thus the moral order is re-established. The 'catharsis' for the reader or listener is thus effected in part through constructive satisfaction as well as through pity and fear."[63] Coffman, while asserting that "any attempt to explain in a sentence why there was no great tragedy in the eighteenth century and why it was not a vital concept would be a gross over-simplification," concludes that "the deistic conception of an ordered universe wound up like a clock and the doctrine of perfectibility carried into the nineteenth century, certainly were the factors."[64]

Freud has stated that the "three most terrible shocks to man's personal esteem were firstly Galileo's discovery that the earth moved round the sun, secondly, Darwin's theory of evolution and thirdly, the discovery of the real nature of the unconscious."[65] But in spite of these discoveries man remains what he ever was "Man has not really changed much ; it is only our greater understanding of his moods and manners that has changed a bit. Nor has our idea of Fate really changed. It is only the face of Fate that alters. That face is no longer marked by an oracle ; Fate no longer comes down as a god in a machine."[66]

So we find that in the modern age of Science and Psychology, the elements essential to tragedy are practically the same as they were in the ancient times. The only difference is that their 'face has altered'. For example, the modern counterpart of fate becomes the 'biological past,' heredity and the unconscious with which man comes in conflict and which are mysteries to him. The order of existence is no more to be sought in the inscrutable gods and the dark Fate but in the forces at work in the human psyche.[67] Tragedy re-establishes the order of existence by bringing man in touch with the hinterland of his mind, by reconciling him with his hereditary limitations, because "all his life man is forced to wrestle with the unconscious in an attempt to reconcile its demands with those of his conscious ego.... Man is in fatal error when he assumes that his conscious ego can fulfil all his needs without acknowledgement of the power of the unconscious, the modern equivalent of the gods."[68] Man's submission to the unconscious, as his fatalistic submission to "the will of God" in the ancient times, means his withdrawal from reality and action. This lack of submission inevitably involves conflict and tension.

O'Neill fully supports this psychological conflict in tragedy,

He says that the proper subject of tragedy is man's struggle with his fate, which is his unconscious. "The struggle," he says, "used to be with gods but is now with himself, his own past, his attempt to 'belong'."[69] In his letter to Arthur Hobson Quinn, O'Neill remarks, "I am keenly conscious of the Force behind—Fate, God, our biological past creating our present, whatever one calls it—Mystery certainly—not of the one eternal tragedy of Man in his glorious, self-destructive struggle to make the Force express him instead of being, as an animal is, an infinitesimal incident in its expression .. it is possible to develop a tragic expression in terms of transfigured modern values and symbols in the theatre which may, to some degrees, bring home to members of a modern audience their ennobling identity with the tragic figure on the stage."[70] The inscrutable forces that shape human destiny are the dark layers of man's psyche.

It would be proper to add here that the unconscious is not the only force with which man is struggling today. George R. Coffman reminds us that "to-day Fate is the Social Order, the Inequality of classes, the Economic Cause of a Submerged Fraction..... Whatever we call him (Fate) he still operates to defeat man ; and as long as the dramatics reflects the maladjustment about him we will still have tragedies for the stage."[71]

To conclude, psychoanalysis has enlarged our conception of man. Science has told us a great many things about man and Nature and man's efforts to have an apparent supremacy over Nature. But the ancient conception of man as a helpless creature before some inscrutable and insurmountable force remains infact still. A knowledge of man's psyche, with its formidable unconscious layers and certain startling truths about man's inner self made known to us by psychology and Darwin, would naturally focus the dramatist's attention upon this aspect of man's being. This means that the centre of dramatists engaged in the representation of man's 'real self' would shift to character study and analysis, involving a shake-up of Aristotle's conception of the supremacy of plot over character. But let us make it clear that it is difficult even according to Aristotle to have the one (plot or character) without the other, for the true tragic effect. The central Aristotelian conception of the tragic hero, however, has found full support in psychoanalytical discoveries.

The conception of 'hamartia' or the 'tragic flaw' of Aristotle is the psychological counterpart of the Sin of Pride, the pride of the conscious ego that it can satisfy itself in spite of the unconscious. This, Doris V. Falk says, "in the Greek theatre brought an inevitable destruction of the hero by jealous gods and is analogous to that compulsion to attain the impossible which in a life situation causes destruction of the self."[72] According to Aristotle, the tragic hero is guilty only of miscalculation or a wrong judgement, but Fate compels him to take a path which brings his doom. Similarly, in the present case the unconscious, his heredity compels the hero to do a thing which may bring about his destruction.

Because of the changed or 'transformed' conception of man's real self, fate, and the forces governing his life, many critics think pessimistically about the future of genuine tragedy in the modern world. Since the eighteenth century the conception of magnitude of the hero in tragedy has been modified to include common people among the dramatis personae. Alan Reynolds Thompson[73] notices certain influences in the modern times which may deprive modern tragedy of a hero of magnitude either in the Aristotelian sense or in the neo-Aristotelian or neoclassical heroic sense. The influences hostile to high tragedy noticed by him are democracy, commercialism, science and psychology. Destiny has lost its time-honoured mystery and can now be explained in terms of the psychological unconscious, heredity, or social and environmental forces. But Richard B. Sewall rightly remarks that "the affair with gods has not, in the minds of all our artists, been reduced to an affair with the social order or the environment or the glands. (And) certainly where it comes so, the muse of tragedy walks out ; the universe loses its mystery and (to invoke catharsis for a moment) its terror.

The above discussion has clearly shown that even in the psychological exposition of tragedy, which obviously is not concerned with tragedy as a literary form, many Aristotelian principles are stated and re-defined, though some of them only in indirect hints.

FOOTNOTES

1 Parker, D.H. ed., *Schopenhauer : Selections* (London, 1928), p. 172.

2 *Ibid.*

3 Copleston, F., *Arthur Schopenhauer, Philosopher of Pessimism* (Burns Oates and Wasbourne Ltd., 1946), pp. 79-86.

4 *Ibid.,* p. 89.

5 *Schopenhauer : Selections,* p. 172.

6 *Ibid.,* 172.

7 *Ibid.*

8 *Ibid.* "...the demand for the so-called poetical justice rests on an entire misconception of the nature of tragedy, and indeed, of the nature of the world itself," p. 172.

9 *Ibid.* p. 173.

10 *Ibid.* pp. 128-9.

11 *Arthur Schopenhauer, Philosopher of Pessimism,* p. 108.

12 *Schopenhauer : Selections,* p. 134.

13 Refer to the *Essays in Criticism,* Vol. IV, 1954, Sewall, Richard B., "The Tragic Form," p. 251, for more details on this point of Nietzche's conception of tragedy.

14 Nietzche, *The Birth of Tragedy,* tr., Housman, W.M.A., (London' 1923), p. 23.

15 *Ibid.,* p. 24.

16 *Literary Criticism : A Short History,* p. 563.

17 *The Birth of Tragedy,* p. 25.

18 *Ibid.*

19 *Ibid.,* pp. 25-7.

20 *Ibid.*, p. 27.

21 *Ibid.*, pp. 34 and 61.

22 *Ibid.*, p. 163.

23 *Ibid.*, p. 164.

24 *Ibid.*, p. 167.

25 *Ibid.*,

26 *Ibid.*, p. 170.

27 *Ibid.*, p. 182.

28 *Ibid.*, p. 159.

29 *Ibid.*, p. 193.

30 *Ibid.*, p. 182.

31 *Ibid.*, p. 135.

32 *Oxford Lectures on Poetry* (Macmillan, London, 1955), p. 71.

33 *Ibid.*, p. 72.

34 *Ibid.*, p. 73.

35 *Essays and Studies by Members of the English Association,* Vol. VIII, 1922, Moore, G.C., ed., "Tragedy." p. 17.

36 *Oxford Lectures on Poetry,* p. 83.

37 *Poetry of Experience,* p. 217.

38 Raphael, D.D., *The Paradox of Tragedy* (George Allen and Unwin Ltd., London, 1959), p. 24.

39 See *Horizon,* Vol. XVI, 1947, Trilling, Lionel, "Freud and Literature," pp. 182-200 for Freud's influence on many writers in the modern age.

40 Brown, J.A.C., *Freud and the Post-Freudians* (Penguin, 1962), p. 6.

41 *Ibid.*, p. 7.

42 See *The Psychology of the Unconscious,* p. 76.

See also *Jung's Psychology and its Social Meaning,* p. 13.

43 *Ibid.*

44 *Jung's Psychology and its Social Meaning,* p. 9.

45 See Symonds, Percival M., *Dynamics of Psychotherapy,* (New York, 1957), for a detailed discussion of this point, pp. 312-16.

46 Jung, C.G., *Two Essays on Analytical Psychology,* tr., Hull, R.F.C. (London, 1953), p. 260.

47 Jung, C.G., *The Practice of Psychotherapy,* tr., Hull, R.F.C., (London, 1954), p. 59.

48 *Ibid.*

49 *Two Essays on Analytical Psychology,* p. 260.

50 Allen, Clifford, *Modern Discoveries in Medical Psychology* (Macmillan, London, 1937), p. 93.

51 Lucas, F.L., *Literature and Psychology* (London, 1951), p. 276.

86

52 *Ibid.,* p. 274.

53 *Ibid.,* p. 19.

54 *Ibid.,* p. 80.

55 *Ibid.,* p. 81.

56 *Ibid.,* (footnote)

57 *Ibid.,* p. 278.

58 *Essays in Criticism,* Vol. VI, 1956, Morrell, Roy, "The Psychology of Tragic Pleasure," p. 26.

59 *Ibid.*

60 *Ibid.,* p. 27.

61 *Ibid.,* p. 31.

62 *Sewanee Review,* Vol. L, 1942, Coffman, George R., "Tragedy and a Sense of the Tragic," p. 29.

63 *Ibid.,* p. 31.

64 *Ibid.,* p. 31.

65 *Modern Discoveries in Medical Psychology,* p. 118.

66 *Sewanee Review,* Vol. L, 1942, "Tragedy and a Sense of the Tragic," p. 32.

67 Falk, Doris V., *Eugene O'Neill and the Tragic Tension* (New Jeresy, 1958), p. 6.

68 *Ibid.,* p. 6.

69 O'Cargill, N.B., Fagin, W.J., and Fisher, ed., *Eugene O'Neill and His Plays* (London, 1962), p. 111.

70 *Ibid.,* pp. 125-6.

71 *Sewanee Review,* Vol. L, 1942, "Tragedy and a Sense of the Tragic," p. 32.

72 *Eugene O'Neill and the Tragic Tension,* p. 140.

73 *Essays in Criticism,* Vol. IV, 1954, "The Tragic Form," p. 351.

CHAPTER IV

Final Assessment of Aristotle's Theory of Tragedy

The foregoing chapters have made it clear that Aristotle's theory of tragedy has been variously interpreted and modified through the ages. Every age has tried to justify or disapprove of these principles by applying them to the tragedies currently in vogue or sometimes even by adapting the tragedies to these principles. It is a simple truth of literary criticism that a principle of art enunciated in a particular age has its direct bearing on the literature of that age. It is interpreted, elucidated, sometimes narrowed or even enlarged in the context of later ages in which it 's being reconsidered in relation to creative writing. Literature is the image of life and life means dynamism. Hence it would be dogmatic to claim that a literary principle derived from the literature of an age with its peculiar outlook of life, culture, religion and moral values, would be literally applicable to the literature produced in later ages in different or altered social contexts. Take the example of Aristotle's conception of plot as the soul of tragedy. His emphasis on it, besides its artistic importance, seems to be the result of the image of life represented in the tragedies of his time.[1] For the Greeks, life, external as well as internal, was governed by the moral laws emanating from gods. Their gods were real and they believed in the objective existence of these gods and their supernatural manifestations. Thus, belief in a life of objective reality by implication necessitated its representation in literature, an emphasis on form, on plot or action.[2] This continued until the Middle Ages when God and angels were still real and objective and man's happiness depended upon his being in harmony with a divine order of the universe.

During the Renaissance and the centuries following, the stress shifted from the supernatural reality to the human world, even though the two were united. In the ancient tragedy man's affairs with gods, in which he was involved, were important and not the study of man as such. With the Renaissance and the spread of humanism, the dignity of man was established and his nature and affairs became important and man became the measure of all things. Hence a shift from action to character became inevitable. Another development followed the vogue of democracy, pushing the common man into the centre of tragedy, which in the ancient and Elizabethan ages had been mainly concerned with personages of high rank and great social events.

In the ancient time man was in conflict with gods, with fate and with the supernatural and his destruction, as shown in tragedy, represented the re-establishment of the divine order of the universe.[3] In the Elizabethan times man came in conflict with the natural laws—the moral order of the universe which also involved an inner division between blood and brain, reason and passions. In the modern times, he is in conflict with his unconscious impulses, his heredity and the social and economic forces around him. Appearances and externals of human life change but the essence remains; so Aristotle's theory, if it is interpreted liberally and undogmatically, can cover a good many tragedies of the modern age. If this were done, we shall find that Aristotle did enunciate some principles of art which have universality and a useful applicability to the tragedies written even today. "Aristotelian aesthetic theory," says John Gassner, "is bound to be viewed in our time with the perspectives laid down by modern Romanticism and Realism, terms under which we may include the creative and critical approaches of Symbolism, Expressionism, Surrealism, and modern psychological and social literature."[4] Its relevance, however, to the literature of later ages cannot be gainsaid. In the words of Dowlin, "even now it exercises a greater influence, perhaps, than any other single work of criticism."[5] Let us now briefly summarize Aristotle's principles of tragedy which have stood the test of time and also those which were almost strictly applicable to the tragedies of his time only.

Aristotle's conception of plot in tragedy with the principle of the unity of action, its harmonious organic structure, and its economy, is true, one would agree, with respect to any genuine tragedy. His principle of the 'probable' in 'action', which has a reference to the inner structure of the play and which emphasizes the principle of cause and effect in the plot, has been accepted by all who intend to write effective tragedies. Aristotle's exclusion of the accidental, the irrational and the gratuitous from the plot has engaged the attention of some of the critics who disputed the soundness of this principle on the score that in real life these elements are present and tragedy which represents life should not exclude them.[6] But Aristotle's principles are the principles of art, the essence of which lies in the creation of order out of the chaos of life. An artist gives a selective representation of life and is not obliged to picture the whole of life photographically. It should be borne in mind that the primary function of tragedy is to provide a pleasure which is peculiar to this genre. This means the representation of life in tragedy, the manipulation of plot and the delineation of characters etc., should be effected in a way which may be conducive to the production of this pleasurable effect.

Then Aristotle's principle of 'peripeteia' holds good even today and in fact is of great importance for the production of the proper tragic effect. We pity the hero when his plans go awry and produce results just the opposite of his intention.

This element explains the working of fate in all its forms—ancient as well as modern, though Aristotle does not state this. Again, Aristotle's 'anagnorisis' applied strictly to the revelation of the identity of persons or situations, which the hero had challenged or revolted against in the passion of his vehement reaction, is essentially valid even today. Even now, tragic drama is generally the hero's struggle for self-realization and for discovering the spiritual meaning in life, a revelation which may come to him only in the end. The play begins with an ignorance of the spiritual aspect of life or a larger meaning in life and the whole action leads the hero from darkness to light, from ignorance to 'self knowledge,' though "it is achieved at the price of his ruin."[7] In psychological actions the hero begins with the ignorance of his inner self and the movement of the play amounts to his search for this life which may or may not fructify. All these forms of revelation may be brought under the Aristotelian conception. Then the element of conflict so essential in our view for dramatic action is also implied in Aristotle's theory of tragedy. This is clear from Aristotle's remark that the proper tragic effect is produced when the protagonist is hurt consciously or unconsciously by a person or persons near and dear to him (Chapter XIV of the *Poetics*). This conflict generates the action which develops to a complication and then declines to resolution or denouement.

So far as Aristotle's conception of the hero in tragedy is concerned it apparently contradicts the modern view of man and limits the range of tragedy. But if we interpret Aristotle's concept more liberally it will be found to contain implications of a larger meaning. The concept means in general terms that the tragic hero should be larger than life. He is like us, no doubt, yet he is also different from us in his concern with a large problem, in his exceptional power of action, in his extraordinary capacity to suffer, and vehement refusal of a servile submissiveness to his circumstances and the forces

working against him.[8] His magnitude of character lies in his
great spiritual and intellectual superiority over all others. He
struggles with a universal human problem or even with a
problem (as in the modern times), social or economic, confronting the people of his class. He rises above his personal,
petty and selfish concerns and strives as if to find a solution
for all.[9] Next, the hero should neither be too good nor too
bad ; he must be appropriate to his position ; he must be
consistent throughout the structure of the play, etc. That
the hero should be neither virtuous nor depraved, we have to
accept, if the desired tragic effect is to be produced. But
then one may ask, what about the Archbishop in the *Murder
in the Cathedral* and the hero in *Macbeth* ? Professor E.E.
Stoll considers that it is difficult to reconcile such heroes
with the Aristotelian conception.[10] But one thing can be
remarked here that it is the elevated quality of the character
which matters in tragedy even though the hero is bad in some
respect. Even in his depravity there should be a grandeur
and touch of humanity which do not go with meanness.
Then even an entirely virtuous man, a saint can be a hero in
a tragedy provided he is pictured as human and in some way
like us. This 'human' quality of his would naturally make
him subject to human frailty which in no case would detract
from his virtue and thus would make him a possible character
for tragedy. One is reminded here of Thomas Browne's
remark in the final chapter of *Urn Burial* that we must place
a premium on the aged martyrs who held their shaking hands
before the fire and humanly courted martyrdom through their
terrible ordeal. The necessary quality in him, whether he is
good or bad, should be, as Raphael remarks, "some grandeur
d'ame, a greatness in his effort to resist."[11] He should have
the power to react to the circumstances. A purely innocent
and passive sufferer will be unable to produce the proper
tragic effect. He would elicit only a sentimental emotional
response from the audience.

Then critics have alleged that Aristotle's conception of character leads to the portrayal of types in tragedy and not individuals. This, they think, is because of Aristotle's statement regarding the 'appropriateness' and 'consistency' being essential in tragedy and also because of his laying too much emphasis on plot. F.L. Lucas says that the principle of "appropriateness" would hardly apply to the modern life which is full of "subtleties, complexities and eccentricities undreamed of by Aristotle."[12] So would his conception of 'consistency' not apply to the modern man whose personality is elusive and hardly integrated and which prides itself on its multiplicity.[13] But these elements in character were probably admitted by Aristotle in the interest of the rational order which the artist must impose on life in order to illuminate it. A hero who is a mere bundle of contradictions, a weather-cock to his momently changing moods, may be consonant with the tenets of psychoanalysis but will never be likely to produce the delight peculiar to tragedy as a form of Poetry. Fortunately for us such psychological tragedies form only a small fraction of the twentieth century tragic drama. We have, even to-day, a large number of tragic plays where the protagonists are not only representative figures but they also fully conform to the Aristotelian demand for 'consistency' and 'appropriateness'. Aristotle's conception of character, concludes Butcher, "contains profound truth, and a capacity for adaptation beyond what was immediately present to the mind of the writer."[14]

A greater opposition has been provoked by Aristotle's view of the supremacy of plot over character. It has been said now by many, turning Aristotle upside down, that there can be a tragedy without plot but not without character. This misunderstanding arises, partly at least, from interpreting Aristotle too literally. Here 'action' does not mean, as is thought by many, merely external events ; but, as Butcher says, it includes "mental processes and the motives which underlie the outward events or which result from them."[15] So, "character" in this connection does not mean only dramatis personae but the habit, the bent and tendency, the mental states, the will and emotion of the dramatis personae. 'Ethos' and 'Dianoia' together constitute a dramatic character and not 'ethos' alone. Aristotle's extreme statement that there can be no tragedy without plot but there can be one without 'character' does not mean that he proposes to dispense with character altogether. Humphry House remarks that Aristotle meant by "tragedies without characters" the plays "in which personages go through a change of fortune (probably a change from happiness to misery, rather than the opposite) in which they suffer and act, but act without showing why, without adequately revealing the habit, bent and tendency of their characters and without showing their characters in act, without showing their minds working upon the means to the actualization of their desires."[16] Butcher has agreed[17] that the plot is the differentia of drama and character evolves through 'action'. Then, so far as the emotional effect of tragedy upon the audience is concerned, it is true that plot is more important. But the modern conception of man with the complex inner reality would press its case for character coming first in tragedy. Gassner remarks that it would be an absurd question to ask which comes first, the egg or the chicken. He rightly argues that character depends upon plot for its manifestation in the theatre at least : "We may ask, besides, how character or psychological reality can manifest itself effectively, especially in the theatre, without a sequence of revelatory responses, decisions taken or evaded, and externalized feelings and thoughts. Does not this sequence, too, constitute 'action' or 'plot' ? To what extent is the mental action of discussion, especially when Shaw presents it, *not* action ? Or is the self-revelation of characters not action when Shakespeare writes a soliloquy in *Hamlet* or Strindberg a dramatic monologue in

The Stranger ? Is not even a succession of moods as in Maeterlinck's *The Intruder*, 'action,' and is not the organization of the mood—with a beginning, middle, and end 'with a rising intensity and a final discharge of tension—plot ?"[18]

Thus, if a liberal interpretation is allowed, it would be agreed that it is the inevitable interplay of character and plot which leads the tragedy to its final goal of emotional 'catharsis' in the audience. Even today as ever before, human nature likes story, action, where the most artistic part is the organized sequence, which serves to convince us that even now its validity remains.[19] "In the twentieth century," let us quote Shipley, "marked by continually intensified national and class struggles, and by corresponding intellectual and emotional conflicts, tragedy naturally remains securely wedded to the Aristotelian theory of the supremacy of action."[20]

The other polemical element in Aristotle's conception of tragedy is 'catharsis'. We may interpret it as a medical metaphor, or as "calm of mind, all passion spent" which has been disapproved by George Santayan,[21] who says that "there is rather something in the nature of an exalting effect." Hegel interprets it as reconciling discordant cosmic truths ; psychotherapists find in it a method for releasing the suppressed emotions of their patients to bring normalcy in their emotional life. Lascelles Abercrombie argues[22] (in the manner of F.L. Lucas)[23] that Aristotle's conception of 'catharsis' tends to presuppose a diseased emotional state of the audience, if the medical metaphor or the analogy of the effect of ecstatic music in *Rhetoric* upon the people who were possessed, is taken into consideration as a basis of our understanding this concept. But he concludes that "tragedy certainly does produce an enjoyable and wholesome effect, by rousing in us emotions which in real life would be unpleasantly and perhaps dangerously disturbing."[24] He further remarks that whatever the controversies, "Aristotle's explanation of the function of tragedy was an attempt in the right direction."[25]

Dr. I.A. Richards says that tragedy effects a reconciliation of the two impulses of opposite nature : "Pity, the impulse to approach, and Terror, the impulse to retreat, are brought in Tragedy to a reconciliation[26] which they find no where else, and with them who knows what other allied groups of equally discordant impulses. Their union in an ordered single response is the catharsis by which tragedy is recognized.... This is the explanation of that sense of release, of repose in the midst of stress, of balance and composure, given by Tragedy, for there is no other way in which such impulses, once awakened, can be set at rest without suppression."[27] Dr. Una Ellis-Fermor also has seen a balance of opposing forces in the effect of tragedy, the balance being between "the view that the world is controlled by an alien and a hostile destiny and the view that somehow this apparent evil may be explained in terms of good."[28] Butcher opines that in 'catharsis' the audience by empathy forgets his petty, selfish and daily routine reality of life and is "lifted out of himself," and in the artistic process of heightening, "he becomes one with the tragic sufferer and though him with humanity at large."[29] In this process lies the true pleasure of tragedy [30]

Whatever the terminology of the interpretations of 'catharsis,' the fact remains that tragedy does have a pleasurable effect upon the audience which is peculiar to this form of literature. Tragedy produces, all of us would readily agree, the emotions of pity and fear and that by the end of the last Act in the play the emotional stir in us is calmed, there comes "some incomprehensible repose"[31] and a pleasurable effect is accompanied with this. F.R. Leavis remarks, taking the term in its wider implications : "If 'calm' may properly be predicated of the tragic experience, it is certainly not 'calm of mind, all passion spent' in the natural suggestion of that phrase. According to what seems valid in the current notion of the tragic, there is rather something in the nature of an exalting effect. We have contemplated a painful action, involving death and the destruction of the good, admirable and sympathetic. and yet instead of being depressed, we enjoy a sense of enhanced vitality."[32] Whether the term was borrowed from the current medical terminology or was amenable to a wider, moral and spiritual interpretation, is difficult to decide, but one thing should be clear that Aristotle's approach was aesthetic, not moral. If any moral effect may emerge from tragedy, it is only by implications which gives it a secondary place. The principle holds true in case of any genuine tragedy which has been or may be written.

It is for the production of this effect that Aristotle defines the nature of action, hero, style, etc. in tragedy. He disapproves of a tragedy which depends for its effect upon any theatrical, histrionic or scenic device and lays stress on the artistic handling of plot and the elements integral to the structure of the play which has been misinterpreted by critics like John A.M. Rillie[33], who find in the conception of Aristotle an enunciation of the principle of melodrama and not of tragedy.

Aristotle's remarks on style and diction which should neither be unduly rhetorical nor mean, but suitable to the purpose and varying according to the change in situations, have been accepted at all hands. His principle of style does not show any rigidity about the exclusive use of verse or prose but stresses only the proper and effective use of words, structure, rhythm, etc.

Here it would be proper to remind ourselves of what Bernard Weinburg has described[34] as a right approach to Aristotle, that he (Aristotle) took these elements of tragedy in their totality for the production of its proper effect. It would be a wrong approach to him to take up isolated elements of tragedy and try to find out how far these are conducive to the production of the tragic effect.

Now let us point out those elements also in the Aristotelian conception of tragedy which would not be readily accepted today. His conception, for example, of the element of 'appropriateness' and 'consistency' in the tragic characters cannot be strictly applicable to the hero in the modern psychological and social context of the world in which multiplicity, incongruity and inconsistency in man's personality would attract a tragedian much more than the integrated and balanced personality of man. But as shown earlier, consistency of the hero within the structure of the play would always be deemed good for a greater tragic effect. Then, the element of chorus has been in many cases replaced by elaborate stage direction and is not suitable to the present context of symbolic and expressionistic technique, though some playwrights have used it successfully.

Thus, only if an undogmatic and liberal approach is adopted (which Aristotle had intended)[35], then alone a reasonably correct appraisal of the principles in the *Poetics* can be made. But there are still critics who would frown upon us at the very mention of the application of Aristotle's principles to the tragedies written in an age with radically changed situations. Sewall remarks, "no artist according to Croce will submit to the servitude of the traditional definition: that a tragedy must have a subject of a certain kind, characters of a certain kind, and plot of a certain kind and length. Each work of art is a world in itself, "a creation, not a reflection, a monument, not a document."[36] But this would mean substituting one dogmatism for another, and Sewall is aware of the danger that "such text-book categories and their tendency (as of measuring every tragedy strictly with Aristotelian scale), if carried too far, would rationalize art out of existence."[37] If we accept Croce's stand, then it would tend to mean that every piece of art is to be judged by the critic himself independent of any generally accepted scale of judgement, the danger of subjective criticism would become inevitable. An equally obvious inadequacy can be shown in the case of an exclusively objective criticism also which bases its judgements on some so-called accepted principles of art. Huntington Cairns remarks that "the first task that confronts literary criticism, if it wishes to correct its present chaotic condition, is to determine whether it can give valid judgements or not. It can only do that by formulating propositions in terms of which literature should be judged and endeavouring to ascertain whether those propositions are consistent, whether they have been properly deduced from other propositions,"[38] and see that they are tested "both dialectically and against the practices of writers."[39] We cannot have propositions, scales of judgement which are of absolute character. "They will always be provisional and subject to the corrections required by the discoveries of the creative impulses."[40]

Whether or not we proclaim that we are following Aristotle's principles in analysing tragedies, the fact is that we do follow them, some unconsciously, some undogmatically, and some fanatically. But if a reasonable and liberal approach is adopted in interpreting Aristotle, we would find a large scope and a great usefulness for the applicability of his principles to a great many tragedies. We can safely conclude that Aristotle's conception of tragedy admits of variations and entertains no rigidity. Thematic as well as structural variations from one age to another and from one writer to another would have to be accepted. Aristotle's principles would be most useful as a guiding beacon to critics and playwrights and not as a deadweight on their critical judgement and creative impulse.

We are now in a position to illustrate the points discussed above by a critical analysis of a set of modern tragic plays, representing the principal types, which will occupy the ensuing chapters of our study.

FOOTNOTES

1 See Carry, M., and Haarhoff, T.J., *Life and Thought in the Greek and Roman World* (Methuen, London, 1940), for a detailed picture of the life represented in the Attic tragedies, pp. 239-56.

2 See *The Times Literary Supplement,* Jan. 7, 1965, Review, Lattimore, Richmond, *Story Pattern in Greek Tragedy* (Athlone Press, 1964), p. 12.

3 See Kitto, H.D.F., *The Greeks* (Penguin, 1957), pp. 194-204.

4 *Aristotle's Theory of Poetry and Fine Art,* Gassner, John, Introduction, p. xlviii.

5 *The Review of English Studies,* Vol. XVII, 1941, Dowlin, Corneli March, "Plot as an Essential in Poetry," p. 166.

6 *Ibid.*

7 Steiner, George, *The Death of Tragedy* (Faber and Faber, London, 1961), p. 169.

8 Scholes Robert, ed., *Approaches to the Novel : Material for a Poetics,* Free, Northrop, "Fictional Modes," (Chandler Publishing Co., San Francisco, 1961), p. 32.

Also refer to the *Paradox of Tragedy,* p. 30.

9 *Times Literary Supplement,* Aug. 14, 1953, Review, Weisinger, H., *Tragedy and the Paradox of the Fortunate Fall,* p. 522.

10 *Shakespeare and Other Masters* (Cambridge, 1940), p. 69.

11 *The Paradox of Tragedy,* p. 26.

12 *Tragedy : Serious Drama in Relation to Aristotle's Poetics,* p. 132.

13 *Poetry of Experience* (Langbaum remarks that "the whole Aristotelian analysis, leading through congruency and appropriateness to the primacy of action over character, breaks down, once we regard the characters as, in the democratic sense, people rather than as hierarchica categories of people." p. 221.)

14 *Aristotle's Theory of Poetry and Fine Art,* pp. 332-3.

15 *Ibid.,* p. 337.

16 *Aristotle's Poetics* (Rupert Hart-Davis, London, 1961), p. 74.

17 *Aristotle's Theory of Poetry and Fine Art,* pp. 343-6.

18 *Ibid.,* Introduction, p. liii.

Also refer to *Approaches to the Novel,* Crane, R.S., "The Conception of Plot," pp. 160-62, for a comprehensive conception of an enlarged interpretation of plot in any piece of art.

19 Refer to Forster, E.M., *Aspects of the Novel* (Pelican, 1964), pp. 91-94.

20 *Dictionary of World Literary Terms* (Littlefield, Adams and Co., New Jersey, 1962), p. 422.

21 *Scrutiny*, Vol. IV, 1936, "Tragic Philosophy," p. 127.

22 *Principles of Literary Criticism,* (Vora and Co., Bombay, 1962), pp. 107-9.

23 *Tragedy: Serious Drama in Relation to Aristotle's Poetics,* pp. 47-8.

24 *Principles of Literary Criticism,* p. 110.

25 *Ibid.,* p. 109.

26 *English, The Magazine of the English Association,* Vol. VI, No. 34, Spring, 1947, Leech, Clifford, "The Implications of Tragedy," pp. 178-9.

27 *Principles of Literary Criticism* (Routledge and Kegan Paul, London, 1961), pp. 245-6.

28 *The Frontiers of Drama,* (Methuen, London, 1946). Her standpoint has been critically examined by Clifford Leech in the article mentioned above, pp. 179-80.

29 *Aristotle's Theory of Poetry and Fine Art,* pp. 265-7.

30 *Lectures in Criticism,* Ransom, John, "The Literary Criticism of Aristotle," pp. 26-7. (Here Ransom says that pity and fear are painful, disturbing emotions in our life and tragedy "mitigates these emotions" He does not like the analogy of the purgation emotions in tragedy : "I can't help but find this figure of purgation inept, it is too hard to apply it and see how the clearing out of the painful emotions must follow from artificially prompting them, there must be subtler mechanism at work. Yet who will disagree with him, once the point is made, and deny that somehow composure is restored to the auditors of proper drama and even to its readers.")

31 *The Death of Tragedy,* p. 9.

32 *The Common Pursuit* (Chatto and Windus, London, 1958), p. 127.

33 *Review of English Studies,* Vol. XIII, 1962, "Melodramatic Device in T.S. Eliot," pp. 267-70.

34 *Comparative Literature,* Vol. V, No. 2, 1953, "From Aristotle to Pseudo-Aristotle," pp. 98-103.

35 *Poetics,* IV-2.

It is clear from his remark : "Whether Tragedy has as yet perfected its proper types or not, and whether it is to be judged in itself, or in relation also to the audience—this raises another question."

36 *Essays in Criticism,* Vol. IV, 1954, "Tragic Form," p. 345.

37 *Ibid.*

38 *Lectures in Criticism,* Introduction, p. 4.

39 *Ibid.,* p. 6.

40 *Ibid.*

CHAPTER V

Critical Examination of Modern Tragic Plays

Ibsen's Ghosts

The Ghosts is a play in three Acts. As the play opens, we learn that Oswald, the twenty-six year old son of Mrs. Alving, has come back home from Paris where he was sent for education at the early age of seven and where he later set up as an artist. Oswald's father, Captain Alving, has been dead several years and Mrs. Alving, with the help of Pastor Manders, is in the process of liquidating the estate of her deceased husband. Her husband had been accepted by the local society as a respectable gentleman, a charming officer, a faithful husband and a loving father. But, in fact, he was a rake, a libertine, an aimless man and an addict to drink. He seduced Joana, the parlour-maid, and begot Regina, now a young girl, under the patronage of Mrs. Alving. Engstrand, the supposed father of Regina, married her mother, Joana, who died shortly. He is at present employed as a carpenter in the construction of the Orphanage which Mrs. Alving is getting ready as a memorial to her husband. He is anxious to take Regina with him in order to make capital out of her beauty and youth, while the latter is averse to the move. Oswald is inclined to her as she is to him in utter ignorance of their actual relationship with each other. From the conversation between Mrs. Alving and the Pastor we gather that Oswald was sent to Paris by his mother in a bid to shield him from the evil influence of his father, but during his stay in Paris, the mother did her best, through her letters, to build the image of an ideal father, in the mind of her son. She did not want her son to know about the reality of her husband's life. All this she has done to bury the dead past and live in a life of joy with and through her son. Now she thinks that by dissociating herself from all that her husband has left behind, she would be able to crown her effort. The Orphanage erected to the memory of the dead man, out of his own capital, is part of that design to free herself from the conventional bondage which she has always been anxious to repudiate. The evolution of the plot, however, is a process of the bitterly ironical revelation that the ghost of the past cannot be laid up and the tie with the dissolute husband has bitten into her flesh and can be dissolved only with the end of her life and of all she cherishes most.

This story has been planned with an artistic compactness and great economy, which proclaim artistic maturity.[1] *The Ghosts* is a play of "ripe circumstances" or a drama of "retrospective analysis." The play begins in the midst of a crisis, at the point when the Orphanage is ready for opening. What has happened before is revealed through conversations with a consummate skill and in the most 'probable' manner: for example, Mrs Alving's running away from her husband to Manders after barely a year of her married life and her subsequent resignation to the demands of the conventional morality and social decorum, keeping up the form of union from which the soul has departed. The entry of Oswald evokes a spontaneous exclamation from the Pastor who is surprised at the striking resemblance of the young man to his father, a re-incarnation, as it were, of the father in the son. Oswald's 'joy in life' picture of Paris shocks his sensibilities and the situation is intolerable when Mrs. Alving also chimes in with her son, 'my loneliness' etc. Then Pastor Mander asserts his authority with : "It is your priest that stands before you, just as he hid once at the most critical moment of your life." He chides her in a manner which immediately reminds Mrs. Alving of her past : "Just as once you forsook your duty as a wife, so since then, you have forsaken your duty as a mother....Your duties as a mother were irksome to you, so you sent your child away among strangers...." etc. Mrs. Alving now feels compelled to lay bare the very truth of life with which she has lived with her husband, who never gave up philandering. She sent her son away from her, not because she wanted to rid herself of the irksome duty of a mother, but because she wanted to keep her son away from her husband's environment.

The main structure of the plot and its development are characterised by rapidity of movement, directness and intensity of action, economy and compactness of the manipulation of events.[2] The action begins with the preparation for the opening of the Orphanage. We are soon informed that Mrs. Alving is constructing this Orphanage to retain the fiction of respectability of her husband's name and, more than this, to release herself and Oswald from their ties with Captain Alving. In the beginning of the action itself we get an impression that Mrs. Alving has been struggling for attaining the 'joy of life' through independence from the influences of her husband and is now hopeful of peace through Oswald. But the whole of the subsequent development of the story is an ironical revelation, stroke after stroke, that she cannot escape the sinister touch of her own past. The climax of the action reaches rapidly when Mrs. Alving finds Oswald and Regina in the kitchen when Oswald is trying to enact the sordid sex-drama of his father. This symbolizes Oswald's inheritance of his father's sensuality. Here the 'reversal of situation' and 'recognition', as envisaged by Aristotle, take place simultaneously. The appearance of Captain Alving's 'disease' in Oswald at a time when Mrs. Alving is taking great pains to release herself and Oswald from all ties with the depraved Captain, is a very strong premonition of the inevitability of Mrs. Alving's defeat. She realizes now that the thing she has been struggling to avert is too strongly present in her son. She discovers the truth now when she sees "the couple in the conservatory—over again." She realizes that her submission to the marriage—yoke was the fatal mistake and constitutes the doom for her and Oswald, the sole anchor of her hope. After this climax, the action moves on to another calamitous event, the burning down of the Orphanage. This apparently might indicate the end of Captain Alving in the life of Mrs. Alving and Oswald. But this is followed by the most startling and cruel revelation for poor Mrs. Alving, the revelation that her son's life is blasted by the virus of his father's disease. Here the heroine's struggles and her heroic efforts to achieve her goal come to a tragic end. Her conflict with a force which now appears to be far stronger than she had guessed, ends in her crushing defeat. The full force of her complicity in the thoughtless crime done to her son comes out in the sardonic taunt of the agonized young man—"what a life." She is eventually brought down to the horrible realization that her crippled son wants a different 'sun or light' altogether for his release from the strangle-hold of his depression—'the Sun' for which he cries is the light hidden in the womb of death for which he had already made a proper and effective provision.

The plot of the play is a complete whole. It has a beginning, a middle and an end and the action develops logically and naturally. The action begins at a definite stage in Mrs. Alving's struggle to free herself from her husband's ties. This is when the Orphanage is ready for opening. This struggle seems to end in failure as the thing she has been trying to eradicate is present in the very source of her future happiness. But she does not give up her efforts and thus keeps the action moving on the principle of cause and effect. The action ends with the shattering of the heroine's hope for the fulfilment of which she has been struggling. At the close of the action no cause remains for any further extension of the plot. Besides the plot being a complete whole as demanded by Aristotle, it has 'magnitude'. As we have shown the action develops naturally though rapidly from the beginning of the play. We do not have any impression that the length of the plot was too short to allow the logical development of the action to take place, or too long to blur the main issue of the action and admit of irrelevant events to mar the tragic effect and detract from the compactness of the action The "retrospective method" of action used in the play is a proof of this. This method has been used to keep out of the main body of the 'action' those events which are essential, but detrimental to the structural unity of the action.

The play has a 'complex' plot which, Aristotle says, is preferable to the 'simple' one, in as much as the 'reversal of situation' and 'recognition,' which are essential to this type of plot, are present here. The 'reversal of situation' occurs when Mrs. Alving learns with a great shock, from the behaviour of Oswald, her sole sustainer of future happiness, that the ghost of her husband is abroad to blast her complacency. The action naturally from now onward develops rapidly to the conclusion of the final shattering of Mrs. Alving's hope. The 'reversal of situation' brings out the truth for Mrs. Alving and for us also that her living with her husband—her adherence to matrimonial morality—has already sealed her fate. Then the 'reversal of situation' is steeped in dramatic irony. For example, Oswald comes to the room where Mrs. Alving and Pastor Manders are sitting and conversing, with his father's pipe in his mouth. Mrs. Alving asks him not to smoke in the room there, because she does not want to see even the most insignificant trait of his father in Oswald. He goes to the kitchen to smoke. Mrs. Alving then hears a voice from the kitchen, "Oswald; Are you mad; Let me go." This shows that Mrs. Alving who did not like to see even a trace of external affinity of her son with his father, sends him to the kitchen as if to provide occasion for the most emphatic demonstration of the fatal tie that links the miserable youth to his 'gay' father.

Now this 'complex' plot, according to Aristotle, has two definite stages in its development—'complication' and 'unravelling.' The 'complication' includes the action from the beginning to the climatic point where it becomes clear that Mrs. Alving's life-long struggle may end in failure. The 'unravelling' of the action is simply the further unfolding of the depth of the dead man's involvement in the young son who is all but wrecked for his whole life. The plot, indeed, does not end on a note of reconciliation, 'calm of mind, all passion spent,' but on a point of the truest and most tragic realization for the mother, that she has been an active though unconscious instrument in destroying the life which she gave in union with her 'tainted' husband, to her luckless son. Then the plot is almost perfect in point of the Aristotelian unity of action. The action of the *Ghosts* from the beginning to the end is a continuous and developing one. Beginning in the midst of a crisis, it grows rapidly but logically. "The play deals with a series of closely related events, primarily revelations, which demonstrate Mrs. Alving's tragic folly in having obeyed the dictates of convention many years before."[3] Events which have happened before the time when the action begins, are narrated at most appropriate places. Nothing in the plot is superfluous, uncalled for, gratuitous or forced in the structure. The three main events coming at the end of the three Acts, with their lurid flashes of revelation on the mind of alarmed Mrs. Alving are not three unconnected incidents. They are the three major movements in the same single current of the action. The action has the "simplicity and directness of a Greek drama; there is an entire absence of any decorative detail ; gaunt, severe and unrelenting the story grows upon the stage from the first whisper of Regina to the final murmur of Oswald."[4] Nothing can be extracted from the action without doing a substantial harm to the structure. The whole structure is built on the principle of 'probability,' or 'necessity'. Even the two "coincidences, for example, the fire in the orphan asylum erected in honour of Alving and the discovery of the illness of Alving's son, are related to the revelation that Mrs. Alving's conformity to convention in returning to her husband had been a disastrous error of judgement."[5] Thus these events which might otherwise appear accidents have symbolical significance[6] and are integral to the structure which leads to Mrs. Alving's revelation of the truth. Thus the plot has an "absolute economy of action and an inevitable approach of the climax."[7] The intensity of the action has been enhanced by the observance of the unities of time and place. The whole action takes place in Mrs. Alving's country house and the duration of the action does not exceed the limits of 'a single revolution of the sun.'

Thus here we find almost all the elements of an artistic plot in tragedy as described by Aristotle. The *Ghosts* has an almost perfect plot. William Archer says that the *Ghosts* has "naturalness of exposition, suppleness of development and... a general untheatricality of treatment."[8] It has the directness, intensity and simplicity of a Greek tragedy.

After the consideration of plot, we come to the next important element in the *Ghosts*, which is the nature of the tragic protagonist. Mrs. Alving is the chief character in the play with an admirable capacity for suffering. She has lived with her syphilitic husband and has "suffered a good deal in this house. To keep him at home in the evening—and at night—I have had to play the part of boon companion in his secret drinking-bouts in his room up there. I have had to sit there alone with him, have had to hob-nob and drink with him, have had to listen to his ribald senseless talk, have had to fight with brute force to get him to bed" (Act I). The very narration of her sufferings makes Manders tremble. She suffered all this because, she says, "I had my little boy, and endured it for his sake."

She has pinned her hope for happiness in her son. She has taken great cares in keeping the boy away from her husband, lest "he would be poisoned if he breathed the air of the polluted house." She has undertaken to do a heroic job. She has "an uneasy conscience" because of her fear that "it was impossible that the truth (of her husband's depravity) should not come out and be believed. That is why the Orphanage is to exist, to silence all rumours and clear away all doubt." (Act. I). She says that she "had another very good reason" for this : "I did not wish Oswald, my own son to inherit a penny that belonged to his father." She would not allow anything of his father to "pass into his hands." "My son shall have everything from me, I am determined," declares Mrs. Alving. It is in this determination of the heroine to live happily with and through Oswald that we perceive the main sting of her tragic defeat. In the very first Act we see that she has discovered the Ghosts. "The couple in the conservatory over again" hints at her inevitable confrontation with the force of heredity which would eventually defeat her. But she does not yield to it and puts up a desperate fight with despair. The Orphanage—the symbol of the fiction of her husband's respectability and of her freedom from the ties of her husband—burns down. But even this does not deter her in her struggle ro achieve her goal. The Orphanage has burnt down; Mrs. Alving says. "I have something else to think about now." Now she thinks that if she unburdened herself of the secret of Regina's birth and of Mr. Alving's depravity to Oswald and Regina, everything would be set right and the vicious circle of hereditary sin would be broken. But the desired result does not come. Regina, knowing the truth of her life, goes away and refuses "to stay here in the country and wear myself out looking after invalids " She says, "And I have got the joy of life in me, too, Mrs. Alving,... if Oswald takes after his father, it is just likely, I take after my mother." And she goes away. Oswald sinks into a complete mental collapse. Thus, it is clear that Mrs. Alving has great power for suffering and capacity for struggling to achieve her goal, which at once raises her stature and makes her larger than life. Now though Aristotle does give illustrations of heroes like Oedipus and his conception of the tragic hero, who has 'high rank', may mean social status, yet in spirit the principle implies that the hero should have uncommon spiritual strength, extraordinary capacity to suffer, indefatigable power to react to his situation, and to feel undeterred by his failures in his attempts. It is by virtue of these qualities in him that the hero becomes larger than life, even though he may have just a bourgeois social status. Mrs. Alving undoubtedly becomes larger than life in her capacity to suffer and her unrelenting struggle to achieve her goal. At the same time she is the most human character to engage our sympathies. Her passions and desires of a happy life are shared by humanity at large. The quality of human goodness in her is exemplified by her genuine concern even for the welfare of Regina, the living memento of her late husband's depravity which has been the cause of her ruin. Mrs. Alving suffers undeservedly hence we pity her and feel sympathy for her. She suffers, though not exclusively, because of her mistake or moral timidity the element of 'hamartia' in her. She takes a wrong step in her life in going back to her husband from whom she had run away. She keeps up the decorum of a devoted wife with the legal husband who is really out of the pale of her love and sympathy. Thus she suffers, and her suffering, though not wholly unmerited in regard to her 'hamartia,' excites our pity because she struggles with a force—heredity—which blindly crushes her hopes.

Sverre Arestad[9] has remarked that Mrs. Alving "while

possessing admirable qualities, lacks those qualities which would have made her a heroic character." And "without a protagonist of heroic proportion, high tragedy is unthinkable, and perhaps too, successful tragedy of any kind." Now whether the character is of heroic proportions or not, depends upon the answer to the important question we may ask in this respect. The question would be whether man is the master of his destiny. How far he, of his free will, may determine how he shall live and how he shall die? The struggle of the hero should lead to an answer to this question. The hero should not merely be just a poor creature struggling hopelessly and as a tool of circumstances. Mrs. Alving makes efforts to find a solution out of the present situation for the "joy of life" for herself, and at the same time, she reveals abundant compassion for the two young people—Regina and Oswald—whose destinies have been crossed and whose lives will be forfeit if no solution were found. She is thus struggling with an enormous problem. "The enormity of her problem, in fact, the hopelessness of attaining any kind of solution to it, is symbolized by the captain's legacy to her through her son."[10] Wherever Mrs. Alving turns, she finds an obstruction and she fails. But she tries again. In this relentlessness of will lies her heroism.

Pastor Menders is the root cause of Mrs. Alving's tragedy. He is the constant barrier in her way of achieving a solution to the problem of her life. She tries within one year of her marriage to dissociate herself from her husband and runs away to Manders whom she loves. Manders preaches to her, upbraids her and sends her back to her husband to live miserably ever after. Her second effort towards the solution of her problem lies in her erecting the Orphan asylum. Significantly this too burns down owing to Manders carelessness—"Manders should be the cause of such a thing !" exclaims Engstrand. Mrs. Alying now proposes to try another means and her face glows with hope because she thinks she has got the solution. Oswald describes the conditions at home, contrasting them with the conditions in Paris where the "joy of life" serves as the basis of man's philosophy of life. Mrs. Alving is now convinced that she need not conceal the truth from Oswald and Regina of Captain Alving's depravity and its influence on their lives. She suddenly realizes its efficacy: "I see it now for the first time. And now I can speak. Now I can speak. Now, my son, you shall know the whole truth. Oswald! Regina!" But when Mrs. Alving is preparing to unburden herself to the children, Oswald utters very symbolically significant words : "Hush !—here is the parson." These words symbolize Manders' being the epitome of obstructions for Mrs. Alving which she ought to get over. Pastor Manders, remarks Arestad, "represents the jumbled web of imponderables which the individual must grasp either intellectually or intuitively.[11] Mrs. Alving's failure to conquer Manders proves her inferior to the task which has been set for her, or which she herself has undertaken. After a life-time effort, "she is as helpless against him (Manders) as she was on the fateful day twenty-five years earlier when he sent her back to her husband. She is now forced to the admission that the human being is but a mote, tossed about on the currents of circumstances."[12] A tragic hero should not be "tossed about on the currents of circumstances;" he should rather rise above these circumstances; he should not act as their tool but as an individual who reacts to them and is capable of putting up a fight with them. Mrs. Alving falls short of the tragic stature; she "represents the hopelessness of man caught up in an impersonal mechanistic order of thing. Her conflict arose as a result of her effort to coerce from this fortuitous, fickle order, a semblance of meaning which would have been compatible with the dignity of man."[13] But she fails to accomplish her mission.

Again, the character of Mrs. Alving is represented in the deterministic order of the world, where, Arestad says, she is given no opportunity of choice which is essential for a tragic hero. The tragic hero does not merely resign himself to the current of the circumstances, and loses his individuality. He has certain alternative choices open to him. He chooses one and sticks to it whole-heartedly. It is in this conviction in the choice that the hero gains extraordinary power of action and his failure resulting from this exalts his stature and establishes the dignity of man. But if tragic nobility of character depends upon the fact that "the hero falls by choosing wrongly, then in the necessity of accepting responsibility for his choice and of learning through suffering lies the ennobling effect of tragedy."[14]

So we can say that Mrs. Alving does have the tragic proportion in her character. She realizes in her defeat, her mistake that her wrong choice, her error of judgement, has done irreparable harm to her. She struggles with heredity, the counterpart of the Greek Fate. She is foiled in her attempts more than once but her tenacity of purpose holds, and she tries relentlessly to retrieve her chance of life till, in the end, she is vanquished past hope. In her defeat which comes after her strenuous struggle, Mrs. Alving is exalted, though the true tragic emotion of exaltation is subdued and we fail to exclaim, "Look at her ; she never had that grandeur and dignity as now she has in her defeat." The 'problem' posed in the play is too rational and psychological to enforce the protagonist's spiritual splendour in the tragic defeat or failure. Mrs. Alving, however, exhibits one great trait in common with the noted tragic figures of all ages. It is her capacity to develop from the web of her experiences a growing insight into the meaning and mystery of life.

The sharpened insight changes radically her earlier attitude towards her past and its connection with the present: "Ghosts. When I heard Regina and Oswald in there, it was just like seeing ghosts before my eyes. I am half-inclined to think we are all ghosts, Mr. Manders. It is not only what we have inherited from our fathers and mothers that exists again in us, but all sorts of old dead ideas and all kinds of old dead beliefs and things of that kind. They are not actually alive in us ; but they are dormant, all the same, and so we can never be rid of them....There must be ghosts all over the world." Here we have a revelation of a universal truth attained intuitively ; here Mrs. Alving's character is exalted to a level where she begins to feel concerned with a problem, which, she has discovered, is a universal one.[15] It is this trait of Mrs. Alving which Clara F. McIntyre[16] would accept as the distinguishing feature of the *Ghosts* as a tragedy.

Thus Mrs. Alving's goodness, her essential humanity, the element of 'hamartia' in her character as the cause of her suffering, her consistent adherence to her purpose which she has espoused whole-heartedly, her heroic struggle and her defeat—the end of the life of hope in the end—are the features which conform to the Aristotelian conception of the tragic hero. She is demonstrably inferior to Oedipus and Electra in social and spiritual stature, yet the dilemma which confronts her is akin to that of her Greek counterparts and in her own way she emerges a sadder and wiser mortal out of her tragic ordeal. She eventually accepts the painful truth that 'death alone is the Lucina' of her tragic life.

Mr. Thompson in *Melodrama and Tragedy*[17] insists upon the 'universality' of the subject-matter as the distinguishing feature of a tragedy. The *Ghosts* has been bitterly criticized for its subject-matter which many critics hold is not universal. Critics like Clement Scott have attacked the play for its preoccupation with an obscene problem of sex and disease which is unsuitable for any serious literary treatment.[18] Ibsen's contemporaries condemned the *Ghosts* because of their misunderstanding of the play. They took Oswald as the hero of the play and not Mrs. Alving and "accused Ibsen, therefore, of indulging primarily in a grossly indelicate physiological-clinical study in degenerate heredity."[19] But Oswald is, in fact, only incidental to the purpose of the dramatist and his disease and his father" depravity as such are not the main problem of the play. The main problem of the play is inheritance and the effort of man to get over it to attain happiness. Now, nobody would agree with Clement Scott's interpretation of the subject-matter that "it is an essay on heredity and contagious disease, and probable incest cut into length—not a play at all."[20] Thomas H. Dickinson remarks[21] that "it is best in such cases, if no attempt is made at defence—since the attacks are irrelevant, defence will only give away the artist's case." Again, as Goethe has said, no subject-matter is unsuitable for poetic treatment : "no real circumstance remains unpoetic so long as the poet knows how to use it."[22] Even the religious stage of Athens decided lust and incest to be the most powerful motives of high tragedy.

S.H. Butcher observes that Ibsen's plays are parochial and the subject-matter is not universalized. And unless the subject-matter admits of being universalized, "fear cannot be combined with the proper measure of pity."[23] He thinks that "within the limited circle of a bourgeois society a great action is hardly capable of being unfolded."[24] "A parochial drama," Butcher further says, "where the hero struggles against the cramping conditions of his normal life, sometimes with all the ardour of aspiring hope, more often in the spirit of egoistic self-assertion which mistakes the measure of the individual's powers, can hardly rise to tragic dignity.[25] An Ibsen play, according to Butcher, always "moves on the flat levels of existence" and "always retains traces of an inherent littleness." George Steiner also finds that the *Ghosts* deals with temporal remedies. "Tragedy", he says, ' speaks not of secular dilemmas which may be resolved by rational innovation, but of the unaltering bias toward inhumanity and destruction in the drift of the world."[26] "Where the causes of disaster are temporal, where the conflict can be resolved through technical or social means, we may have serious drama but not tragedy."[27]   More pliant divorce laws, declares Steiner, "could not alter the fate of Agamemnon; social psychiatry is no answer to Oedipus."[28] But the crisis in the *Ghosts*, as also in all Ibsen's plays, could be resolved by a saner and more reasonable approach to marriage morality.

Now an objective interpretation of the *Ghosts* will make it clear that so far as conventional morality and its effect upon individual freedom and happiness are concerned, the play does have a temporal and parochial problem and it does seem to indicate that happiness and freedom in the true sense of the terms can be attained only when the conventional sense of morality is buried. But if we give a moment's thought to the problem, it becomes clear that as the action moves we feel concerned at the heroine's conflict with heredity rather than with conventional morality as such, though the latter is, no doubt, the cause of the former. It is this force of heredity which makes man helpless. So the problem here is deeper enough. No law will ever be able to solve the problem of heredity. It is not merely the question of the inheritance of "venereal disease" and "sensual depravity" but a host of hereditary traits which may always baffle posterity. Moreover, in the *Ghosts* "heredity itself is conceived in a manner that suggests the Greek idea of fate and retribution rather than the dull pronunciamentos of a eugenics forum; Oswald's hereditary disease is virtually the domestic Ate of the Alvings."[29] At the end of the play we feel awed at the inevitability of Mrs. Alving's failure in her struggle with a force which is the counterpart of the Greek conception of fate.

Considered in this light, the subject-matter becomes "so significant, and its meaning capable of such extension, that through it we discern the higher laws which rule the world,"[30] and that higher law is heredity as fate and gods were in the Greek tragedies. The action is extended far beyond "the private life of an individual"[31] and Mrs. Alving's utterance on her sudden realization of truth, the ghost she saw in Oswald, assumes a larger application and is extended to the world at large.[32] Alrik Gustafson rightly says that the play may have a "melodramatic" theme for many superficial students. But the 'scenes in which Mrs. Alving appears are by and large invested with the note of high tragedy in the old Greek sense and arouse our sympathy in a manner consistent with the greatest traditions of pure tragedy."[33]

Thus, the subject-matter of the *Ghosts* is serious and universal as demanded by Aristotle, which naturally leads us to the consideration of the tragic effect of the play upon the mind of the audience. Mr. Sverre Arestad's explanation of the failure of the tragic effect of the *Ghosts* stresses some fundamental points and needs to be quoted in detail :

"In larger part, our failure to enjoy the tragic experience in the *Ghosts* is due to the breakdown of an established moral order, which in turn undermined the formerly accepted value ... In a valueless naturalistic order the protagonist was in fact deprived of the freedom of individual choice (he could choose, but any choice was meaningless), which would appear to be a necessary action for successful tragedy."[34] He further says : "the dramas written within the naturalistic tradition leave us with feelings of defeat and dissatisfaction, for we are merely witness to man as a tool of senseless, impersonal natural forces, and we are denied the tragic catharsis and thereby fail to experience emotional equilibrium. Paradoxically, Ibsen's failure to create successful naturalistic tragedy cannot be ascribed to the middle-class protagonist.... It would seem from a study of Ibsen's concept of tragedy that successful tragedy is dependent in the final analysis upon the age-old conditions, with their basis in moral values, where individual initiative, reflected in freedom of choice and of action obtains."[35] Again, Arestad argues that the play has failed to reach the goal it has set before it, because "neither Mrs. Alving's tragic quest nor the poet's vision of human life

has been fulfilled."[36]   This is clear when Mrs. Alving returns
to her husband; she has to face a situation out of which
develops her search for an understanding of human existence.
"Before the play ends this search terminates in a meaningless
nothingness for her and for us, for the whole fabric of her
desired world collapses about her in a nightmarish void,
from which she can derive no comfort and no guide for the
fateful decision that has been forced upon her."[37]

It is undeniable that the full tragic effect of exaltation, of
'catharsis,' is not felt. But we do feel a subdued sense of
exaltation at the close of the play, which is brought home to
us by her defeat after her heroic struggle, by the singleness
of her aim and whole-hearted effort to realize it. It is hard
to agree with Arestad[38] that the tragic effort is not realized
because the thesis of the *Ghosts* remains so strong in the
mind of the audience as their curiosity is left unlulled : "Will
Mrs. Alving or will she not give Oswald the poison which
will reduce to physical death the mindless and spiritless lump
of human flesh that is now her son."   Such doubts arise only
when a wrong step is taken in considering Oswald the hero
of the play and his disease the central theme of the play. So
far as Mrs. Alving, who is the protagonist is concerned, it is
enough for the tragic purpose when it is made clear to us that
Oswald's tottering into debility has completely shattered her
hope for the joy of life.

This brings us to the style of the play. Aristotle says that
the style of a tragedy should be clear but not mean. It should
be appropriate to the emotional context and vary with the
change in emotion. Considered in this light, the style of
the *Ghosts* is most effective, and clear without being mean
and dull. When we have a problem as plain and direct as
that with which the *Ghosts* deals, the style to be effective has
to be straightforward and precise. This purpose has been
served most effectively by a subtle treatment of dialogue in
the *Ghosts*.[39]   "Having determined to use modern social

problems as the materials of his plays," remarks Gustafson, Ibsen "saw the necessity of using everyday, idiomatic prose as the appropriate form for his dialogue."[40]

Many critics[41] think that prose is unsuitable for tragedy because it is an inadequate medium for expressing the emotional element of tragedy. But if we judge the dialogue of the Ghosts from the point of view of its dramatic effectiveness, whether it helps the action move properly and is capable of carrying the emotional weight which is intended and also whether it reveals the working of the minds of the characters of the play, we find that the style of the play is most effective and almost perfect. "The language is as pure as that of any classic, for every line is a gem of literature. There was not one word too much."[42] Mr. Zucker has remarked that "in the tragedy, one of heredity, there was little action, the dialogue conveying almost entirely the story, the working out of a mental process."[43]

One can take any passage from the play, to illustrate the straightforwardness, clarity and effectiveness of style. Precision and immediacy of effect have been achieved by, besides the consummate skill in the choice and use of words, the symbolic use of language which never becomes abstruse. At the end of the play the use of the word 'the Sun,' for instance, becomes symbolical and intensely charged with meaning. It begins on the literal plane, "Oswald, what a lovely day we are going to have ? Brilliant sunshine," and takes a symbolic significance in Oswald's cry "Mother, give me the Sun—the sun, the sun."

The artistic economy and suggestive force may be illustrated from a single episode. 'The fatal kinship between Oswald and his depraved father is enforced by the simple repetition of a few words. The words used in relation to the father's misdemeanour, "the door was standing ajar ; Let me go, Mr. Alving! Let me be!" may be compared to Oswald's case, "leaving the door ajar...Oswald! Are you mad? Let me go!" The style becomes intensely effective in the symbolical significance it assumes in the end.

F.L. Lucas, commenting on Yeats' criticism of Ibsen's style as lacking in "beautiful and vivid language," remarks that "it is hard to judge the style of an author known to most of us only in translation,"[44] and even then it is undeniably true that "a strange poetry still clings" to his language. George Steiner has also commended Ibsen's prose. He says, "Ibsen's mature prose is as tightly wrought in cadence and inner poise as is good verse. As in poetry, moreover, the force and direction of meaning often hinge on the particular inflections and array of sounds. These resist translation. And so there is in the versions of Ibsen's play available to most readers a prosaic flatness."[45]

Thus, we see that the *Ghosts* has a well-knit and compact plot which illustrates all the Aristotelian elements of the tragic plot. The play, though beginning with a conflict, with a temporal, parochial problem—conventional morality—becomes universalized[46] through Mrs. Alving's heroic struggle to be happy and the force of heredity coming in collision with her attempt to be happy. The heroine is a good lady. She suffers because of her error of judgement in going to her husband and living with him. She has admirable strength for enduring calamities. She struggles heroically to achieve her aim, but is defeated in the end by a force which she finds too strong for her efforts. She is a common, average human being, but in her struggle and heroic suffering her stature is raised. She is human and like us, hence our pity for her undeserved suffering. She is larger than life and her struggle typifies a universal problem of man's struggle for happiness in the face of formidable odds, and hence her final defeat is capable of arousing fear of a tragic sort. The prose style of the play is remarkably effective and has the extraordinary power of movement and adaptability to varying situations. It is clear, precise, straightforward and suggestive. The

Ghosts, thus may quite properly be regarded as a modern version of the ancient Greek tragedy.

FOOTNOTES

1 See Stuart, Donald Clive, *The Development of Dramatic Art*, (Dover Publications, Inc., New York, 1960), p. 580.

2 See Dickinson, Thomas H., *The Contemporary Drama of England*, (John Murray, Albemarie Street, London, 1920), p. 42.

3 Gassner, John, *Form and Idea in Modern Theatre* (Dryden Press, New York, 1956), p. 32.

4 Roberts, R. Ellis, *Henrik Ibsen, A Critical Study* (Martin Secker, London, 1912), p. 117.

5 *Form and Idea in Modern Theatre*, p. 66.

6 See Bradbrook, M.C., *Ibsen the Norwegian* (Chatto and Windus, 1948), p. 89.

7 *Henrik Ibsen : A Critical Study*, p. 115.

8 Quoted in The *Contemporary Drama of England*.
See also Shaw, G.B., *Dramatic Opinion and Essays with an Apology*, Vol. II, "Ghosts at the Jubilee" (Brentano's, N.Y., 1907).

9 *PMLA*, June, 1959, Ibsen's Concept of Tragedy," p. 266.

10 *Ibid.*, p. 290.

11 *Ibid.*, p. 291.

12 *Ibid*.

13 *Ibid*.

14 *The Times Literary Supplement*, Aug. 14, 1953, Review, Weisinger, Herbert, *Tragedy and Paradox of the Fortunate Fall*.

15 Knox, B., ed., *Tragic Theme in Western Literature : Seven Essays by B. Knox and Others* (Yale University Press, New Haven, 1960). "Mrs. Alving is defeated, no doubt, but her critique of social convention stands."

16 *PMLA*, Vol. XLIV, 1929, "The Word 'Universality' as applied to Drama," p. 927.

17 See *PMLA*, Vol. XLIII, 1928, pp. 810-35.

18 See *Philological Quarterly*, Vol. XIX, 1940, Zucker, A.E., "Southern Critics of 1903 on Ibsen's Ghosts," pp. 393-99, for a detailed summary of the condemnation of *Ghosts* when it was first staged.

19 Clark, B.H., and Freedley, George, ed., *A History of Modern Drama*, "The Scandinavian Country," by Alrik Gustafson (D. Appleton-Century Comp., Inc., New York, London, 1947), p. 11.

20 Ward, A.C., ed., *Specimens of English Dramatic Criticism, XVII-XX Centuries,* "Daily Telegraph 14th March, 1891," (Oxford University Press, 1946), p. 186.

21 *The Contemporary Drama of England* (John Murray, Albemarie Street, London, 1920), p. 41.

22 *Essays by Divers Hands,* Vol. XII, Morgan, Charles, "The Nature of Dramatic Illusion," pp. 67-8. In this connection the untenability of the condemnation of the subject-matter of *Ghosts* becomes quite obvious if we think that many tragedies with more 'shocking themes' than this have been written in the past (such as Hippolytus; Phedre) but the mythological clothing given to such theme does not incite any resentment.

23 *Aristotle's Theory of Poetry and Fine Art,* p. 270.

24 *Ibid.*

25 *Ibid.*

26 *The Death of Tragedy,* p. 291.

27 *Ibid.,* p. 8.

28 *Ibid.*

29 Gassner, John, *Masters of Drama,* (Dover Publications, U.S.A., 1954), p. 371.

30 *Aristotle's Theory of Poetry and Fine Art,* p. 270.

31 Knight, Wilson, G., *Ibsen,* (Oliver and Boyd, Edinburgh and London, 1962) : "What at first seems to be a problem-play shades through the purely tragic into a conclusion touched by a gleam from beyond mortality," p. 50.

32 *A History of Modern Drama,* These utterances are also an attack upon the society where people are trying to "clock immorality in respectability the complications of which are world removed from a mere study of "degenerate heredity." These words "lift the play above a mere consideration of the operations of natural law upto the whole superstructure of ethical concepts," p. 12.

See Gascoigne, Bamber, *Twentieth Century Drama,* (Hutchinson University Press, London, 1963), p. 164.

33 *A History of Modern Drama,* p. 12.

34 *PMLA,* June, 1959, Isben's Concept of Tragedy," p. 289.

35 *Ibid.,* p. 297.

36 *Ibid.,* p. 290.

37 *Ibid.*

38 *Ibid.,* p. 289.

39 See Nicoll, A., *British Drama,* (George, G. Harrap and Comp. Ltd., London, 1927), p. 344.

40 *A History of Drama*, p. 10.

41 *The Times Literary Supplement,* Aug. 7, 1959, "A Hope for Tragedy," p. 459.

42 *Philological Quarterly*, Vol. XIX, 1940, Zucker, A.E., "Southern Critics of 1903 on Ibsen's Ghosts," p. 395.

43 *Ibid.*, p. 396.

44 *Tragedy : Serious Drama in Relation to Aristotle's Poetics* p. 156.

45 *The Death of Tragedy,* p. 298.

46 *Ibsen :* "In *Ghosts* veil after veil was removed till we were brought up against the simple fact of humanity's inability in our era to establish contact with the positive powers of its existence....', p. 57.

CHAPTER VI

Synge's Riders to the Sea

Riders to the Sea is a one-act play, so the events of the play are few and simple. It deals with the struggle between the dauntless members of a sailor's family and the inexorable Nature symbolized by the sea which has already taken a toll of four lives. The play opens under the shadow of the death of the fifth son (Michael) of the old woman, the protagonist of the play, whose dead body has not yet been recovered from the sea. But a bundle of clothes "got off a drowned man in Donegal" has arrived and confirmed the worst fear about him. Thus, only one of the six sons of Maurya, namely, Bartley, now remains It is turning into a wild night. "That wind is raising the sea and there was a star up against the moon, and it rising up in the night," the old bereaved mother says. But the last son will not be deterred from crossing to the mainland. We are as certain of some disaster overtaking Bartley as the old mother herself. As Bartley leaves the house he instructs his sister : "If the west wind holds with the last bit of the moon let you and Nora get up weed enough for another cock for the kelp. It's hard set we'll be from this day and no one in it but one man to work." To these words the old woman replies, "It's hard pressed we'll be surely the day you're drowned with the rest " And when Bartley has gone the old woman says, "He's gone now, and when the black night is falling I'll have no son left me in the world." At the nightfall Bartley's dead body is brought in to her from the sea. This is all the story of the play.

There is little that transpires in *Riders to the Sea*. The play is like the last act of a tragedy.[1] The scene of the action is the small kitchen of a fisher-family. It opens with a description of the things kept in the kitchen which at the same time gives a picture of the life of the fisherfolk and symbolically suggests the precariousness of these people, only an inch removed from death. Nora comes in with a bundle under her shawl. It is a bundle of "a shirt and plain stocking...got off a drowned man in Donegal," which the young priest has given her. Our curiosity is aroused to know whose clothes have been recovered from the sea, because the very second sentence at the beginning of the play has informed us that Maurya is lamenting some one's death or apprehended death. "She's lying down, God help her, and may be sleeping, if she's able." Without any delay Nora says that the young priest has suspected that the clothes were Michael's : "If it's Michael's, they are, you can tell herself he's got a clean burial by the grace of God, and if they're not his, let no one say a word about them, for she'll be getting her death... with crying and lamenting," even for the son of another woman. It is nine days since she has been crying and keening for Michael, her last but one son, and making great sorrow in the house. Now instead of telling us more about the 'shirt and the plain stocking' for which we have become curious, Cathleen talks about the last son of Maurya, who would go to the Gateway horse-fair on the mainland. What Nora says to Cathleen in reply to the latter's query if the young priest could dissuade Bartley from going to the fair across the sea when the "tide's turned to the wind ; and there is great roaring in the west," makes us fully aware of the havoc the sea has been making in the lives of the people, and our suspicion about the 'clothes got off a drowned man' becomes strengthened at the deep concern of the girls at Bartley's also going across the sea. The priest has said, says Nora, "It' won stop him, but let you not be afraid. Herself does be saying prayers half through the night, and the Almighty God won't leave her destitude with no son living." By now, when it is hardly twenty lines in the play, the atmosphere of the play is established and our sympathy for the anxious family fully engaged.

We now see Bartley getting ready to go to Connemera even though the weather is bad and the mother opposed to his design. She tells him that any time the dead body of Michael might be washed ashore and then there won't be anybody to make his coffin. She has already bought the white board and the rope to give Michael a deep burial. But Bartley won't be dissuaded. Wishing the blessing of God on his sisters and mother, he goes out. Maurya who knows the sea and we also who by now have known the rapacious monster, are sure that Bartley won't return. The girls send her after him with the foregotton cake ; she may go down by the short way to the spring well, and give it to him as he passes, and with it her blessing also. The moment she is gone, the girls get down the bundle from the left. From Nora's stitches on the stocking they discover that the clothes were Michael's, who, as the priest said, had had a clean burial. Meanwhile Maurya returns with the cake in her hand. She could not give it to Bartley nor could she bless him. She saw "the fearfulest thing." She stood at the spring well and Bartley came first on the red mare, and she tried to give him Godspeed, but something choked the words in her throat; she looked up then at the grey pony, and there was Michael upon it in fine clothes on him and new shoes on his feet.

Now it has become clear that Maurya will have no son left to her. The action has reached its climax here. Michael is dead. Bartley has gone off and we have the clearest premonitions that now the white board and the new rope that Maurya bought for Michael will have to be used for Bartley. We are only awaiting his dead body to be brought in. Maurya is lost in the recollection of her old griefs ; she laments the

death of her husband, her husband's father and her six fine
sons (because she has included Bartley also in the list), some
of whom were found and some were not found—they are
brought in, and the story of Maurya's conflict with the sea is
completed when the latter has claimed her all. Thus we see
that the plot is thin but it has its clearcut development from
the beginning to the end. The story begins with the news of
Michael's death though it retains our suspense until almost
the end of the play, the confirmation of the news being
delayed dramatically. The action ends with the dead body
of Bartley being brought in to his mother, who has been
counting all the while on its inevitability.

The plot has a beginning, a middle, and an end. The
events are not presented in the sequence of their happening.
What has happened before in the life of Maurya due to the
malignity of the sea, is narrated in the middle of the plot.
The action begins with an indication that four out of the five
sons of Maurya have fallen victim to the fury of the sea. As
the action moves further we learn that the sea has been
playing havoc on the lives of the members of Maurya's family
which ends only with the death of the last son of Maurya.

The plot of *Riders to the Sea* represents the malicious and
destructive action of the sea upon the life of Maurya, through
her sons and husband and her husband's father. As there is
no 'active' struggle, on the part of Maurya against the malig-
nant Nature, the elements of 'peripeity' and 'anagnorisis' are
absent. Maurya, in the end of the play, attains to her stoic
calm of mind not because she has recognized the truth, which
she knows too well, but because her continued suffering and
perpetual anxiety for her sons ending with the loss of her last
son has induced in her a feeling of resignation. She feels a
sense of relief, so do we, in witnessing the inevitable happen.
One may now, ask, how the tragic effect is produced without
the element of 'peripeity'. We may say that the tragic effect
is produced because of the obvious inevitability of the end of

the conflict, the creation of the tragic atmosphere and the poetic and the highly dramatic dialogue of the play.

But what about the 'magnitude' of the plot of *Riders to the Sea* ?[2] Aristotle demands a certain length of the plot of a tragedy because in a very short play the development of action is not possible. It is not possible in a short plot to depict the working of the mind of the characters, their motives and the steps they take to do a thing or avoid doing it. The play is required to have a certain magnitude "so that the sequence of events according to the law of 'probability' or 'necessity' may admit of a change from bad fortune to good, or from good fortune to bad." In *Riders to the Sea,* one act play as it is, the action does not show Maurya's active struggle with the sea because it is, all through, the sea which is active and Maurya seems to be an unprotesting sufferer.[3] The action of the play, like the last act of a tragedy, represents the consequence of the events which have gone on for a long time. Owing to the peculiar nature of the story Maurya is deprived of the opportunity of an 'active' struggle with the force with which she has come in conflict. A tragic hero should have the opportunity to fall honourably after his struggle to evade or overcome his fate, or circumstances confronting him. This can be done only when the action has a 'magnitude' to allow its development on the basis of the principle of cause and effect. Barrett H. Clark remarks that "the most momentous developments in tragedy occur between the acts: What we see is almost entirely the points during the period of development."[4] *Riders to the Sea* shows only one stage, the final one—in the development of the situation of Maurya's forced struggle with the sea. The play, therefore, is "a short flight of poetic perception, the brief excursion rather than the exploration of an action."[5]

Though the plot lacks 'magnitude' and the action only flashes on the imagination of the audience illumining it with the "slice of life" caught at its most intense moment, the other requirements of plot-construction as desired by Aristotle are most artistically met. That is, a complete whole as has been shown earlier, the unity of action, the most important of all the features of a tragic plot, are artistically preserved. The action, however, small it is, is pruned of all that is unnecessary. Even the young priest talked of by the two girls is never shown in person. The plot is by and large uneventful and whatever 'events' are there are logically harmonized into an organic unity. The news of Michael's death Bartley's foretold doom and the already-occurred deaths of Maurya's husband, of her father-in-law and four sturdy sons are not presented in the chronological sequence of their happening but are interwoven into the structure in a dramatically effective way. The clothes of a drowned man suspected to be those of Michael's but not confirmed, have come. Attempts made to open the bundle to identify them, are given up, because Maurya comes in. Then without having finished the confirmatory verification of Michael's clothes, we are invited to feel concerned at Bartley's doom. When Bartley has gone off but before his dead body is brought in, the clothes are identified as Michael's. Before the dripping corpse of her son is brought in to her, Maurya laments vocally the several deaths she has suffered already. The series of deaths seems to have been completed when finally Bartley's dead body is carried in to Maurya. The action is intense and rapidly developing within its narrow limits. The progress of the action is 'swifter partly for the reason that there is less to be revealed by the dialogue....It is given swiftness also by the marvellous intensity Synge has given it; the temper of the play is like a white flame, in which everything that is irrelevant, or ordinarily below this terrible significance, has been burned up."[6] This masterly unity of action, compactness and intensity have been achieved by the immense significance with which the details of the setting have been invested. Look at the vast meaning and significance, from the opening words, with which the "shirt and the plain stocking," "the white rock and the tide," "the pig with the black feet" and "the bit of a new rope" are clothed. A deeper meaning than the surface one is infused into the shirt and the plain stocking that are all the remains of the dead son for his old mother, the white rocks and the tide that are to destroy the only son left, the pig that must be sold to the jobber by the old woman now that her last son has gone, and the 'bit of the new rope' that would be required now to lower Bartley's corpse into his deep grave. "The fine white boards bought for a big price in Connemera take a visual significance, almost intolerable, as they stand against the kitchen wall. Synge never wrote a play,—never surely, has a play been written— in which such a complete intensification of the dramatist's materials is achieved."[7]

Now this tragic intensification on the printed page, says Powe,[8] is sublime, but it does not bear this visual embodiment without reduction, on the stage. The swiftness of the action in *Riders to the Sea* becomes the cause of the structural defect in the play. The action of this play "does not succeed, in advancing step by step with reality, for in its half hour's occupation of the stage we are asked to suppose that Bartley should be knocked over into the sea, and washed out where there is a great surf on the white rocks, and his body recovered and brought back again, when he himself allows for half an hour to ride down only. This unreality is an undesirable difficulty in the theatre."[9] This is because there is one single scene here, and the action has been condensed even to the detriment of 'probability' The whole play is written on one note, "the note of the dirge, the dirge of the tides that sound their menace of the sea through Innismaan" which causes destruction on the lives of the islanders. The story of the finding of the clothes which tell of the death at sea of the last but one of Maurya's sons, and of the death on the very shore itself of the last son, is in its very nature a dirge and demands a slower movement than is possible when the incidents have been crowded in a space of time far shorter than their probable duration of actual occurrence. Aristotle says that a successfully well written tragedy should be effective on the stage as well as in the closet. The lack of 'probability' in the action, especially in the end may not be so much felt when one is reading the play, because the peculiar poetic atmosphere which has been created by the poetry of the language does not allow us to bother about it. But on the stage this will appear detrimental to the 'probability' of the action, because probably even the most cunning stage devices would not be able to bring home to us the impression of the atmosphere which from the very beginning of the play tells us of the inevitability of Maurya's tragedy.[10]

Maurice Bourgeois says that "*Riders to the Sea* is elegy all through, but elegy in a highly dramatic form." It is because, as Darrell Figgis has remarked,[11] it is only "set in the atmosphere of tragedy...there is not tragedy in *Riders to the Sea* because it is all tragical." In the present play we have the minimization of external action. A mother gets information of the death of her last but one son, and she watches the last one riding straight into death and being brought back as a corpse. This is nearly all that happens. The play has been interiorised and it is through atmosphere plus characterization that the tragic effect is produced.

Thus in *Riders to the Sea* we see that action has been reduced to the minimum, magnitude is lacking and yet the tragic effect, as we shall see presently, is produced. Aristotle's principles of the plot being a complete whole, and of the unity of action are present here. But Aristotle's supremacy of plot over everything else in tragedy is obviously out of place here, because the desired tragic effect is produced he'e by the composite impact of atmosphere and the dramatic dialogue used in the play besides, of course, the plot, however thin it is, and the character of Maurya. But "the action, though it will ceaselessly and unobtrusively widen and advance without a jar to the logically fatal and indubitable conclusion, can hardly be progressive."[12]   Nevertheless, it should be kept in mind that the plot, though lacking in some of the requisite standards, is the basis of the play.   It throws sufficient light on the inner self of Maurya, the heroine of the play.

Maurya is a fisherman's aged wife, whom the sea has already bereft of her husband, and four sons.   She is awaiting the news of the fifth son's death.   The last son has also gone without leaving Maurya and us in any doubt about his doom. From the very opening of the play she impresses as a pathetic old woman.   She is always keening and we are made aware of her great suffering from the very beginning of the play. Before she enters upon the scene at all, one daughter says, "Where is she?" and the other answers, "she's lying down, God help her, and may be sleeping, if she's able."   She is human and like us, in her feelings and emotions.   In her laments over the death of her sons, we have an expression of the sentiments which stir our soul : "If it was hundred horses, or a thousand horses, you had itself, what is the price of a thousand horses against a son when there is one son only."   When Bartley goes out to cross the sea, she goes after him by the shortest way near the spring well to give him the forgotten cake and also her blessing.   But she fails, and returns with full conviction that her last son also is going to be snatched away from her by the sea.   Thus, her struggle to save her son against the malicious force whose destructive action upon her family is too well known to her, her perpetual suffering and lamenting and her humanity (the priest says that if the clothes he has brought of some drowned person were not Michael's, the girls need not tell Maurya anything about them, because she will lament over the death of another woman's son) make her an object of our deep sympathy.   As her suffering seems to be passive, and she is innocent, one might logically conclude that Maurya falls short of the features of a tragic heroine. She does not choose wrongly and suffer because of any 'hamartia'. She does not have the capacity to fight with fate, or we can say that the force is too immensely strong for her even to put up a fight with it. But we can say that she is not weak, because she does not feel unnerved by the repeated shocks from the sea. In her extraordinary capacity to suffer and endure sufferings lies her strength. It is this capacity which at the end of the play exalts her stature above that of the average humanity when she throws a heroic and defiant challenge at the sea : "They're all gone now, and there isn't anything more the sea can do to me...." It is in this exalted moment that she experiences a "terrible calm"[13] in her freedom from anxiety : "I'll have no call now to be up crying and praying when the wind breaks from the south....I'll have no call now to be going down and getting Holy water in the dark nights after Samhain, and I won't care what way the sea is when the other women will be keening...It's a great rest I'll have now...and great sleeping in the long nights after Samhain, if it's only a bit of wet flour we do have to eat, and may be a fish that would be stinking."

Raymond Williams has remarked that Maurya is simply a victim of the cosmic force and her acceptance of the inevitable without any active struggle "is not whole, but rather a weary resignation."[14] W.B. Yeats in his *Oxford Book of Modern Verse* has said that "passive suffering is not a theme for poetry."[15] In this connection Miss Una Ellis-Fermer's judgement that it is the sea which is the protagonist, because it is most active as contrasted to Maurya's passivity, is significant.[16] But it can be said that Maurya's conflict with the cosmic force, which is in the manner of the Greek tragedy, does not belittle her stature of a tragic heroine even though she is 'passive'. Her capacity to suffer constantly at the hands of a force which she defies in the end of the play does exalt her in our eyes. She, in fact, is triumphant in the end in having rendered the sea powerless to assail her any more. Moreover, the problem she is grappling with and the 'immensity of issues' she is facing have the same situation which high tragedies of ancient Greece had. At the end of the play, says Maurice Bourgeois[17], "when Maurya re-enters with haunted eyes, a lonely, stately figure as majestic as the sea itself, her disclosure comes to us, if not altogether as a surprise, certainly as an irresistible tragic shock." Maurya is engaged in an unavailing strife with the cosmic force which is blind, irresponsible, unfathomable and resistless. Her conflict with the malicious sea makes her great and raises her to tragic proportions because nothing stands between her and the fierce onset of the ineluctable circumstance.[18] One thing should be borne in mind that it is not necessary that the tragic hero should have a high stature from the opening of the play until the close. It is enough if he is able to show the height of his stature even for a moment at an intense occasion of his life. In fact, this stature, tragic proportion or dignity of the soul of the hero, whatever one calls it, comes at the end of the play which is the consequence of the development of the action. This is what happens in the present play.

Thus, it cannot be said that Maurya has fallen far short of the tragic proportions of an Aristotelian heroine in essence. We see that she is confronted with the cosmic force and yet is "so firm set and integral in her nature that in spite of all its victories over her, she is still herself and will remain herself, not distracted, nor frenzied."[19] It is through her husband and her six sons that the sea has been assailing her. It seems as if she herself in her own nature is invincible. That is why in the end when the sea has claimed its last toll from Maurya, she stands defiant towards the sea : "there isn't anything more the sea can do to me," and obviously her victory over the sea is established. In this way we find that Maurya, though like us, is larger than life.

It has been said by many critics that as Maurya lacks active struggle and as *Riders to the Sea* is a one-act play where the development of character could not be possible, the tragic emotion of fear could not be effectively produced. Aristotle says that the tragic hero is like us and is yet larger than life. He suffers undeservedly at the hands of a 'superior force' which ultimately destroys his life and hope. The tragic emotion of fear is aroused when we feel that under similar circumstances we may also have not been able to avoid the doom. Now the production of these emotions obviously postulates a development of character under the stress of the action, because a sudden unaccounted for mishap is conducive to theatrical horror rather than to tragic fear. In Maurya's case also we do find a development of her character. This is why we do not find any anticlimactic effect in the end. When the play opens she has already paid a heavy share of her toll to the tax-gathering sea. Now she is left with one son only. She is fully aware of the nature of the sea and the fate of the fishermen on the island. Even then she tries to prevent Bartley from going to the fair across the sea. She has been praying to God for sparing her last son for her : "Herself does be saying prayers half through the night, and the Almighty God won't leave her destitute with no son living." When Bartley goes off to the fair Maurya rushes after him to give him her blessing, but she returns with the clearest forebodings that Bartley also is doomed. Thus she strives to save her son from the sea. She knows that the sea has been assailing her through her sons. When all her sons have been taken away by the sea, she attains to a sense of relief. Now this relief is not a sudden feeling in her but the result of her long conflict with the sea. This does show a development of her character which is probable and natural. Her 'triumph' in the end invites our admiration for her. Her sufferings have made her large-limbed, rugged, stern and rock-set. For no fault of her own, she comes in a direct conflict with the cosmic force ; she suffers owing to the malignity of this force rather than to any error of judgement or any wrong step taken by her. In this way Maurya fulfils most of the Aristotelian requirements of a tragic hero except the one, i.e., 'hamartia'. Even in many of the Greek tragedies, out of which Aristotle drew his models, we find that it is the natural force, gods or the supernatural powers which caused the doom of the heroes rather than the element of 'hamartia' in their character. Most of the Greek tragic heroes moved in their lives under a doom and in *Riders to the Sea*, Maurya's family is also living as if under the shadow of death. In the present play, therefore, it would not be very profitable to seek the proper tragic effect in the plot only or even in the character of Maurya. The emotional effect here comes, to a great extent, from the masterly creation of the atmosphere and the haunting cadences of the prose speech, which harmonize inseparably with the theme.

The theme of *Riders to the Sea* is apparently localized because of its connection with the lives of fisherfolk of the island of Innismaan who earn their livelihood from the sea which in turn takes away their lives. Maurya says, "In the big world the old people do be leaving things after them for their sons and children, but in this place it is the youngman do be leaving things behind for them that do be old." Here it is the life of a youngman to be going on the sea from which he draws the sustenance for his people, and the life of an old woman to be down looking by the sea for the son whom the sea has taken away. Thus, the play has its root in a particular locality and in the life of the people there. But the hard and precarious struggle for existence is, indeed, the lot of common man everywhere. "The reality of work and occupational disaster,"[20] remains a subject which has universal significance. Then man's conflict with cosmic forces in which he is defeated and mercilessly crushed, as is shown in *Riders to the Sea*, is as old as the history of man himself. The sentiments which Maurya expresses are universal and she becomes the universal mother voicing the emotions of the bereaved mothers :[21] "If it was a hundred horses, or a thousand horses, you had itself.

what is the price of a thousand horses against a son when there is one son only ? Then again, "isn't it a pitiful thing when there is nothing left of a man who was a great rower and fisher but a bit of an old shirt and plain stocking...?" These are the expressions of the pathetic reality which is of universal significance.

The success of a tragedy, says Aristotle, depends upon its being able to produce the proper tragic effect of 'catharsis' through pity and fear. In *Riders to the Sea*, we find that this effect is most successfully produced. Maurya is a character like us. She comes in conflict with the cosmic force. This force inflicts untold miseries on her. She suffers undeservedly. Hence our pity for her. We experience the emotion of fear when we feel that even we in our confrontation with such a malicious cosmic force would have met with the same doom as overtook Maurya. In the end, Maurya is resigned to her fate and attains a philosophic calm of mind; all her anxieties being over, she is exalted in her triumphant defiance of the cosmic force. The peculiar pleasurable effect of tragedy which consists in reconciliation, a calm and repose of mind, "all passion spent," is thus attained.

This tragic effect through the harmonious blending of theme and atmosphere is deepened by the singularly characteristic prose of the islanders made poetic and dramatically effective by Synge, and his most dramatically effective use of 'keening'. The Innismaan islanders seem to live as if under the constant threat of death. This acute realization of the hovering nothingness in their lives finds a dramatic expression in the "half-savage, half-musical melopoeia known as the keen. The lilted recitative, with all its threnetic appeal is another very impressive, pathetic note.... Faintly it sounds from the opening of the piece, like some 'unheard melody' perceived by the spiritual ear alone ; but at the climax of the tragedy it rises and swells in entrancing power, and mingles with the moan of the Atlantic which, one knows without words, is dashing its surf beneath the cabin walls."[22] There is a magical and immediate effect of the terror of the sea when we listen to the strange litany of Maurya chanting the names of her dead men-children. "They're all together this time, and the end is come. May the Almighty God have mercy on Bartley's soul, and on Michael's soul, and on the souls of Sheams and Patch, and Stephen and Shawn. . . ." But one should not carry away the impression that this keening is the main source of the tragic effect in the play.

At the close of the play Bartley's dripping corpse is brought in, which may give one an impression of melodramatic effect. But this melodramatic effect, if one insists on it, is amply redeemed by the singularly august, and almost Greek solemnity of the play at the close, "The lyrical fervour of the lament now gives way to a note of resignation which instead of being bathetic as might be expected, actually heightens and intensifies the tragic effect."[23] Maurya's closing words of "half-heathenish," "half-catholic" submission : "no man at all can be living for ever, and we must be satisfied," do not mark an anti-climax but rather bring about an elevation of Maurya's stature and consequently an exalting effect on us. Now we share with the old woman herself the calm of despair, the blank feeling of restfulness[24] that ensues when all that we feared has happened and there is an end : "I'll have no call now to be up crying and praying when the wind breaks from the south. . . .It's a great rest I'll have now, and great sleeping in the long nights after Samhain, if it's only a bit of wet flour we do have to eat, and may be a fish that would be stinking." The effect of *Riders to the Sea,* says A. E. Morgan, "like that of all great tragedy is not to depress but to uplift the spirit and enrich the soul."[25] "It must be stated emphatically that however inexorable and inevitable the tragedy, however deep the gloom, however pagan the fatalism, the play is neither depressing nor pessimistic. Like all great tragedy it ennobles. The terror and pity stir our emotions to purify them. Human nature is shown at its top-most height of glory"[26] and we discern human courage and endurance triumphing over death itself.

Synge has been justly praised for the dramatic dialogue and the exquisite language which is in itself an "unceasing source of beauty, a constant stimulus to fine emotions." Aristotle demands that the language of tragedy should be clear but elevated, commonplace but not mean. Synge knew how to bring this 'elevation' of the commonplace diction and make it a competent vehicle of serious ideas. He has used in the present play a language which has simplicity, directness, precision and picturesqueness. The test of a dramatic language is the immediacy of its effect upon the audience which the present play amply illustrates. The old woman's words are infected all through with this immediacy. Mark, for example, the following passage :

"It isn't that I haven't prayed for you, Bartley, to the Almighty God. It isn't that I haven't said prayers in the dark night till you wouldn't know what I'ld be saying ; but it's a great rest I'll have now, and it's time surely. It's a great rest I'll have now, and great sleeping in the long nights after Samhain, if it's only a bit of wet flour we do have to eat, and may be a fish that would be stinking."

The prose of *Riders to the Sea* has a haunting cadence which is inseparably harmonised with the theme. See, for example :

"It's little the like of him knows the sea...Bartley will be lost now, and let you call in Eamon and make me a good coffin out of the white boards, for I won't live after them. I've had a husband, and a husband's father, and six sons in this house—six fine men, though it was a hard birth I had with every one of them and they coming into the world

and some of them were found and some of them were not
found, but they're gone now the lot of them...There were
Stephen and Shawn were lost in the great wind, and found
after in the Bay of Gregory of the Golden Month, and
carried up the two of them on one plank, and in by that
door."

Professor Nicoll remarks that "there is exquisite music here,
a music that works upon our senses and charms us into
viewing the dark disaster that has fallen on Maurya's little
household not with the dark despair but with deeper vision."[27]

Raymond Williams observes that in *Riders to the Sea* "the
language is an imposed constituent of flavour rather than the
essence of tragedy."[28] But it seems that Mr. Williams has not
been quite just in his criticism of *Riders to the Sea*. We find
that language is not an 'imposed constituent of flavour' here
nor does it have its justification for its own sake. It is harmoniously blended with the theme ; it is dramatic and has the
quality of the immediacy of effect, it produces the proper
tragic atmosphere in the play. Moreover, we do not feel anywhere the imposition of language. It is so natural and 'real'
that we do not have even the awareness that we are hearing
some language, because it is so inseparably blended with
everything else in the play.[29] The words and phrases dance
to a very strange rhythm which produces the effect of mysterious beauty and natural music and works upon our soul in
the manner of symphony.[30] Mark the sentences : "Is the sea
bad by the white rocks, Nora ?...If the west wind holds with
the last bit of the moon let you and Nora get up weed enough
for another cock for the kelp....He's gone now, and when the
black night is falling I'll have no son left me in the world....
I've seen the fearfulest thing any person has seen, since the
day Bride Dara seen the dead man with the child, in his
arms"—how simple yet dramatically effective !

Barrett H. Clark has aptly remarked,[31] "Synge's mastery of words is one of his greatest assets. Like Shakespeare, he can at once suggest environment by purely verbal means." His success lies in his being able to make his dramatic language an integral part of the play in conformity with Aristotle's demand. For example, the sharp contrast between the homely and everyday life and the gruesomeness of death has been clearly drawn when Bartley asks, "Where is the bit of the new rope. Cathleen, was brought in Connemera ?" And Cathleen replies, "Give it to him, Nora, it's on a nail by the white boards. I hung it up this morning for the pig with the black feet was eating it." These words themselves are a part of the action ; for one thing, they suggest atmosphere better than many scene-painters could hope to do.

Thus, we have seen that *Riders to the Sea*, though a one-act play, follows the Aristotelian principle of plot—its 'wholeness,' unity of action and the presence of some conflict as the basis of the action. The plot lacks 'magnitude' and hence a dramatic development of the character of Maurya through an interplay with action has not obviously been fully possible. But Synge has achieved the tragic 'catharsis' in *Readers to the Sea* through pity and fear by a cumulative effect of plot, character, atmosphere and language. Though in his *Poetics*, Aristotle analyses the elements of tragedy separately, yet he wants these to be taken as a whole when the emotional effect of tragedy is being considered. In the present play also we find that unless all the elements, which are harmoniously fused together, are taken into account, the full import of the tragic effect would not be realized. Thus, *Riders to the Sea*, though a short play, is one of the best tragedies written after Shakespeare, which can well be placed along the side of any Greek tragedy.

FOOTNOTES

1 Robinson, Lennox, ed., *The Irish Theatre: Lectures Delivered During the Abbey Theatre Festival held in Dublin in August, 1938,* O'Conner, Frank, "Synge," (Macmillan and Co., London, 1939). "It is literature stripped to the bone...(and) is so bare that it may almost be said to have no dramatic structure. Synge makes no attempt to interest his audience; he keeps them waiting for the completion of an inevitable event," p. 43.

2 Fred, B. Millett, *Reading Drama: A Method of Analysis with Selections for Study,* "Though most writers of tragedy have worked with a canvas more than five times the size of Synge's. yet by a miracle of concentration he has managed to arouse those emotions of pity and fear which, since Aristotle, have been an integral part of our conception of tragedy," p. 103.

3 See Ellis-Fermor, Una, the *Irish Dramatic Movement* (Methuen, London, 1939), p. 169.

4 *A Study of the Modern Drama* (D. Appleton and Comp., New York, London, 1928), p. 341.

5 *Form and Idea in Modern Threatre,* p. 64.

6 Powe, P.P., *J.M. Synge: A Critical Study* (Martin Secker, London, 1912), p. 58.

7 *Ibid.,* p. 59.

8 *Ibid.*

9 *Ibid.*

10 See Hudson, Lynton, *The Twentieth Century Drama,* p. 42.

11 Bourgeois, Maurice, *John Millington Synge and the Irish Theatre,* Figgs, Darrell, "The Art of J.M. Synge," (Constable and Comp. Ltd., London, 1913), p. 170.

12 *Ibid.,* p. 161.

13 See *Masters of the Drama,* p. 557.

14 *Drama from Ibsen to Eliot* (Chatto and Windus, London. 1952), p. 160.

15 *Ibid.*

16 *The Irish Dramatic Movement,* p. 169.

17 *John Millington Synge and the Irish Threatre,* p. 162.

18 *Ibid.*

19 Corkery, Daniel, *Synge and Anglo-Irish Literature* (Cork University Press, Oxford, B.H. Blackwell Ltd., Ireland, 1947), p. 140.

20 *Masters of the Drama,* p. 555.

21 *Synge and Anglo-Irish Literature,* p. 141.

22 *John Millington Synge and the Irish Theatre*, p. 165.

23 *Ibid.*, p. 167.

24 Morgan, A.E., *Tendencies of Modern Drama* (Constable and Company Ltd., London, 1924), p. 160.

25 *Ibid.*

26 *Ibid.*, pp. 170-71.

27 *World Drama* (George G. Harrap & Comp. Ltd., London, 1952), p. 962.

See also Lucas, F.L., *The Drama of Chekhov, Synge, Yeats and Pirandello* (Cassell, 1964).

28 *Drama from Ibsen to Eliot*, p. 160.

29 See Synge's Preface to the *Playboy of the Western World,* where he has given the reason of using a 'real' language.

30 See Synge's Preface to *The Tinker's Wedding,*

31 *A Study of Modern Drama*, p. 339.

CHAPTER VII

Galsworthy's Silver Box

The Silver Box is the story of the suffering of Mr. and Mrs, Jones—people belonging to the lower stratum of society. Mr. Jones is out of job. His employer has dismissed him from service because his wife had conceived before their marriage. Mrs. Jones is employed as a charwoman in the house of John Barthwick—a wealthy man and an M. P. She is trying to feed her three children and her husband, who ill treats her under the influence of wine to which he has resorted, for drowning his bitterness. Her fellow servants in John Barthwick's house advise her to leave her husband who is worthless and inhuman to her. She also has a mind to do so sometimes, yet hesitates to take the final step as she knows that her husband's harshness is due to his unemployment and the lot of their half-fed children which constantly preys upon his mind. She understands the psychology of an unemployed father who wants to work and make his family happy but does not succeed. So she continues living with him as a submissive suffering creature. But an incident occurs in Barthwick's family which prepares the ground for her tragedy. One night when Jack Barthwick, John Barthwick's son, returns home late in the night dead drunk, he is helped in by Jones who happens to be there drunk but not senseless. They sit together, talk politics and drink whisky till the young 'lord' rolls on the sofa fast asleep. Jones looks about in the room in a fit of drunkenness and embittered hostility against the worthless rich and goes out with John Barthwick's silver box and the amount of seven pounds from the pocket of young Jack, which he has pilfered from a lady in the Pub.

Next morning the silver box is found missing. Suspicion naturally falls on Mrs. Jones who has been in Jack's room to sweep it in the morning. She is interrogated by John Barthwick and is obliged to reveal her irregular union with Jones before their matrimony to the disgust of Mrs. Barthwick and her own bitter humiliation. On returning home, she finds her husband still asleep. She wakes him up and eventually discovers the silver box which falls from his pocket. She scolds him for stealing it despite his vehement protests and threats, and struggles to snatch it from him, when the police detective appears there and recovers the silver box from Mrs. Jones whom he takes into custody. He also arrests Mr. Jones for assaulting him while he was trying to force Mrs. Jones physically towards the police station. In the court Mrs. Jones is set free because Mr. Jones confesses his guilt, but he is given one month's rigorous imprisonment despite his vigorous self-defence and denunciation of the iniquity of law which discriminates between the rich and poor victims guilty of identical crimes. The ruthless and blind operation of legal system crushes the helpless innocents also under its iron wheel, because Mrs. Jones is thrown out of her job and her children are faced with starvation.

The plot of *The Silver Box* in the words of Galsworthy is a "sure edifice that rises slowly and moves steadily to its destined end." The play has been divided into three Acts. The development of the plot starts emphatically with the theft of the silver box, which is the device to convey the 'premise' of the play.[1] The confrontation of Jack and Jones in this scene is a meeting of the extremes—the one drinks and steals because he is under no necessity to work, while the other follows the same course because he gets no job for all his effort and will to turn an honest penny, which has naturally embittered him against the worthless rich, whom he can rob with an easy conscience. Soon the action moves quickly to the discovery of the theft and cross-questioning of Mrs. Jones which discover for us the conditions under which Jones and Mrs. Jones were living and their shady pre-marriage relationship. The suspicion of theft is fixed upon Mrs. Jones and the crime of Jack is hushed up by his moneyed father.

Then comes the discovery of the theft of the silver box and its recovery from Mrs. Jones who has snatched it from her repentant but still defiant husband. The arrest of his innocent wife arouses his manliness and he makes a clean breast of his crime and proceeds even to assault. The policeman as he refuses to listen to his protest on behalf of Mrs. Jones. The element of suspense enters the action at this point when Mr. and Mrs. Barthwick, severally but on different grounds, become anxious to withdraw the case. Yet the legal machinery has been set in motion and there is no stopping it till full sacrifice has been exacted from its victim. The trial comes in the final and climactic scene which is, in a way, a ruthless exposure of the partiality, stupidity and callousness of what is miscalled the administration of justice or rule of law in democracy. The brief 'pantomime' between Mr. Barthwick and Mrs. Jones which ends the play is a bitter and eloquent commentary on the incalculable and causeless suffering which the agents of this Justice cause to the helpless innocents of our complex society.

The plot of *The Silver Box* is a complete whole in the Aristotelian sense. The action moves logically and rapidly. It begins with an incident in which identical crimes are committed by two persons—one poor and the other rich, and in the course of its development it reveals the bitter truth of Jack's off-hand but pregnant remark in the first scene that the formula of all persons being equal in the eye of law is a hollow platitude. The plot has a clear-cut development and moves in a simple and straightforward manner. Galsworthy, says Hamilton "constructs his stories with a punctilious sense of form. He is

a deliberate and conscious and very careful artist, and everything he writes conveys that satisfying sense which we receive
only from a completely finished thing."[2]

The plot of *The Silver Box* is 'simple' in the Aristotelian
sense as it lacks the elements of the 'reversal of situation' and
'discovery'. Mr. Jones has had no illusion about his position
in society, nor does he discover any truth which he did not
know before. The same can be said about Mrs. Jones. The
action, therefore, does not seem to have the typical movement
of a great tragedy, where the external movement involves
internal revelation or illumination. But 'conflict' which is the
very soul of a tragic plot is present here. It is between the
hero and the society which takes the place of fate or God
or some uncontrollable force which we find in ancient
tragedy.

The action is 'probable' and develops on the principle of
cause and effect. The plot moves in a natural and simple
manner. The situations are unforced. The playwright's
here may sometimes rightly give an impression of being "too
severely, too nakedly architectural."[3]

The subject-matter of the play relates to the life of ordinary
humanity as we find in *The Tragedy of Nan* and *Riders to the
Sea*. But the striking difference between the present play and
the other two mentioned above lies in the nature of its conflict.
Here we have "poor creatures set against the power of organi-
sed intitutions—especially the power of law—and their struggle
ends in inevitable disaster."[4] The subject-matter is parochial
but rooted in the history of human civilization. It is a problem-
play confine to the bounds of human society and concerned
solely with the relationship between man and man or man and
his environment, rather than the position of man in the scheme
of the universe. In short, the conflict is social, not cosmic.
Such subjects are apparently unsuitable for a high tragedy. The
theme of a tragedy may begin with a problem of local and
contemporary nature but it should rise above the sublunary

level to a height where the problem ceases to be the problem of a particular individual or a small class and opens a wider vista of life. Yet, if we analyse the play carefully, we can discover its real magnitude which is anything but parochial. There has always existed a conflict between the weak and the strong and the former has always been victimised by the latter. So long as our society permits the existence of different levels of social living, the exploitation of one class by the other is bound to exist. Thus, the theme of the play, which begins with a local parochial problem, rises eventually to concern itself with a question which is bound up with the social history of man in general. Hence it is a suitable subject for tragedy. At the end of the play we realize that Jones' tragedy is not the tragedy of an individual but the tragedy of all the underdogs of any society. Jones takes up the problem on his shoulder which does not concern him alone but all those who are in his place and thus he rises above his individual level. He does not dwell solely upon the difficulties that his wife and children would be facing but demands the administration of a justice before which no discrimination is made between the poor and the rich. This, we know, he can never get and therein lies his tragedy. It is a fruitless struggle—as fruitless as that of the hero of a great tragedy fighting against his fate, some blind force or some power which crushes him. Thus, the social machinery devised by man and propelled by human agents, becomes as powerful, pitiless and inhuman as the working of the inexorable destiny which blasts the good and the innocent irrespective of their goodness and nobility of heart and mingles the guilty and the guiltless in one heap of ruin.

Next we come to the characters. Mr. Jones and Mrs. Jones are the characters whom we can take as tragic characters. We can say that they are like us. If we had been in Jones' position, probably we would also have done the same thing, spoken the same words and expressed the same emotions and reacted to the situation in the same manner in which Jones does. He struggles fruitlessly but defiantly with the forces he comes in conflict with. In this reaction to the sorry state of the affairs of society, he forgets his personal concerns and raises his voice for all the people who are the innocent victims of social iniquity and injustice. In this bitter defiance and loud-tongued protest he becomes larger than life. Then like a tragic hero he is completely vanquished by the force he comes in conflict with, though only physically. But what he lacks is the sense of reconciliation with the inevitable. He goes to prison revolting. Besides this, one can say that he lacks the dimension of a tragic hero. He lacks the passions, emotions and the strength of inner self. His individuality is blurred partially at least by the dramatist's design to make him a vehicle of social criticism. He remains, therefore, simply an impersonal type.[5] His sufferings cannot be attributed to any tragic flaw or 'hamartia' natural to character, though his pride, rebelliousness and obduracy arising from his social condition to constitute— 'hamartia'. He becomes more positively individual and assertive when placed by the side of his wife.

Mrs. Jones at once impresses us as a meek, simple and honest lady. She is a dumb, suffering and enduring creature as her husband describes her in his mood of frank antipathy, and has learnt only to bend before the calamities which the inhuman society and adverse circumstances may heap upon her. She is a soul of gentleness, love and self-sacrifice which prove practically ineffectual and serve only to increase her suffering. She has worn herself out to feed her brutalized husband and her innocent children and ventilates her grievances only in whispers to keep the consequences at arm's length. Every spark of individuality is crushed out of her by the cruelty of her lot and she remains before us more as a symbol than a living individual. She stands for all the frail and feminine creatures (in a wider sense of the term) who are born to suffer for their passive virtues and are crushed to nothingness by the forces, human or superhuman, without a word of defiance or a blow 'struck in the face of the wrong.' In a way she recalls Shakespeare's Ophelia and Desdemona and Galsworthy's own Irene in *The Forsyte Saga*, beautiful and white lambs, destined only as sacrifices to the dark forces of life. Her helpless gesture at the end of the play before the hypocritical and heartless M.P., John Barthwick, 'a man of high sentiments and liberal professions,' brings the irony of legal justice in all its nakedness and incalculable poignancy, setting a sharp edge on the dramatist's humanitarianism which is latent in the story itself. The part of Mrs. Jones, thus, is extremely pathetic, a dilution of the Aristotelian sentiments of tragedy (pity and fear) because she is shorn of that 'eminence', not social but moral or temperamental, which may be broken to pieces by hostile forces but which resolutely refuses to bend before them.

Though Mrs. Jones is human and like us, her character lacks growth—there is no development of her stature, no flesh of deeper insight. The plot, as we saw earlier, lacks the two important elements, namely the 'reversal of situation' and 'discovery'. It is because the plot is much more concerned with the presentation and definition of the social thesis, than with the revelation and exploration of human nature and behaviour. The lack of 'peripeity' and 'anagnorisis' in a plot where characters are subservient to the social problem detracts from the tragic effect of the play. When Aristotle called the 'plot' the soul of tragedy and gave to 'character' a secondary place he certainly did not preclude the possibility of human greatness and elevation within even the circumscribed limits of the unalterable sequence of events.

A tragedy is required to have a subject-matter which is not parochial but universal, dealing with the fundamental human problems, emotions and passions. Such a subject requires a hero who has a great soul capable of rising higher even in its fall before the superior force against which it is pitted. If the hero is too small in stature for the job, he will not be able to arouse in us the tragic emotions of pity and fear. In *The Silver Box*, as we have seen, the subject-matter is serious, no doubt, and has in it an element of universality to raise the play to the level of high tragedy, which, however, is not fully exploited. The characters (Mr. and Mrs. Jones) are common, familiar creatures brought against social forces operating blindly against them, but they are too strictly fitted into the frame of the naturalistic setting to cause any sense of liberation and elevation germane to the genuine sense of high tragedy.

As it is a problem play and no attempt is made at character building and the heroine suffers mostly passively, the emotion of pity dominates. Besides this, as George Steiner says,[6] when the solution of the problem, which brings about the tragedy of the hero, can be secured by a simple change of law, the tragic effort is bound to shrink in scope and diminish in its rigour. In *The Silver Box* the tragic effect is not one of reconciliation in the end, of the 'calm of mind, all passion spent'. Mr. Jones is never reconciled with the inevitable in the end and for Mrs. Jones the sufferings in her life have not come to an end. She does not retire from the scene defiant like her husband but stands dumb and helpless at the overwhelming agony. In spite of all this, we do feel the tragic impact of the play on us. This effect, in fact, comes from the sense of waste. We realise that Mr. and Mrs. Jones would have been fruitfully happy, if circumstances had been congenial to them and society just and sympathetic towards them. But they have been wasted away by the selfishness and lack of imagination in those who are running the social machinery.

We feel the emotion of pity at the suffering of Mrs. Jones who is a normally good and innocent human being. We also feel the emotion of terror at the way social institutions, meant for our welfare, are guided by the rich to the undoing of the poor who may fall easy victims to its blind fury for petty and venial crimes. We feel that, however, innocent and, honest we might be in the society of the Barthwicks, we shall meet with the same fate which overtook Mrs. Jones. The 'cathartic' effect of the play is further enhanced by our realisation of the inevitability of the end. We could never have hoped otherwise. This 'cathartic' effect is mingled, no doubt, with our feeling of resentment with which we leave the auditorium.[7] "In the end we are left with an overpowering sense of the inequalities of modern life and of the inadequacy of our social machinery to deal, one need not say, sympathetically but justly, with the miserable specimens of humanity it has produced."[8]

Next, we take up the style of the play. The style of a serious play should be simple, plain but not mean. It should be appropriate and elevated. *The Silver Box* is written in the language of everyday common speech. "The dialogue is crisp and human with all the cadences of speech."[9] It has a close resemblance to actual speech made dramatically effective. The very conversation between Mr. Jones and Jack displays the masterly economy in the use of words. The movement of the action is effected by the dramatic dialogue ; "We're all equal before the law—that's rot, that's silly," sets the action going. The whole plot is rather an expansion of this statement. Then take another example: " 'E got drunk—' E took the purse...but it's 'is money got him off—Justice!" sums up the premise of the play. All that the writer wants to convey has been conveyed effectively through the naturalistic dialogue he uses. The style is appropriate to the spirit of the play and to the characters who speak the language. To take an example (Act II—Sc. 2), the author conveys to the audience powerfully the picture of Jack as dull, good for nothing, and ego-centric by using three words repeated four times: "Crackers, please, dad." The dialogues where Mrs. Jones speaks become charged with emotion and still remain commonplace: "But you see, Betina, he has a very hard time—he's been out of work two months and it preys upon his mind. It's all the drink, and things preying on his mind; he's not a bad man," etc.

Galsworthy achieves a great dramatic effect economically by employing the well-known device of repetition. Thus. Mr. and Mrs. Barthwick complement each other with such remarks as 'you have not the imagination of a fly'. A significant aspect of this artistic economy is the dramatic use of silent and symbolic scenes and gestures. Thus, the cry of Jones' child very emphatically conveys the incalculable consequences of the petty crime committed in a fit of drunkenness and well-grounded spite by the father. The effect this cry produces on Mrs. Barthwick clearly shows that she is not devoid of natural sympathy and tenderness. But the way in which Mr. Barthwick muffles the penetrating cry by shutting the window succinctly summarizes the habitual practice of the rich to raise a wall of protection against the suffering prevalent among the less fortunate members of the society, who may be their neighbours. Equally emphatic and pregnant is the brief 'dumb-show' at the end of the play—Mrs. Jones advancing towards Mr. Barthwick for sympathy and the 'liberal' M.P. hesitating just a moment before beating a hasty and prudent retreat from the unfortunate petitioner. The silent episode speaks volumes about the relationship of the rich and the poor in our society, about the nature and character of the boastful 'lord' and about the bleak prospect of abject poverty which opens before the innocent victims of this social tragedy. Galsworthy has rightly said that it is passion which weaves the plot, because it is passion which provides a flaming soul to the familiar words and a powerful propulsion to the plot.

To sum up, *The Silver Box* is a problem play dealing with the social problem of the unequal dispensation of justice to the rich and the poor. It poses a problem which, on the face of it, is temporal and topical. Such a subject-matter is apparently unsuitable for tragedy, which deals with a subject of universal implications. But the subject has a larger dimension in the sense that it concerns a considerably large section of humanity and has remained one of the most familiar and recurring problems of human society. The protagonist and his wife and children suffer for no 'hamartia' of character but on account of the working of the social machinery. The defiance of Jones and the abject submissiveness of his wife both point to the inexorable force of society because both are the products of conditions resultant from social circumstances. This is why the true tragic function of the arousal of the emotions of pity and fear and their 'catharsis' are modified to a great extent.[10] The emotion of pity dominates over the emotion of terror, which is by no means completely absent, because throughout sympathy for these victims of society we come to apprehend the fearful nature of the social organization which may overwhelm us also with grief and affliction simply because we lack the power and influence to neutralize its blind iniquity. The central problem round which the play revolves contributes to the unity of its effect, and the various stages in the development of the action are so arranged that each logically leads to the other, and the drift of the whole is a slow but steady movement to the inevitable goal. The movement lacks the elements of 'the reversal of situation' and 'recognition' emphasized by Aristotle; yet it does not fall short of that tragic fatality which is uniformly present in all genuine Greek tragedies. The style of the play is simple, bare and familiar throughout and deliberately kept to the level of the language actually spoken by men, yet the emotional effect of crucial passages is very great and the artistic economy in the handling of dialogues and 'silences' reveals the hand of a cunning and conscious artist.

154

Thus, we find here that the principles of conflict as the basis of action, 'probability' and the organic relationship of the different elements of the play, and the function of tragedy as arousing the emotions of pity and terror, which have been enunciated by Aristotle, are illustrated by this play. Though it does not conform fully to the spirit of ideal tragedy as interpreted by Aristotle, it illustrates amply, positively as well as negatively, the validity of the basic principles of the *Poetics.* Then it bears out Aristotle's emphasis on plot as the principal constituent of tragedy, the characters being more in the nature of social types than individuals of marked peculiarities. The tragic vision which is embodied in the present play is social rather than cosmic yet the implication and appeal of the play is universal, because the problem presented is a recurring aspect of the social history of the race and it is destined to abide so long as selfishness remains the guiding motive of the men and women of power and influence.

FOOTNOTES

1 See Egri, Lajos, *The Art of Dramatic Writing* (Simon and Schuster, New York, 1960), p. 1.

2 Hamilton, Clayton, *Conversations on Drama* The Macmillan Company, 1925). p, 129.

3 *The Contemporary Drama of England,* p. 213.

4 Cunliffe, John W., *Modern English Dramatists* (Harper and Bros., New York, London, 1927), p. 99.

5 See Clein, Ellehauge and Munksgaard, *Striking Figures Among Modern Dramatists* (Copenhegen, 1917), p. 32.

See also *The London Mercury,* Vol. XXVIII, 1933, Sparrow, John. "John Galsworthy, pp. 51-2.

6 *The Death of Tragedy,* p. 8,

7 *The London Mercury*, Vol. XXVIII, 1933 : John Sparrow says that having witnessed the *Silver Box* the audience leave the theatre "with the good resolutions that the dramatist intended. But they have not seen a tragedy. If they had, the good resolutions might never have been made. Playgoers leaving the theatre after *King Lear* have not uppermost in their mind the resolve to show more gratitude to their parents. What is more, the persons in *Lear* are remembered when its lesson (if it can be said to have one) is forgotten; while the lesson of.... *The Silver Box* stays in the mind long after the characters have disappeared," p. 51.

8 Cunliffe, John W., *Modern English Dramatists*, p. 100.

See also *Masters of the Drama*, p, 617.

9 *The Contemporary Drama* of English, p. 213.

10 See *The Times Literary Supplement*, August 14, 1953, Review, *Tragedy and the Paradox of the Fortune Fall*, p. 522.

CHAPTER VIII

Sherriff's Journey's End

From Galsworthy's *Silver Box* to Sherriff's *Journey's End*, a war play in three Acts, the transition is easy, proper and logical; because in this play also our attention is fixed upon a serious social nuisance which cannot be attributed to the mistakes or errors of individuals, but to the collective pugnacity and lust for power, which have been common to the influential members of society, savage as well as civilized. Thus, though the immediate concern of the play is the World War of 1914-18, yet its significance is universal.[1] Eliot has rightly said that all wars are one war, because they are alike in their destructiveness and their brutalizing effect on the human victims. In this connection the citation from *Alice's Adventures in Wonderland* is very significant :

> How doth the little crocodile
> Improve his shining tail,
> And pour the waters of the Nile
> On every golden scale?
> How cheerfully he seems to grin
> And neatly spread his claws,
> And welcomes little fishes in
> With gently smiling jaws!
> (Act II, Scene ii)

The action of the play is serious and grave, even though the plot does not fully conform to the Aristotelian demand of the 'complex' action in tragedy. The narrative element is thin but the plot has a definite movement, internal as well as external, which intensifies the element of unity, because the various parts of the movement are bound together by the law of 'probability' and 'necessity'. The external movement has two broad divisions, the first representing the lull before the storm of actual attack, and the other, the advent of the attack itself and the destruction wrought by it. The lull is simply a calm before a destructive storm, so that the sense of suspense born out of an impending disaster hangs over it like a dark and sinister pall. This element is emphasized in the remark of Raleigh, "It seemed so frightfully quiet and uncanny—everybody creeping about and talking in low voices. I suppose you've *got* to talk quietly when you're so near the German front line —only about seventy yards, isn't it?" (Act II, Scene i). The lull is at last broken by the noise of the actual raid which can best be described in the words of the author himself :

"...suddenly, there comes the dull 'crush' of bursting smoke bombs, followed in a second by the vicious rattle of machine-guns. The red and green glow of German alarm rockets comes faintly through the dug-out door. Then comes the thin whistle and crash of falling shells; first one by itself, then two, almost together. Quicker and quicker they come, till the noise mingles together in confused turmoil." (Act III, Scene i).

More important, however, than the external movement is the inner movement represented by the psychological and spiritual journey of Stanhope, the central figure in the play. His career is the epitome of the actual stages through which young and innocent spirits have to pass as they move through the fiery ordeal of war. In this connection we recall the words of Osborne, the friend and colleague of Stanhope, with reference to the nature of the strain on his commander : "He came out straight from school—when he was eighteen. He's commanded this company for a year—in and out of the front line. He's never had a rest. Other men come over here and go home again ill, and young Stanhope goes on sticking it, month in, month out." (Act I). The strain naturally has been terrible and the nature of Stanhope has altered under it past recognition. In his school he was a virtuous hero hard upon those of his companions and fellow students who betrayed any weakness for drinking or smoking. The point is clearly brought out in Raleigh's account of Stanhope at School : "I know old Dennis's temper! I remember once at school he caught some chaps in a study with a bottle of whisky. Lord! the roof nearly blew off. He gave them a dozen each with a cricket-stump.... He was so keen on the fellows in the house keeping fit. He was frightfully down on smoking—and that sort of thing." (Act I).

But under the strain of war this impeccable man has been compelled to drown his killing depression and loneliness in the wine bottle so that his hard drinking has become a standing scandal among the officers under him. Stanhope himself makes a clean breast of this tragic fact in his reply to young Raleigh, who had the boldness to protest against his senseless drinking even after the death of his friend! "To forget, you little fool—to forget ! D'you understand ? To forget! you think there's no limit to what a man can bear?" (Act III, Scene ii). This journey of Stanhope is not only a process of brutalization but also one of alienation. One after another all the graces and privileges of life have been taken away from him till he becomes a lonely figure, dark and apparently lifeless amid the noise and crush of the furious war. In this respect the snap-shot presented by the author himself after the death of Osborne is quite pertinent to recall :

"Stanhope is staring dumbly at the table—at Osborne's watch and ring. Presently he turns his haggard face towards Raleigh, who sits with lowered head, looking at the palms of his hands. Stanhope moves slowly across towards the doorway, and pauses to look down at Raleigh. Raleigh looks up into Stanhope's face and their eyes meet. When Stanhope speaks, his voice is still expressionless and dead." (Act III, Scene ii).

'Reversal of situation' and 'recognition' in the strict Aristotelian sense may not be found in the plot of the play, yet the spiritual journey of Stanhope brings about one important development in him which is the gift of intense suffering. This development is an almost preternatural insight which borders upon insanity. Stanhope himself wonders at this change which he describes at length to his trusted companion Osborne : "D'you think this life sharpens the imagination! Whenever I look at anything now a days, I see right through it... I was looking across at the Boche trenches and right beyond—not a sound or a soul; just an enormous plain, all churned up like a sea that's got muddier till it's so stiff that it can't move. You could have heard a pin drop in the quiet; yet you knew thousands of guns were hidden there, all ready, cleaned and oiled—millions of bullets lying in pouches—thousands of Germans, waiting and thinking." (Act II, Scene i).

Stanhope, the protagonist of the play, has the requisite qualities of a tragic hero even though his suffering is not due to any 'hamartia' in his character. His tragic story is fully capable of exciting our pity because his searing experiences may aptly be described as 'unmerited suffering,' and this pity readily blends with fear born out of our conviction that any human being in Stanhope's position would have sufferred identical tortures and met with the same tragic end. Yet, we hasten to add that this tragic end is not entirely depressing or crushing, because it shows us very clearly the courage, bravery and mental ingenuity of men who are living in the midst of death and are undergoing the physical and mental strain quite apt to dehumanise and intimidate them.[2] In the earlier part we have been presented with a vivid and realistic picture of the life of soldiers and officers in the trenches, who are following their usual routine under the dark threat of death and destruction, their minds being brimful of devices which are calculated to beguile their worries and the strain of duty and make their life tolerable. Among them, Stanhope, the protagonist, stands first and foremost, because he has constantly stuck to his post amid all the ravages and destructions and in spite of the essentially human fear which lurks in his brave heart, this fear being so natural in the face of death. This interesting point is brought out in his crucial encounter with his fellow officer, Hibbert who refuses to face the grim ordeal and is bent upon escaping it even by feigning sickness, " I know what you feel Hibbert..... Because I feel the same—exactly the same! Every little noise up there makes me feel —just as you feel.. .. I hate and loathe it all. Sometimes I feel I could just lie down on this bed and pretend I was paralysed or something—and couldn't move—and just lie there till I died—or was dragged away." (Act II, Scene ii).

But it does not mean that one should shirk one's duty where one has to work with a team of trusted and fearless companions : "Take the chance, old chap, and stand in with Osborne and Trotter and Raleigh. Don't you think it worth standing in with men like that?—When you know they all feel like you do—in their hearts—and just go on sticking it because they know it's—it's the only thing a decent man can do." (Act II, Scene ii) But more remarkable than this grim determination to discharge one's duty amid the terrors of war is Stanhope's success in retaining his essential humanity even under the petrifying touch of war. This human touch forces itself upon our attention at certain points and raises the tragic career of Stanhope to a higher spiritual plane. For example, in a burst of anger he declares before Raleigh—"My God ! You bloody little swine ! you think I don't care—you think you're the only soul that cares.". (Act III, Scene ii). But the crowning touch of this essential humanity comes out towards the close of the play as young Raleigh is brought mortally wounded before Stanhope who actually pours the milk of human kindness upon his dying admirer and hero-worshipper. The whole effect of this tragedy is epitomized by the author himself :

'Stanhope lowers Raleigh's hand to the bed, rises, and takes the candle back to the table. He sits on the bench behind the table with his back to the wall, and stares listlessly across at the boy on Osborne's bed. The solitary candle-flame throws up the lines on his pale, drawn face, and the dark shadows under his tired eyes. The thudding of the shells rises and falls like an angry sea.''

(Act III, Scene iii)

Then comes the stern call of duty which must be obeyed and which means the end of this terrible journey, but even in this hour the demand of humanity cannot be ignored altogether. This conflict is vividly painted in the brief stage-direction, "Stanhope pauses for a moment by Osborne's bed and lightly runs his fingers over Raleigh's tousled hair. He goes stiffly up the steps, his tall figure black against the dawn sky." (Act III, Scene iii). The indication is quite, clear that this will mean the end of his journey, i.e. Stanhope's departure from this lonely life into the quiet embrace of death, because as he moves forward, the "whine of a shell rises to a shriek and bursts on the dug-out roof. The shock stabs out the candle-flame; the timber props of the door cave slowly in, sandbags fall and block the passage to the open air.'' (Act III, Scene iii)

It must be remembered, however, that the end of this journey is not tragic in the strict sense of the term because it is on this event that Stanhope has concentrated all his hope for rest and the regaining of all the things which life in the trenches has gradually deprived him of.[3] The point is underlined in his significant exhortation to Hibbert, "think of the chaps who've gone already. It can't be very lonely there—with all those fellows. Sometimes I think it's lonelier here." (Act II, Scene ii). The remarks bring out the significance of the famous Shakespearean line which supplied the title to this play—"The Journey's End is the lovers' meeting." Thus, the play may be described as a high tragedy because while it dilates upon all the terrors and tortures which man is destined to undergo for the follies of his race and the cruelty of adverse circumstances, yet there is in him an invincible potentiality of goodness and nobility, which even the most difficult trials of life cannot completely extinguish. It is this dual vision of human littleness and of human greatness which has formed the foundation of great tragedy, ancient or modern.[4]

This brings us to the style of the play which is realistic and colloquial for the most part and seems to contradict the Aristotelian requirement of dignity combined with simplicity. Yet, a closer attention to the play will convince us of one essential fact which is underlined by Aristotle in the course of the discussion of tragedy in the *Poetics*. The fact is contained in the famous remark of the Greek philosopher that the tragic effect does not depend upon spectacle and other external aids, because it is implicit in the story itself the bare narration of which should tend to produce the emotions of pity and fear. Thus, the apparently realistic and humdrum style becomes charged with great force and effect when we remember the rich suggestions behind the common words.[5] We may take, for example, the apparently casual and light-hearted remark of Osborne to Hardy : "The ones (beds) in the other dug-out haven't got any bottoms to them. You keep yourself in by hanging your arms and legs over the sides. Mustn't hang your legs too low, or the rats gnaw your boots." (Act I).

Then Hardy informs his companions that there are thirty-four gun boots and Osborne at once mutters, "seventeen pairs," but he is quickly corrected by the former, "Oh, no; 25 right leg and 9 left leg." (Act I) It is needless to point out that these ordinary remarks effectively bring home to us the nature of the hardship and of the ravages which modern warfare involves. But there are passages where the terrible effect of war is clearly and most emphatically expressed in the emotional outbursts of characters. The best illustration is provided by the moving words of Hibbert, "Stanhope! I've tried like hell—I swear I have. Ever since I came out here I've hated and loathed it. Every sound up there makes me all—cold and sick. I'm different to—to the others—you don't understand. It's got worse and worse and now I can't bear it any longer. I'll never go up those steps again—into the line—with the men—looking at me—and knowing—I'd rather die here." (Act II, Scene ii) Then there are brief and vivid passages in the form of stagedirection which contain the picture of the furious raid in miniature, where we have the simple style raised to the height of poetic dignity by the harmonious fusion of sound, sense and quiet lyricism. We have already quoted these passages substantially and it is not necessary to repeat them here.

In this way we can say that Sherriff has managed to produce a moving tragic play, with many essential qualities of great tragedy, out of the materials supplied by life under the stress of modern warfare, which, we are often given to believe, represents the conquest of machine over the natural human attributes of man.

FOOTNOTES

1 See *Types of English Drama,* p. 683,

2 See *English, The Magazine of the English Association,* Vol. VI, No. 34, Spring 1947, Leech, Clifiord, "Implications of Tragedy," p. 182.

3 See Nicoll, A., *British Drama,* (George G. Harrap and Co., Ltd., London, 1962), pp. 277-8.

See also Kreiger, Murray, *The Tragic Vision* (Holt, Rinehart and Winston, New York, 1960), p. 2-9.

4 See *PMLA*, Vol. XLIV, 1929, McIntyre, Clara F., "The Word 'Universality' as applied to Drama" p. 927.

5 See *The London Mercury,* Vol. XXXIII, 1936, Clarke, Austin, "The Problem of Verse Drama Today," p. 37.

CHAPTER IX

Masefield's Tragedy of Nan

The Tragedy of Nan is the story of an orphan girl whose father has been hanged for stealing a sheep. Since her father's death she has been living miserably with her aunt and uncle. Mrs. Pargetter, Nan's aunt, has made her niece's life a virtual hell by constantly finding fault with her and harping upon her father's fate, and, cruellest of all, dubbing her as a hanged man's daughter. See finally takes away her lover, i.e., Dick Gurvil, the only source of happiness to the cheerless girl, to get her brainless daughter married to him. Nan is forsaken by everybody in the world around her. She sometimes broods over the idea of committing suicide, but desists from doing so in the hope that her lover Dick Gurvil would one day marry her and put an end to her torture.... But this never happens. At the crucial moment of loneliness and despair she finds great consolation in the poetic half-distracted murmurings of the old Gaffer about the Severn harvest tide as it rushes up its narrow bed, sweeping all before it. Gaffer, a martyr of love is a fiddler and has come along with other invitees to Mrs. Pargetter's to attend a feast given by the latter. The tide exercises a strange fascination on Nan's mind. At first she thinks of herself in its grip with shuddering horror : "A strange fish in the nets tomorrow. A dumb thing knocking agen the bridges. Something white. Something white in the water. They'd pull me out. Man would. They'd touch my body. I couldn't. I couldn't." Then the news comes that the innocence of her father has been established by the confession of another man, and the Government has sent to her fifty pounds as compensation for the "misapplication" of law—for the wrong done to Nan and her father. It seems a bitter irony to give fifty round pieces of yellow metal for the life of a man. This irony is made more bitter when Dick Gurvil, who was really put of more by Nan's poverty than by the supposed stain on her father, comes back to her with the proposal to marry her and throw over Jenney. To test him, she proposes to give the money she has received to Mrs. Pargetter as a salve to her wounded pride and when he hesitates, she finds him out as the selfish, sensual, treacherous man that he is, and stabs him to death to spare other women from his wiles and meanness. As the other members of the family open the door in answer to his outcray, the sound of the tide is heard rushing up the Severn and Nan goes out to meet this messenger of her death.

The plot of *The Tragedy of Nan* is based on the pattern of *Oedipus Rex* in as much as the event forming the basis of the action has already occurred and the progress of the play simply shows the suffering undergone by the heroine on that account. The plot develops into a sequence of events leading to the tragic end of the heroine in a manner logical and inevitable enough to satisfy the Aristotelian demand for 'probability' or 'necessity'.

As the play opens we are introduced to the main problem of the play, i.e., Nan's sufferings. The theme of the play tends to illustrate the saying that children are visited by the sins of fathers as we find in many of the important Greek tragedies. Nan's father is supposed to have been a sinful man because he was hanged for committing a petty theft. She was left alone after her father's death and was given shelter by her uncle but this patronage itself is extremely humiliating. Mrs. Pargetter hates her and calls her a "gallus bird" because she is "always, so prim and well be'aved" and "always elping 'er friends." She is alway plotting against her and wants to turn her out of the house. Mrs. Pargetter dislikes Nan because she prizes family respectability above everything else and Nan happens to be the daughter of a socially looked-down-upon man. But the hollowness of her idea of family respectability becomes clear in an ironical way when we learn from her own husband that once upon a time she herself was "sweet on 'er dad."

In this environment of malicious cruelty Mr. Pargetter's attitude towards Nan seems to be of great consolation. But it is rendered ineffectual by the machinations of his domineering wife. By the end of the first act even this illusion of Mr. Pargetter's support to Nan is shattered. Mr. Pargetter remains just a neutral disinterested observer of the tragedy of Nan. Moreover, this neutrality is turned into positive anger by the accidental breaking of the mug, the mug which he valued greatly, an accident which his wife is quick to capitalize.

We also learn before the curtain falls on the first Act that preparations are being made to receive some guests at a dinner to be given by the Pargetter which, among others, would be attended by Gurvil.

By the end of the first Act the stage is set for Mrs. Pargetter's cruellest stroke to Nan. She prepares to snatch away Nan's only object of hope, i.e., Gurvil. Nan can forget all her miseries only if she gets her lover. This we learn from Nan's confession of her deep love for Gurvil to her "friend," Jenney, who under the pretext of friendship elicits her heart's secret to convey the same to her scheming mother. This small episode shows Nan's hunger for sympathy in an atmosphere of stark antipathy, open or cloaked. Even the brainless Jenney can show a vileness of heart quite worthy of her mother's daughter. Thus, this sole hope of poor Nan is ominously shadowed by the cloud of Mrs. Pargetter's dark design.

When the curtain rises on the second Act, we find Gurvil confessing his deep love to Nan, which sounds deceptively sincere. Nan tries to tell him about her past regarding her father, but Gurvil won't listen to her and promises to many her for her own worth. But we remain doubtful because we know that Mrs. Pargetter will try to take Gurvil away from Nan for her daughter at all cost. And she has a big trump card to defeat Nan with, which is the past of Nan's life, i.e., her father's guilt. Our suspicion comes true when we find Dick Gurvil learning from Mrs. Pargetter about Nan's father and about his own father's decision to disinherit him in case he married any such 'unworthy' girl as Nan. He at once shrinks from accepting Nan, and prefers a brainless girl with some economic stability and free of any social blemish to a girl who is beautiful, intelligent and loving but is known as the daughter of a hanged man. Now everybody has forsaken Nan. The last prop of her hope is gone. Here the plot reaches its climax. We realise that Nan's course of life is almost clear. Where should she go now ? In the previous Act we heard her saying : "O Dad I wish I were dead." Should she then commit suicide ?

Being forsakan by all and rendered lonely, Nan now gets a new insight into the affairs of life. Here the 'reversal of situation' and recognition take place simultaneously. The plot develops into a turn contrary to what Nan has been striving for and she discovers the truth, i.e., that the present world in which she has been living is rotten and people around her have cold, selfish hearts. There is no meaning in hoping anything from this wicked world. This is why Nan now decides to join the world of old Gaffer where there is no cruelty, hypocrisy, treachery and jealousy—where one's happiness is not crossed by the sins of one's parents and the malice of one's 'friends'. Thus by the close of Act II the plot has made it clear that the only world for Nan is that of Gaffer's imagination and the only way out of the present state of affairs is the Severn tides.

This feeling is further accentuated in Act III. Now she

feels a sense of nothingness in her life when her "love be dead" and the inevitability of her going to the grave becomes clear, and she already has this realization that she was in the grave because her "heart was broke." Nan's desire to be swept away by the tides and Gaffer's description of these leave no doubt in us about Nan's fate. Gaffer says that whenever the tide comes in the river Severn, someone is washed away : "It be full moon to-night maidy. There'll be a high tide to-night. For some one of us.... It'ad some one every time. It'ad my vlower one time. O, it be a gallows thing, the tide." Who would be the victim of the tide to-night ? Will it be Nan ? May be, Nan will surrender herself to it as she has no more interest in her life on this earth. She has begun to speak the language of old Gaffer and feel the mysterious impact of the tide on her, though still with a slight shudder : 'Fast, Fast. A black line. And the foam all creamin' on it.... A bright crown upon it. And hungry...... The claws of the tide. ... And to-night it be the harvest tide.... A strange fish in the nets to-morrow. A dumb thing. Knocking agen the bridges. Something white. Something white in the water. They'd pull me out. Men would. They'd touch my body...."

After the action has made it clear to us that Nan's future course of life is decided now, we are brought back once more to the world of Pargetters and Jenneys. Nan has discovered the real self of Jenney and makes her "girl friend, little Judas friend" see her wretched self which is a "little, mean, cold lying thing" who "cannot love nor hate." At this time the action apparently seems to take a turn for a happy conclusion when Parson Drew and Captain Dixon come and inform Nan that the actual culprit has confessed his guilt of stealing the sheep for which her father was hanged. They have brought fifty pounds as compensation to Nan for this 'misapplication' of law. Unlike others around her, Nan evinces no pleasant surprise because she has had little doubt about her father's innocence. The award of fifty pounds to her is nothing but an ironic play of fate with her and it adds to the cup of bitterness which fate has already prepared for her. This serves to enhance the pathos for the girl who, knowing that her father was innocent, had to suffer for his supposed guilt. Now there comes a sudden change in the attitude of Dick who tells Nan of his new conviction to marry her. The shrewd girl cleverly tests him by her proposal to give all the money she has just now received to Mrs. Pargetter as a peace offering. The mean, materialist Dick falters. Nan shows Dick his real self, a mean and sensual materialist, and stabs him to spare other women from his wiles. Nothing is now left for Nan but a willing surrender to the Severn tide. Thus, Nan, a hapless, innocent girl, caught in the toil of fate, is eventually transfigured into an awe-inspiring force of destruction which strives to sweep away all evils and wiles around her before sinking into the embrace of death.

The plot has the unity of action, time and place, the last two helping the first, which is the prime requirement of the tragic plot. It has a beginning, a middle and an end. The action depicts the consequences of heredity upon the next generation and the heroine's pertinacious but unavailing conflict with her environment. The basis of the action, the guilt of Nan's father sets the tragedy in motion under the impact of which Nan discovers the sordid meanness in the persons around her and find ng no meaning in her existence decides to be one with the rising tides of the Severn. When Nan goes to meet the Severn tides, we realise that it is but logical and inevitable that the Severn tide is the only way out for Nan. When she has gone, nothing remains in the plot for further development, for which we could be curious. The plot develops logically and shows the principle of cause and effect and no where do we find any incident of crude realism. Incidents like Nan's taking up the knife and threatening Mrs. Pargetter to kill her, her compelling of her 'Judas friend' to eat the rotten meat herself which she had brought for the old Gaffer, and her stabbing Dick after she has convinced not only herself, but also the victim of his meanness, are all integral to the plot. Her decision to woo the Severn tide is the last stage in the development of the story of Nan's suffering. She has been prepared for it by the cumulative effect of the events preceding, each one of which serves only to intensify her sense of man's malice to man and the utter futility of life itself. She is thus psychologically attuned to the magic vision and enchanting voice of old Gaffer, a true lover and love's martyr like herself, who is already lost to the normal ways of the humdrum world and is intoxicated with the beauty and peace of that other world to which all that we love and prize are wafted by the tides of death.

The unities of time and place help the compactness of the plot[1] and bring about an artistic simplicity in the structure. The entire action of the play takes place in one place—Pargetter's house—and the time taken for the whole plot does not cover even twenty-four hours. But it should be remembered in this connection that nowhere is the 'probability' of the action in any way affected. These unities underlie the structure and are not imposed upon the plot. The movement of the plot is slow but steady. All the situations head towards the inevitability of the end. There are some incidents which might appear crude, petty and even unsuitable for any serious treatment to a sophisticated reader. But, as we shall see in the following paragraphs, the ordinary stuff of this tragedy is imbued with tragic seriousness and the protagonist, though an ordinary girl, is transfigured into a being of tragic height with a deeper insight into the realities of life than the people around her are capable of.

"*The Tragedy of Nan*," says[2] A.E. Morgan, "is the greatest example of the possibility of moulding great drama from the simple material of rustic life." The story concerns the lives of the peasants in the first decade of the nineteenth century. But the dramatist has no inclination to deal with any social problem of the day. He is occupied with the elementary passions of human beings. It may appear to a superficial observer that the play deals with the low, sordid story of a poor girl crushed to death by beastly and merciless cruelty. But "if it were that and that alone it would indeed be a repulsive play."[3] The play deals with inhuman cruelty meted out to a poor orphan, which, if narrated in its skeleton, would appear an unsuitable subject for tragic treatment. But the calculated and callous cruelty that *The Tragedy of Nan* depicts "has hardly ever been depicted with greater power,"[4] than Masefield has shown here. Nevertheless, this cruelty and inhuman behaviour of the people toward Nan is only the substratum of the play and not the essence of the tragedy. The essence of tragedy is to be found not in the ignoble and cruel environment in which the heroine has been living, but in the soul of Nan herself. She is hemmed in with a ring of implacable circumstance created by the combined forces of Mrs. Pargetter's wicked meanness, her cruelty and ignoble machinations, Dick's materialistic sensuality and selfish treachery, the hardness of Jennet's narrow and mean heart and the too easy acquiescence of her not unkind but weak uncle. The subject-matter of the play is universalized and raised to the height of tragic pathos when we begin to feel the sense of waste in the wreck of a fine soul like Nan's. Nan might have grown gradually to a beautiful and happy maturity under the mellowing influence of love and affection, the rich profusion of which in her is evinced by her lavish sympathy for old Gaffer.

John Gassner has remarked that *The Tragedy of Nan* is not so much a modern play as a timeless evocation of brutality and poetry; "the most sordid reality and a grisly nightmarish element were compounded in this peasant drama into something memorable."[5] The dramatist has successfully transformed the folk life into a subject-matter of high tragedy. The subject-matter assumes a universal significance because the grandeur of Nan's soul and her insight into the truth of life soar beyond this sordid reality. "The play" says Allardyce Nicoll, "gains an added grandeur by its use of heredity as a fatal force, consuming children's lives for the sins of their parents."[6] Here the "concrete facts of an unhappy state are magnified to a universal and quieting significance."[7] Some have seen in these "concrete facts of an unhappy state" only a sordid story of crime. But "the critics," says John W. Cunliffe, "generally recognize it, not only as the best thing Masefield has done in drama, but as a leading modern example of domestic tragedy worthy for its artistic restraint and imaginative power to be compared to Synge's *Riders to the Sea*."[8] Masefield's own statement of his conception of tragedy is clear and emphatic and takes full account of the crude commonplaces as a worthy ingredient of true tragedy. "Tragedy," he says in his Preface to *The Tragedy of Nan*, "at its best is a vision of the heart of life. The heart of life can only be laid bare in the *agony of dreadful acts*." He says that the tragic effect can be attained by a combination of reality and poetry and we find that the golden thread of poetry runs throughout *The Tragedy of Nan*, which would otherwise have been sickeningly oppressive. "The sound of the river brings the eternal note of sadness in, and the babblings of the almost clairvoyant old Gaffer, to whom Nan brings her sorrows, provide an eerie obligato. The unearthly music of water and of Gaffer's unintelligible words blend with the harsher music of peasant dialect as spoken by the other characters into a tone-poem."

The next point to be considered in our analysis of the play is the character of Nan as a tragic heroine. She is outwardly an ordinary girl, daughter of a man hanged for stealing a sheep. She has been given shelter by her uncle and aunt not for love and sympathy but for ensuring the concealment of Mrs. Pargetter's previous secret relations with Nan's father. Nan's life is a perpetual torture to her. Her aunt hates her for no fault of her own. Her uncle is almost indifferent to what has been happening about her in the family. The third

member of the family, Jenney, though an idiotic girl, pretends
to be friendly with her but only to betray her after she has
elicited Nan's secret (though it was no longer a secret now)
of her object of love which Mrs. Pargetter would snatch away
for her daughter. Her lover Dick Gurvil also betrays her and
that too when she has reached the peak of her emotional
exaltation. Even the disclosure of her father's innocence
comes to her as an added bitterness which fate has already
meted out to her. Her long sufferings have transfigured her
into an object of our admiration. Hers is not passive suffering
(though in the first Act this impression may come to many)
which would detract from her tragic greatness. The
essence of the greatness of a tragic hero lies in his capacity
to react to his situation. Nan eventually does react to
her situation. She even threatens Mrs. Pargetter to
kill her, when the latter tears the collar of her coat given to
her by her loving father. She forces Jenney to eat the poiso-
nous mutton pie herself which she had brought for old Gaffer.
She can even kill Dick Gurvil, whom she once loved, when
she is convinced of his treachery and materialistic consideration even in love. At last she goes to embrace death without
any hesitation once she is convinced of the futility and depravity of the life around her. It should be borne in mind that
Nan's capacity to react and her spiritual strength are not stati-
cally present in her. They are rather the result of her character
which develops within the plot. In the beginning she is
somewhat passive but as the situations surrounding her
develop, she is transformed into a girl of extraordinary capacity
for action and one who attains an insight into the truth of life
which average people don't have. Besides all this, Nan is
human and like us. She has desires and emotions natural to
all human beings. Like all girls she has a desire to marry and
beget children : "But it be wonderful for to 'ave little ones.
To 'ave brought life into the world. To 'ave 'ad them little
live things knocking on your 'eart, all them months. And then

to feed them. 'Elpless like that'." These words spring from the deepest core of the heart which is full of motherly instincts. But her stature is raised above the common humanity around her and even humanity in general in her acquisition of the true insight which enables her to see things in clear perspective in relation to the higher reality of life and realise the futility and nothingness of the life based on materialism. She imbibes clairvoyance and speaks the uncommon language of old Gaffer, which others around her befogged by lust and money, cannot understand.

The tragic dignity of Nan's character is discernible when we find her forsaken by all and standing like a lonely rock, unsubmissive to the people around her and her adverse circumstances. Like old Gaffer, she also is transfigured by suffering. More than him, she becomes, as it were, a divine instrument, the saviour of innocent girls symbolized by her killing of Dick who is the breaker of women's hearts. She becomes ruthless as she gets an insight into the reality beneath the appearance. It might be argued that Nan's tragedy involves the suffering of an innocent person which is not conducive to the production of true tragic emotions. But a closer scrutiny will reveal an element of 'hamartia' in her gullible nature and her proneness to believe everybody. She confides the secret of her love to Jenney who is a spy on her. It is because of her simple nature that she is not able to understand Dick fully in the beginning. But as in a Greek tragedy, her suffering does not ensue from her good and simple character alone because fate, which in the present case is 'heredity' and hostile environment combined together to blast her life.

The tragic sense of Nan's character arises from the utter failure of her effort to woo one after another—the persons around her, for sympathy, help, love and support in a desperate bid to mend her broken life and ensure at least a moderate peace and happiness which is the birth-right of every rational creature. She finds ultimately a spiritual affinity with Gaffer

176

and decides to woo death which remains the only alternative
left in her life. Yet she offers a sharp contrast to Gaffer, the
martyr of true love, who is emotionally dead to the affairs of
this world and can dream and talk only of his dear one and of
the happier realms where her soul has taken its abode. Nan,
on the contrary, is embittered by the treachery and meanness
of her fickle-minded lover and is determined, as it were, to
obliterate all traces of human infidelity around her. She
becomes a tragic force as ruthless almost as Medea and Lady
Macbeth. "Broken, Nan stands lonely as a truly tragic figure
companioned only in spirit by the half-mad old Gaffer, whose
peculiarly beautiful meanderings add a touch of high passion
to the theme."[9]

This leads us to the consideration of the tragic emotions
peculiar to this play as a type of tragic drama. Nan is human
and like us. She suffers for no fault of her own. We pity her
for her sufferings. This pity in the beginning tends to be
sentimental because we find her amidst people who are hostile
to her, enduring all the cruel perpetrations. But if we take
into account Nan's confrontation with heredity and environment which are the modern equivalent of Greek fate and consider Nan's strength of mind and soul and her unrelenting
struggle with her situation, this impression does not remain
long with us. Later on, in the play, we find the element of
terror more dominant than pity, when she is transfigured into
a superhuman being—into an agent of divine Nemesis as it
were, destined to effect a purgation of the world of crooked
hypocrites like Dick. We feel the emotion of fear when we
realise that the forces of heredity and environment are too
powerful and pitiless to be overcome or neutralized by human
goodness and innocence. The tragic emotions arising from the
play are accentuated in effect by the sense of waste that we
feel here. "This girl might have grown gradually to beautiful
happy maturity under the mellowing influence of love and
kindness. The pressure of besetting fate forces her soul to

an unnaturally fast growth. The influence of sorrow may be beneficent but if it overtakes the spirit too suddenly and too violently, it may overwhelm. Her cup of sorrow is too deep and too bitter. Instead of sweetening her nature and tempering her sympathies it swells her heart with tragic intensity. Suddenly she stands erect no longer a girl but a woman impelled by all the force of thwarted passion. How she would have loved we may judge from the gentle affection, which she lavishes on the old Gaffer, the only object on which she can bestow herself. There is something infinitely touching and infinitely beautiful in this exhibition of maternal love, for it is with a mother's solicitude that this clings to and cares for the old man."[10]

The true test of tragic effect is a proper purgation of these emotions—a genuine 'catharsis,' to use the much discussed term. There must be a sense of reconciliation in which all the emotional din and upsurge are buried. This reconciliation is the last stage in the development of the plot. In the present case Nan's efforts to exist in this world are all foiled. The plot as it has developed until the end of Act II makes it clear that death is the only way out for her. But at first she shudders at the idea of meeting death by drowning : "A strange fish in the nets tomorrow.... They'd pull me out. Men would. They'd touch my body. (Shuddering) I couldn't. I couldn't". But as the action moves on, her fear melts away and she is ready to meet death half way. Nan in the end is reconciled with her tragic lot. This inevitability of her end is calculatde to induce in us a "calm of mind, all passion spent." We feel this emotional repose when we realise that this world—crooked, cruel and unsympathetic that it is,—is not for Nan and she must seek the shelter of the grave. There does not seem to be any other solution to Nan's problem of life in the present set-up of circumstances. Nan comes in conflict not with a temporal cause which, as George Steiner has discussed,[11] is not conducive to the production of tragic effect,

Greed, lust, jealousy and cruelty in man are as old as Adam's fall from heaven to earth and no human effort can remove them completely from the heart of human beings. The soul recoiling from them falls into the embrace of death, a fact emphasized by the mystifying utterances of Gaffer interwoven into the main body of the action itself.

"Tragedy," says, Masefield (in a passage already quoted), "at its best is a vision of the heart of life. The heart of life can only be laid bare in the agony and exaltation of dreadful acts. The vision of agony, or spiritual contest, pushed beyond the limits of dying personality, is exalting and cleansing. It is only by such vision that a multitude can be brought to the passionate knowledge of things exalting and eternal." Here it seems that Masefield desires the "dreadful acts" to be shown in the body of the action as is the case with the 'Oedipus' story which, as B.H. Clark[12] remarks, Masefield probably had at the back of his mind. "The heart of life" can only be "laid bare through dreadful acts," says Masefield. But this does not mean that "dreadful acts" in themselves are exalting and cleansing. It is the business of the artist to utilise this material in art to give aesthetic pleasure by charging the raw material with a significant import. This is true of the present play where crude raw materials of the life of an ordinary girl are artistically moulded to yield the effect which is "exalting and cleansing." Masefield in his paper on 'Playmaking' (in *The Taking of Helen and Other Prose Selection*, 1924),[13] says that "the foundations of drama is this, that human action is hypnotic; if you do something, you will hold the attention of men." This statement, which is amply illustrated in his *Tragedy of Nan*, makes a good case for Aristotle's conception of the supremacy of plot over other elements in tragedy. Masefield follows Aristotle very closely in his representation of conflict—spiritual or otherwise— as the very kernel of the tragic plot upon which everything else depends. "The vision of the agony or spiritual conflict" which does not remain particularised but rather becomes universalized—"is pushed beyond the limits of dying personality. "In *The Tragedy of Nan* this conflict, though beginning as a particular episode, assumes universality as the heroine herself is changed into a universal figure and rises above the mundane considerations of life. Thomas H. Dickinson[14] says that "to the classic Idea of catharsis there is added now the demand that this cleansing conduces to more knowledge of eternal things on the part of the race. Darwin has been added to Aristotle.... Tragedy must search the vision of the heart of life in order to elevate its reality. This *The Tragedy of Nan* does. The substance of the play is one with the substance of life. But the spirit of the play elevates the substance to Tragedy."

The next point for consideration is the style of *The Tragedy of Nan*. B. H. Clark rightly says[15] that though *The Tragedy of Nan* has been "wrought out of the folk ways of England," it has considerable merit of high tragedy... "His lyric passages are uplifting... in his sorrowful story of Nan, his greatest play and high watermark in English poetic composition for the stage." In *The Tragedy of Nan* Masefield uses the rural dialect for the folk story that he has chosen for his play. The prose that we hear from the characters in the play is simple and clear. It is fully capable of furthering the movement of the action. Take, for example, the following conversation :

Nan — "When I was grateful you called me a 'ipocrit.

Mrs. Pargetter — Oh ! When was you grateful, as you call it ?

Nan — When I first came 'ere. I did my best, I did. I thought you'd like me if I work 'ard, and 'elped you.

Nan — I used to make you tea afore you got up of a morning. I wash up the dinner things, so as you could 'ave your nap of a afternoon,...."

... ...

Nan	—	Jenney. I'll thee why I didn't kill myself.
Jenney	—	Lord, Nan, don't 'ee.
Nan	—	I want 'ee to bear with me. Jenney : I'll tell 'ee why I didn't kill myself. I thought...there...It's only nonsense. Did you ever think about men, Jenney? About loving a man? About marriage?

...   .

| Dick | — | Do 'ee care for me? Do 'ee love me Nan? |
| Nan | — | You don't know! You don't know! You don't know about me. |

...   .

| Dick | — | When shall us be married? When shall us come together? |
| Nan | — | Ah, my love! Now is enough. Now is enough. |

...   .

| Nan | — | Now loose me, darling I have had my moment   I have been happy..." |

The style is appropriate to the crude realism of domestic life. But with the appearance of Gaffer at the crucial point, the style assumes an extraordinary beauty. In fact (as we have already said) it is the golden thread of poetry, running through the play, which relieves this play from becoming sickeningly oppressive. "The unearthly music of water and of Gaffer's unintelligible words blend with the harsher music of peasant dialect as spoken by the other characters into a majestic tone poem. For one brief moment in the British theatre realism became sublimated into folk poetry, and common speech acquired a golden tongue as in Ireland."[16] There is piercing beauty in the half-cracked old Gaffer's pathetic recollection of his wife who died fiftynine years ago :

"She looked out of the window, my vlower done. She said,

'The tide, the tide. The tide coming up the river.' And a she rose, my white vlower done. And she burst out a—a laughing, a—laughing. And 'er fell back, and my white vlower done. Gold 'air on the pillow. And blood. Blood of my girl. Blood of my vlower."

In *The Tragedy of Nan* Masefield has followed Synge[17] in the matter of style. The diction employed here is plain and homely. "But in the third Act, although it never attains the form of verse, it rises to great heights of lyrical beauty. It is essentially poetic in its captivating rhythm and in the weird and mysterious beauty of its imagery. In particular the conversation of Nan and Gaffer when her soul resounds to his while he tells her of the power and beauty of the tide is surely nothing if it is not poetry."[18] The conversation between Nan and Gaffer, besides being highly poetic and impregnated with suggestiveness, becomes almost mystical.

The secret of the greatness of *The Tragedy of Nan* lies in tha fact that the elements of tragedy here are interdependent and contribute to the totality of the effect of the play. This is in the true Aristotelian spirit. These elements separately do not have much significance. But their total impact upon the mind of the andience is that of true tragic pleasure.

To sum up, *The Tragedy of Nan* can successfully be analysed on the Aristotelian criteria of tragic composition. Its plot is simple and has the unity of action; it is compact and an integrated whole. It can conveniently be divided, as Aristotle demands, into two clear-cut parts, 'complication' and 'unravelling'. The first part begins with the opening of the action and reaches the climax where the two elements—the 'reversal of situation' and 'discovery' which constitute a complex plot—occur simultaneously. The climax is reached when Nan stands like a lonely rock, forsaken by all but erect and possessed of an extraordinary insight into the affairs around her and, above all into the nature of life, and the course of her own destiny. The second part begins from the climax and ends with Nan's embracing of the Severn tides. In the end the plot does not leave any curiosity in us unsatisfied or any complicated knot untied. Then the character of Nan, initially and ordinary girl forced into unfavourable conditions, attains to tragic heights as the action develops. In this connection we need to consider the greatness of her soul, her power of action and the deep insight which she achieves later. She becomes larger than life when she rises, transfigured, above the petty concerns of life around her and becomes almost a divine agent for purging the world of unworthy souls like Dick Gurvils. As required by the rules of the *Poetics*, she is human and like us but she has a greater power of endurance and is much more capable of action than normal human beings. Aristotle says that innocent suffering is not conducive to the production of genuine tragic effect. The element of 'hamartia', therefore, has been considered necessary by him. This element also can be found in the present play in Nan's gullible nature and her wrong step blindly taken in disclosing the secret of her heart to her 'Judas friend', Jenney. But it can be added here that this does not alone constitute her tragedy or we can say that even without her confiding her secret of heart to Jenney, the course of action would have remained unaltered. This shows that the world is not worthy of open and simple Nans in whom the presence of such virtues as simplicity and openness of heart could become a weakness fraught with tragic consequences. Thus, the subject-matter of the play has been universalized, Masefield is not concerned with any social problem or such temporal things. The problem posed here is one of universal significance. The tragic effect of 'catharsis', has been successfully achieved and Masefield's consciousness of it is clearly proved by the Preface to the play. The end of the play which has been made inevitable by the development of the action based on the principles of 'probability', or 'necessity', brings about an emotional repose in the audience, watching and at times partaking of the sufferings of Nan. The style of the play is plain and homespun for the most part, yet becomes highly poetical and charged with suggestiveness in the last Act, with its generous infusion of the broken mutterings of Gaffer and his tranced conversation with Nan about his 'white vlower', the Severn tide and the golden rider.

One unique feature of this tragedy, in the light of the Aristotelian canons, is the emphasis de iberately laid on action more than on anything else for producing the tragic effect of 'catharsis' But this should not be misconstrued to mean the neglect or negation of character and other elements. It is the interplay of plot and character which determines success in producing the tragic effect. Thus, *The Tragedy of Nan*, which has been wrought out of the English folk-life in the early nineteenth century, is a high tragedy of considerable merit. Masefield wrote this tragedy with the full consciousness of the changed conditions as is clear from the 1911 Preface to *The Tragedy of Nan* :

"The poetic impulse of the Renaissance is now dead...our playwrights have all the powers except that power of exaltation which comes from a delighted brooding on excessive terrible things."

One would readily agree that this exalting effect has been achieved in the present play.

FOOTNOTES

1 See *A Study of Modern Drama*, Masefield, John, 'Playmaking' in *The Taking of Helen and Other Prose Selections*, p. 300.

2 *Tendencies of Modern Drama*, p. 260.

3 *Ibid*, p. 264.

4 *English, The Magazine of the English Association*, Vol. VI, No. 34, Spring, 1947. Malcolm, J.E., "Maeterlinck and Static Drama": "In the realm of Drama it is not murder and treason, jealousy or revenge, that should be the subject of modern tragedy.... The object of modern drama should be to reveal the grandeur and beauty of everyday life, the mysterious sources and powers of that life more clearly than they normally appear."

5 *Masters of the Drama*, p. 621,

6 *British Drama*, p. 375.

7 *The Contemporary Drama of England*, p. 217.

8 *Modern English Playwrights: A Short History of the Drama from 1825*, p. 181.

9 *British Drama*, p. 374.

10 *Tendencies of Modern Drama*, p. 264.

11 *The Death of Tragedy*, p. 8.

12 *A Study of the Modern Drama*, p. 297.

13 *Ibid*.

14 *The Contemporary Drama of England*, p. 217.

15 *A History of Modern Drama*, p. 188,

16 *Masters of Drama*, pp. 621-2.

See also *The Times Literary Supplement*, 'A Hope for Tragedy.' (August 7, 1959), p. 459.

17 See *Tendencies of Modern Drama*, p. 264.

18 *Ibid*.

CHAPTER X

O'Neill's Hairy Ape

The Hairy Ape presents a psychological conflict—a struggle within the soul of man himself. Here the external conflict only serves to induce the inner conflict which develops simultaneously with it. The present play is an attempt to depict the torment of a soul in conflict with itself, the torment which it feels at its alienation from its environment. The suffering of man, O'Neill shows here, springs from two sources—from his conflict with Fate which is none other than his own 'unconscious', and from his own sense of pride; ultimately free and independent as he is, he is responsible for most of the grief he brings upon himself through this pride.

O'Neill interprets the ancient Greek idea of Fate and the destruction of man in conflict with it in psychoanalytic terms. He follows Jung, who says that man has a longing for a life of meaning and purpose. He wants to have a sense of order in the universe to which he may 'belong'— with which he may live in harmony as he did in his primordial stage of existence. He needs a universe which he can trust. Jung calls this psychological fact—true though not provable objectively. The constant and claimant desire in the mind of man for a sense of order in the universe and its expression in archetypal symbols constitute the psychological truth of the existence of such an order. This order of existence which O'Neill calls 'Fate,' 'Mystery' or the 'biological past', is to be found in the forces working within human psyche. Following Jung, O'Neill claims that man's actions and problems spring not only from his 'personal unconscious', but also, and in a more significant manner and to a considerable extent, from his 'racial' or 'collective unconscious'. This means that the desires, motivations and actions of man are controlled and guided by the entire history of the race which might date back thousands of years. O'Neill conceives of this force—the 'unconscious'—as autonomous which exists independent of man but finds expression through him. The tragedy of man arises from his struggle with this 'unconscious' in order to reconcile its demands with those of his conscious ego. Man meets with destruction when out of his Pride, he begins to think that he can fulfil all his needs even by refusing to acknowledge the power of the 'nnconscious'—'personal' as well as 'collective'. The 'unconscious' takes the place of Fate, the gods, or the supernatural agencies of ancient Greece which used to foil the 'conscious' efforts of man's ego. In the present play the conflict is a psychological one. The hero struggles to find a solution to the spiritual problem : 'Where does he belong?'— the problem of understanding the meaning of life which man has been struggling to solve from times immemorial.

The Hairy Ape, which illustrates this ancient aspect of tragedy in the modern psychoanalytical terms, is the story of a stoker in a transatlantic liner, who is strong, sturdy and proud of his place in the liner. He is happy and confident that he 'belongs' there. He is visited in the stokehole by Mildred Douglas, the daughter of a big capitalist, who is frightened at his grimy appearance. Mildred's revulsion at his appearance seems to be an unbearable insult to him; his illusion of the sense of 'belonging' is shattered and he bocomes impatient to avenge himself on the insulting lady. He throws up his job and goes out to find a place where he can 'belong' and also to take revenge upon those who have destroyed his self-confidence by their superiority. He is eventually arrested and jailed. In the prison he hears that the I.W.W. are planning to blow up the factories of Mildred's father. He goes to them and offers his services, but he is taken to be a spy there and is pushed out of the I.W.W. office. Having been thrown out by his own men, he goes to a zoo to seek fraternization with animals. But he is not accepted there also, because the gorilla there crushes him to death.

The play aims at presenting to us mainly the psychological conflict in Yank who is struggling against himself. For this, eight short scenes, like eight snap-shots, have been presented to show Yank's position in different places and reveal his character. The first scene shows Yank in the stokehole. Here is a strong, and proud man with a deep conviction of the sense of 'belonging' :

"We're better men dan dey are, ain't we? Sure ! One of us guys could clean up de whole mob wit one mit. Put one of 'em down here for one watch in de stokehole, what'd happen? Dey'd carry him off on a stretcher. Dem boids don't amount to nothin'. Dey're just baggage who makes dis old tub run? Ain't it us guys? Well then we belong, don't we? We belong and dey don't.... Hell in de stokehole? Sure! It takes a man to work in hell— Hell, sure dat's my fav'rite climate. It eat it up. I git fat on it! It's me makes it hot! It's me makes it roar! It's me makes it move! Sure, on'y for me everything stops. It all goes dead, get me? De noise and smoke and all de engines movin' de woild, dey stop. Dere ain't nothin', no more? Dat's what I'm sayin'. Everything else dat makes de woild move, somep'n makes it move. It can't move without somep'n else, see? Den yuh get down to me. I'm at de bottom, get me! Dere ain't nothin' foither. I'm de end! I'm de start! I start! somep'n and de woild moves! It—dat's me! de new dat's moiderin' de old! I'm de ting in coal dat makes it boin; I'm steam and oil for de engines; I'm de ting in noise dat makes yuh hear it; I'm smoke and express trains and steamers and factory

whistles; I'm de ting in gold dat makes it money! And
I'm what makes iron into steel! Steel dat stands for de
whole ting! And I'm steel-steel-steel! I'm muscles in
steel, de punch behind it".

This long speech of self-glorification stemming from conviction leads all the company to yield to Yank's superiority and
the scene closes with a picture of Yank—a sturdy, proud man
who is the leader of the workers in the stokehole where he
properly 'belongs'.

Scene II is significant as a contrast to the picture of Yank
in the previous scene. In contrast with activity, exuberance,
vigour, contentment and conviction in life presented in the
first scene, here we have dullness, emaciation and a 'fretful,
nervous and discontented' life 'bored by anaemia'. Besides
this, the scene brings an element of suspense implicit in
Mildred's decision to visit the stokehole. She has a sense of
"disdainful superiority" and so has Yank a sense of the superiority of his strength and position in his own world.
Something significant might happen when these two
meet. This brings us to the third scene where Mildred is
standing in the stokehole and Yank is busy plying his work
with his back towards her, completely unmindful of her
presence there. When he turns his face towards her she is
horrified at the grimy appearance of Yank. She turns her
face from him and calls him a 'filthy beast' and faints at the
unbearable sight though she professes to be interested in the
study of the life of the poor and the working class people.
Yank "feels himself insulted in some unknown fashion in the
very heart of his pride... he hurls his shovel after them at the
door which has just closed." His pride, the very kernel of his
being, is wounded. He cannot get the peace of his mind
unless this wrong is redressed through revenge.

This brings us to Scene IV. Paddy suggests that Yank
should take recourse to law, to Government, to God which,

one after another, he rejects with ' abysmal contempt." When
Paddy interprets the words "filthy beast" as "hairy ape" to
Yank, the latter becomes furious and his conviction of
'belonging' is visibly shaken, though he is still trying to
console himself that he 'belongs'. The shake-up is too violent
for him to put up with. He is waiting for Mildred to come
down to the stokehole again to knock her down dead. But
she won't come because Yank "sacred her out of a year's
growth... She'll never come. She's had her belly full, I'm
telling you. She'll be in bed now, I'm thinking, wid ten
doctors and nurses feedin' her salts to clean the fear out of
her" (Scene II). The scene closing with this, makes the two-
fold conflict in the play clear : Yank's determination to avenge
himself upon the one who has insulted him (external conflict)
and his search for his place of 'belonging,' his struggle against
his ownself (the inner or the psychological conflict).

But the solution to Yank's problem of revenge is not so
easy. He has not to fight Mildred Douglas alone but all the
Mildreds who treat the Yanks in that fashion. Long tells him:
"I wants to convince yer she was on'y a representative of 'er
clarss. I wants to awaken yer bloody clarss consciousness.
Then yer'll see it's 'er clarss yer've got to fight, not 'er alone.
There's a 'ole mob of 'em like 'er, Gawd blind 'em!" Long
shows these people to him coming from the church in the
Fifty Avenue Scene. He has further accentuated Yank's
spiritual agony by telling him that he was only the slave of
this mob which don't 'belong' : "and you and we comrades,
we're 'is slave!... We're all 'er slaves. And she gives 'er
orders as 'ow she wants to see the bloody animals below
decks and down they takes 'er." Yank is shaken, "Say!" wait
a moment! Is all dat straight goods? As the mob is coming
out of the church, he speaks contemptuously about each man
or woman. He collides with a 'civilised' man, engages in a
brawl and is arrested. From this point onward we see Yank's
twin conflicts developing rapidly. He fails to avenge himself

on Mildred, the representative of the big class of the rich people and is convinced that he cannot 'belong' to the world of the refined, polished, civilised and materialistic people of the town. But he does not give up his search for the place where he can 'belong' nor does he give up his efforts to take revenge upon these rich people. In the next scene, while he is in the prison cell, he hears about the I.W.W. office and offers his services to them. But he is taken there as a spy of the police, an "agent provocator" and is thrown out of the I.W.W. office. He finds that he does not 'belong' there also. The plan, the Secretary of the I.W.W tells him to follow, is too insipid and meaningless for him. "Take some of these pamphlets with you to distribute aboardship They may bring results. Sow the seed, only go about it right. Don't get caught and fired..." etc. But Yank finds that this is no solution to his problem. The I.W.W. will not endorse his purpose of blowing up the factories and the Secretary calls him a "brainless ape." Yank is disappointed here also : "So dem boids think I belong, neider." Thus, Yank's plans are all frustrated in spite of his best efforts. Until now he had been saying that he 'belonged,' though his conviction was long shaken up in the stokehole with his encounter with Mildred Douglas, but he went on fighting desperately which is in fact a fight against himself : "Steel was me and I owned de woild. Now I ain't steel, and de woild owns me. Aw, hell ! I can't see—it's all dark, get me? It's all wrong! (He turns a bitter mocking face like an ape gibbering at the moon)."

It is here at last that Yank feels defeated when he has been forsaken by all. It is a turning point in the plot. Yank asks : "Say, where do I go from here." He cannot go back to the stokehole where his status is neither human nor truly animal. The only thing he can now try is to seek fraternity with the apes—to seek his primeval fraternity with the animals. He goes to a zoo where he confesses to the gorilla the falsehood of his illusion of 'belonging' which he had :

"On'y I couldn't get in it, see? I couldn't belong in dat." He opens the door of the cage. The gorilla comes out and 'hugs' him 'murderously'. Crushing him to death he goes back into the cage leaving him there. This leads Yank to the realization that he does not 'belong' to the animal world either : "Even him didn't tink I belonged.... Christ, when do I get off at? Where do I fit in"? The play ends with the death of Yank, who, the representative of humanity in the modern age, does not 'belong' anywhere. The only solution for him is the grave, the only place where "perhaps, the Hairy Ape at last belongs."

Thus, we see that the tragic search of Yank begins with his feeling of alienation from his environment—his severance from the world of nature. Tragic tension arises here, says Gassner, from Yank's "struggle against alienation."[1] Yank symbolizes the "eternal conflict between Man's aspirations and some intransigent, ineluctable quality in life which circumscribes and limits him, and frustrates the realization of those dreams which seems to make life worth living."[2] The conflict is a psychological one. The action depicts "man overwhelmed by the force of unconscious primitivism latent ¡in him."[3] It would not be proper to look at *The Hairy Ape* as concerned mainly with an external conflict. Some may consider it as a "tragedy of the American pitted against his environment" or "even of the proletarian pitted against Capitalism."[4] But it is the tragedy of "the universal human being pitted against himself."[5] At first glance, it may appear that Yank is thwarted by the forces of society and by his own limitations. "But I believe," says Edmund Wilson.[6] "that if anyone will read the last scenes in the printed text, be will see that though it is a consciousness of sociable inferiority that gives the first impetus to Yank's debacle and though he himself at first supposes that it is society he has to fight, the Hairy Ape's ultimate struggle for freedom takes place within the man himself." It is this conflict which is important for our analysis of the play and the development of the plot. The entire plot from the beginning till the end is concerned with this conflict. "Thus the plot of the play is a series of short scenes beginning in the hold of the steamer where Yank properly 'belongs' and ending in the zoo, where he is killed, and at last perhaps 'belongs'."[7]

Then Aristotle requires the plot to be a complete whole, and of a certain 'magnitude'. It should develop logically on the principle of 'probability' or 'necessity,' cause and effect and move steadily to the inevitable end. This inevitability has to be built up gradually through the course of the development of the plot. The plot of *The Hairy Ape* begins with a picture of Yank's illusion of his 'belonging'. We do not need to enquire how and why this sense has come, because that is not the problem of the play. The play attempts to shake this illusion and start the hero's search for a place where he may more securely 'belong'. The story develops from this point on the basis of causal relationship. The plot of *The Hairy Ape* ends with the inevitable destruction of Yank in his search for the place of 'belonging'. After the gorilla has crushed him to death, nothing remains in the plot for further development. The action is long enough to allow the progress to an inevitable close of Yank's search in a clear, logical and unambiguous manner. We do not feel anywhere that the action has been compressed to mar the tragic effect or detract from the building up of the inevitability of the end of the plot. Alexander Woollcott remarks: "The scene in the Fifty Avenue when the Hairy Ape comes face to face with a little parade of wooden-faced church-goers who walk like automata, and prattle of giving a Hundred Percent American Bazaar' as a contribution to the solution of discontent among the lower classes; the scene on Blackwell's Island with the endless rows of cells and the argot of the prisoners floating out of the darkness; the care with which each scene ends in a retributive and terryfying closing in upon the bewildered fellow—all these preparations induce you at least, to accept as natural and inevitable and right that the hairy ape should, by the final curtain, be found dead inside the cage of the gorilla in the Bronx Zoo."[8]

The most important element of a tragic plot is the unity of action. By this Aristotle means that the action should be a complete whole and the structural union of the parts should be such as nothing can be taken out of it without sufficient damage to the whole plot (*Poetics* VIII-4). Every incident in the plot should be organically integrated with the whole structure. *The Hairy Ape* consists of eight scenes. As the play is written in expressionistic style, these scenes are singly displayed. They are like small snap-shots to reveal the state of a struggling soul. But unless these scenes are connected by a causal relationship, the structure is bound to be affected adversely. Clifford Leech says that "there is, in fact, as stern a logic in the order of the scenes in *The Hairy Ape* as we found in *Emperor Jones*. First, Yank sees the rich in their Sunday clothes; then he is a prisoner; then he moves outside society's institutions and seeks refuge with the anarchists, the declared enemies of society; than he goes to the zoo. All the time he is moving further away from the world of Mildred Douglas who rejected him; if not there, he must find a lower place where he may 'belong'.[9] The plot "shows Yank's disintegration when his faith in the importance of his superhuman endurance was shattered,"[10] and this has been developed logically.

Then, as required by Aristotle, we find here that the plot can be clearly divided into two parts—'complication' and 'unravelling,' which primarily implies the development of the plot on a definite pattern which is logical and conducive to a natural evolution of the main problem. The action here, as we find in all genuine tragedies, begins with darkness, the hero's ignorance leading him finally to light, to the realization of truth. Here the darkness is the Protagonist's ignorance of his place in the universe—his mistaken conviction that he 'belongs' somewhere. The shock to his placid, though illusory state of 'belonging', resulting from his encounter with Mildred, leads him to a search for his place of 'belonging'. The truth of his position comes home to him when he realises, after the 'murderous hugging' by the gorilla in the zoo, that he does not 'belong' anywhere. We find that the two elements of 'reversal of situation' and 'discovery', which are a necessary accompaniment of climax and occur simultaneously with it, come at the close of the play. The 'reversal' occurs when contrary to the protagonist's expectation, the gorilla kills him and this naturally leads him to the 'discovery' of the truth that he does not 'belong' to any place. *The Hairy Ape* thus has a climactic end. Aristotle's division of the plot into the two parts mentioned above implies that the complication develops until the climax where the further development of the plot into denouement becomes decisively clear. In this regard we find that when Yank is thrown out of the I.W.W. office, the course of the action becomes clear—that it is fruitless for Yank to seek a place of 'belonging' in the human world. This also brings the realization of the truth that there is no place in the human world where man can 'belong' and that his conviction that he was the mover of the little world and the energy behind all movement was illusory : "Steel was me, and I owned de woild. Now I ain't steel and the woild owns me." (Scene VII) This point may be taken as the climax in the Aristotelian sense of the term, because from here the story hurries towards its tragic conclusion. It is here that we realize that now Yank will have to seek fraternity with the animal world. This realization is intensified and made more effective aud strongly felt when Yank learns from bitter experience that he does not 'belong' to the animal world also.

The plot of *The Hairy Ape* has been criticised by many critics. Hogo von Hofmannsthal says that ' the close of *The Hairy Ape*, seems to me to be too direct, too simple, too expected; it is a little disappointing to a European with his complex background to see the arrow strike the target toward which he has watched it speeding all the while."[11] Clayton Hamilton says that "the later scenes of the dramatic narrative are artificial and forced."[12] John Gassner endorses it : "The action, especially in the Fifty Avenue Scene becomes, increasingly frantic as well as unreal, as in the following episode in which Yank, the burly half-animal and half-human stoker, confronts the well-dressed men and women who have come out of the church."[13] But as Alexander Woollcott has argued, this and the succeeding scenes are the "preparations to induce you at least, to accept as natural and inevitable and right that the hairy ape should, by the final curtain be found dead inside the cage of the gorilla in the Bronx Zoo."[14] Clifford Leech agrees that the play has a "less obviously contrived structure" which "adds to the sense of actuality." But he adds that 'there is a stern logic in the order of the scenes in *The Hairy Ape*."[15] Thus, we see that though the plot of the present play is conceived in an expressionistic style, consisting of a series of apparently disjointed scene, it conforms, to a great extent, to the Aristotelian concept of plot-construction.

"This play," says Clayton Hamilton about *The Hairy Ape*, "interests me in its exposition of the character..."

The plot, as it develops, exposes the character of Yank to us. "The expressionist playwright," says John Gassner, "dispensed with the 'middle class' clutter to be found in man's mind and showed only the springs of passion. He did not hesitate to present depersonalised characters, individuals transformed into stark symbols or allegorical types deprived of a personal name....," etc. *The Hairy Ape* is written in expressionist style, no doubt, and the character of Yank is symbolical to some extent. Nevertheless, his character conforms considerably to the criteria put forth by Aristotle for a tragic hero. Accoding to Aristotle a tragic hero should be human and like us but at the same time he should be over life-size. He should have 'propriety' to his station, i.e., he should be a type, besides being an individualized character. He is essentially good but at the same time his fall is attributable, to some extent, to the element of 'hamartia' though the chief role in his fall is·played by fate. There may be many characters in a tragedy, but it is the central figure alone who becomes the character whose affairs from the main focus. When the play ends, it is he (the hero) who lingers in our mind.

Yank is the central charactar in *The Hairy Ape*. He is 'barely articulate, splendidly muscular, (and) dominant in stokehole.'[16] He is proud of his strength and proficiency in the craft he plies. He is human and like us which is attested by the fact that we sympathize with his struggle and his tragic end and admire him for his unrelenting fight against his fate. The inner dissension that he feels and the way he reacts to the insulting comment by Mildred Douglas, show him to be a man swayed by human emotions and sensitive to his environment. Yank, says O'Neill, is "every human being." He becomes larger than life in his domineering character, his superhuman physical power and a deep conviction of his sense of 'belonging'. There is dignity and splendour in his personality, though he does not rise to the spiritual largeness to which a hero ultimately attains. He is defiant in his attitude towards the environment and has an extraordinary capacity to react to his situation. When he determines to take revenge upon Mildred Douglas, the representative of the rich and the ruling class, he undertakes a Herculean task on his shoulder and his struggle assumes a universal significance. "By the faint spark of such intelligence as he has, he gropes out indomitably toward truth. Set against certain specimens of the upper class, he assumes epic grandeur."[17] For instance, take his utterances like: ' What's dem slobs in de foist cabin got to do wit us? We are better . . . we belong and dey don't ....'' Though Yank judges civilization from his own tiny corner, he is often disconcertingly near the general truth which at once raises his stature: "Hell in de stokehole? Sure! It takes a man to work in hell....But us guys, we're in de move, we're at de bottom, de whole ting in us!" The hero becomes larger than life when he grapples with a problem which assumes a universal character, i.e., his struggle to find a place where he can 'belong'. Then the element of 'humartia' in Yank's character is his inability to fit in the circumstance other than what he 'belongs' to. This lack of adjustability, combined with his strong sense of pride in his place in the universe, leads to Yank's destruction. It is because of this and his deep conviction in his 'belonging' that even a slight insinuation shakes his conviction and shatters his state of self-confidence and mental equilibrium. He does not want to live in any intermediate place between the state of 'belonging' and the state of spiritual sterility. Nothing less than what he desires can satisfy him. It is because of such an inner make-up of his being that he launches upon the struggle against the outer world which consequently leads to his struggle against his own self.

Then Yank's character shows a definite development from his state of happiness, self-confidence and 'belonging' through disintegration to the realisation of the truth that he does not 'belong' to any place. The only exit left for him is into death, when he is rejected even by the franternity of animals. Like a tragic hero he falls from a state of happiness to a state of complete destruction through the force of the 'unconscious,' the modern counterpart of ancient Fate and the element of 'hamartia' in his character.

Barrett H. Clark remarks[18] that in *The Hairy Ape*, O'Neill "instead of intensifying a particular man, has symbolised him in the person of Yank." O'Neill himself has said that *The Hairy Ape* "was propaganda in the sense that it was a symbol of man who has lost his old harmony, which he used to have as an animal and has not yet acquired in a spiritual way. Thus not being able to find a place on earth nor in heaven, he is in the middle, trying to make place for himself, taking the 'woist punches, from lot of 'em'. This idea was expressed in Yank's speech. The public saw just the stoker, not the symbol, and the symbol makes the play either important or just another play. Yank can't go forward and so he tries to go back. This is what his shaking hands with the gorilla meant. But he can't go back to 'belonging' either. The gorilla kills him. ...."[19] Yank would thus become a symbol and be deprived of the human individuality which is so essential. O'Neill defends his creation of Yank and claims that he is human first and symbol only in the second place: "I personally do not believe that an idea can be readily put over to an audience except through characters. When it sees "A Man" and "A Woman" —just abstractions, it loses the human contact by which it identifies itself with the Protagonist of the play...the character of Yank remains a man and everyone recognises him as such."[20] Thus, O'Neill's statement gives us to understand that Yank is depicted to represent an idea, a view of life. B. H. Clark says that "Yank has Human attributes, but he is a symbol. Is it possible to make a man and a symbol at the same time? A human being like hamlet or Faust may symbolize certain qualities or characteristics or even sum up a whole philosophy, but when the dramatist deliberately uses a figure in order to make him typify man, or humanity, he necessarily minimizes the human elements in his story. At least I feel this to be true in the case of Yank. He is supernatural, more or less an abstraction, an idea."[21] Supernatural one can be, and still he can be human. But one cannot have a symbol and a man in the same person: "Yank cannot symbolize man and his efforts to 'belong' and yet remain a single individual."[22] A hero can be a type and even Aristotle approves of it, but he cannot appeal to our emotions if he is just a symbol, a mere abstraction.

Though the premise of the play aims at conveying an idea and the hero does stand as a symbol for this, still he has features in his character which make him a human figure. His spiritual sensitiveness and agony, his pride, his lack of adjustability, his deep sense of self-confidence and his unrelenting struggle for the solution of the problem of life—go to make his fall pathetic and awful. He seems to collide with the force which he does not fully comprehend and hence the recognition of the truth produces the desired tragic effect. The purely symbolic character of Yank is redeemed to some extent at least by the universalization of the subject-matter which has immense human appeal.

The subject-matter of the play, if we take the hero's external conflict only into consideration, may appear to be "jejune in thought, a popular sermon,"[23] and unsuitable for tragic treatment. Doris Alexander says, *The Hairy Ape* gives the main outlines of his social theory as no other one play does. *The Hairy Ape* presents an extremely negative view of the state of mechanized America, where the worker best adjusted to the system is a "hairy ape" and where the "Capitalist class" is even more terribly dehumanized, for it has lost all connection with life, is simply a 'procession of marionettes!'" (Scene IV)[24] The theme of the play may appear to an unwary reader as a contemporary social problem—the rottenness of society, resulting from the inhuman economic system. But if we look into it carefully and take into account what O'Neill himself has said about it, we shall find that the subject-matter has a wider universal significance than what it appears to have to a superficial observer. Even the external conflict between Yank and Mildred Douglas and the former's determination to take revenge upon her have a universal significance. The motive of revenge and its frustration have been a suitable topic for tragedy since the ancient Greek times.

O'Neill says that "the subject here is the same ancient one that always was and always will be the one subject for drama, man and his struggle with his own fate. The struggle used to be with gods, but is now with himself, his own past, his attempt to 'belong'."[25] Through Yank, O'Neill has attempted to point out the spiritual state of man's existence in the mechanized world of today. Man was happy when he led a spiritual life—when he was in harmony with nature—when he 'belonged'. The play raises the fundamental problem of human happiness and man's position in the universe. The contemporary social problem is interlinked with the universal problem of man—his search for his place in the universe which once he had but now has lost, The failure of Yank to find acceptance even by the animal community and his being killed by the gorilla may suggest that the only way out for man is death, so desperate is his state. Here the influence of Schopenhauerian thought on the play is perceptible. This brings a pessimistic view of life, which probably O'Neill could not help. But the problem posed here is a universal one—the search of an uprooted soul for its place in the scheme of the universe. *The Hairy Ape*, thus, is "offered as a modern tragedy, correlative with the ancient presentation of man at odds with a supernaturally controlled destiny."[26]

The next point for consideration in our analysis is the tragic effect of the play on the reader or the audience. Aristotle says that tragedy produces the emotions of pity and fear only to allay them. It brings an emotional equipoise in us who have been witnessing the struggle of the hero at odds with a superior force. As we have already seen, Yank is essentially human and like us and his problem is the problem of everyone of us. The suffering he meets with, because of the tension resulting from his conflict,[27] because of his spiritual torture at the shattering of his self-confidence, produces the emotion of pity in us for him. We sympathise with him, and our pity is saved from becoming sentimental by our admiration for his manliness. We feel the emotion of terror at the insuperable force with which everybody may come in conflict—and react in the Yank-way. We admire Yank for his strength, courage and determination to fight the insurmountable force and with his own self.

Graham Sutton says that in "*The Hairy Ape* Yank's illusion is that he and his fellow stokers are the motive force of the world. Call it an obsession rather: for there is an element of deep truth in it that makes Yank both more pathetic and more admirable."[28]

A sense of reconciliation and the 'calm of mind' come at the end of the play through the successful building up of the inevitability of the end. We submit to the end as it is inevitable, and nothing else than what has happened could probably be the end of Yan's struggle. Yank tries to destroy Mildred and her class to avenge himself for his insult. We know that he has undertaken something impossible. But the deep conviction and the intensity of the feeling which prompt him throughout redeem the play from a melodramatic effect. Clifford Leech says[29] that the effect of the melodramatic comes from the idea that "the forces contended are not seen as altogether insuperable," and it is because of this, he claims. that O'Neill in his sub-title of the play calls it a comedy. Here it can be remarked that the term comedy has been used by O'Neill in an ironical sense. It is a comedy for those who take only the surface meaning of the play into account. By them Yank will be considered as rightly punished. One who is foolishly sensitive to insult and who blindly throws himself into the cage of a wild beast, cannot expect anything better than what Yank got. But the problem is far deeper and Yank's encounter with the gorilla and his destruction at his hands have deep symbolic connotations.

The last scene of the play with the force of its visual effect and Yank's monologue makes the condition of a lonely soul felt by us most effectively. Clifford Leech says that if the plot moves "toward an ultimate acquiescence in self-deception not towards the self-knowledge which...is the characteristic of tragedy," we cannot call the play a genuine tragedy.[30] *The Hairy Ape* does begin with a self-deception. By the end of the play Yank has no illusion left about his mistaken sense of 'belonging' and his search for 'daylight' ends in his discovery of the truth which, of course, he does not claim to have found but which becomes obvious to the audience.

The style of *The Hairy Ape* is simple and home-spun—the play is written in the realistic language of the sailors. This dialect which allows abbreviation has been brought to a pitch of effectiveness and great precision as the language in many places becomes expressionistic, e.g., the chorus of the stokers in the first scene:

> "Gif me a drink dere, you!
> 'Ave a wet!
> Salute
> Gesundheit!
> Skoal
> Drunk as a lord, God stiffen you!
> Luck!"

and so on for about[28] consecutive speeches. This expressionist distortion of language may appear sometimes to be enigmatic and coarse to the well-bred people, but it is effective and the words have been caught in all their richness. Alexander Woollcott remarks, "Squirm as you may, he holds you while you listen to the rumble of their content, and while you listen also, to speech more squalid than an American audience heard before in an American theatre; it is true, all of it, and only those who have been so softly bred that they have never really heard the vulgate spoken in all its richness would venture to suggest that he has exaggerated it by so much as a syllable in order to agitate the refined."[31]

"Shut up, yuh lousey booh! Where d'yuh get dat tripe? Home? Home, hell. I'll make a home for yuh! Dis is home, see? What d'yuh want wit home? (Proudly) I runned away from mine when I was a kid. On'y too glad to beat it, dat was me. Home was lickings for me, dat's all...." (Scene i). This simple dialect is raised above the level of its ordinariness by the intensity of emotion behind it. The style becomes lofty but still extremely simple in the monologue of Yank in the last scene. At places it assumes a poetic quality, though the form is prose : "Oh, there was fine beautiful ships them days," says Paddy the old Irish Sailor in Scene 1, "clippers with tall masts touching the sky—fine strong men in them—men that was sons of the sea as if 't was the mother that bore them. Oh, the clean skins of them, and the clear eyes, the straight backs and full chests of them! Brave men they was...we'd be making sail in the dawn, with a fair breeze, singing a chanty song wid no care to it. And astern the land would be sinking low and dying out, but we'd give it no heed but a laugh, and never a look behind....Oh, to be scudding south again wid the power of the Trade Wind driving her own steady through the nights and days....Nights when the foam of the wake would be flaming wid fire, when the sky 'd be blazing and winking wid stars. Or the full of the moon may be. Then you'd see her driving through the grey night, her sails stretching aloft all silver and white ...." (Scene I) He goes on in this reminiscent strain over the beauty of sailing in the past for over one page more.[32]

Then the style varies with the change in situation and from individual to individual. Yank speaks in a style which is broken and highly abbreviated but has great emotional intensity behind it. Long's speeches are oratorical and fit for argument. Paddy's speeches are full of poetic quality when he is recalling the past beauty of their sailing profession. Mildred and her aunt speak in a manner as lifeless and prosaic as their existence itself.

To sum up, *The Hairy Ape* is a tragedy of the man who has lost his ancient harmony with nature. He desperately looks for it in different places in the perplexing, mechanised and dehumanised world of today. He feels that he has become so spiritually dead that he cannot go forward in search for a state of 'belonging'. All that he can do is to go backward to his primeval state of 'belonging'. But even there he will not fit in. The subject-matter of the play, thus, is the same which always was and always will be for tragedy, i.e., the struggle of man at odds with destiny. Here the struggle is between man and his own self, his 'unconscious'—'unconscious' in the Jungian sense, which is the modern counterpart of the ancient Greek gods, and fate etc. Though the play has an external conflict and a political and social undertone, its chief problem is the inner conflict —man's struggle with his own self. The theme is thus universalised. The hero is an ordinary stoker with an extraordinary power of will and conviction and almost superhuman capacity for action. Though his spiritual and mental stature is not as high as that of a great tragic hero, his mental tension and resolute opposition to the force which is beyond his power make him a truly tragic character. He has the element of 'hamartia,' which is his pride of strength and position, his desire for not accepting anything less than what he wants to have and his inability to adjust himself to his environment, which leads him to the tragic search for his place in the universe. The plot of the play is in conformity with the Aristotelian canons. It is a complete whole. It has the unity of action and the elements of 'peripeity' and 'anagnorisis,. It develops logically on the principal of probability' or 'necessity' from the beginning to the end, the 'inevitable close of the play. The tragic effect of the play is undeniable. It produces the emotion of pity because of Yank's inner tension and great suffering and the emotion of fear because he is like us, he is 'everyman' and is struggling to solve a problem which is everybody's problem. At the end of the play we feel a sense of resigned calm because we realise that this was inevitable. But one may miss here the effect of exaltation which great tragedy produces in the end. It is probably because O'Neill's conclusion of the problem is pessimistic. The play suggests that the only way for man out of the present dehumanised society is death. But the effect is not depressing entirely as man never 'submits or yields'. The style of the play is simple, plain and clear but not mean because of the intensity of emotions behind it. It becomes lofty in certain situations and varies with the change of situation or emotion. Thus, practically all the basic tragic elements recommended by Aristotle are present in *The Hairy Ape*, which has successfully modified and modernized some of the basic themes and motives of tragedy.

FOOTNOTES

1 Gassner, John, ed., *O'Neill, A Collection of Critical Essays*, "The Nature of O'Neill's Achievement : A Survey and Appraisal," (Prentice-Hall, Inc., Englewood Cliffs, N.J., 1964), p. 169.

2 *Ibid.*, Whitman, Robert, F., "O'Neill's Search for a 'Language of the Theatre,' " p. 145.

3 *Ibid.*, Muchnic, Helen, "Circe's Swine : Plays by Gorkey and O'Neill," p. 106.

4 *Eugene O'Neill and His Plays : A Survey of His Life and Works*, Wilson, Edmund, "Eugene O'Neill as Prose Writer," p. 466.

5 *Ibid.*

6 *Ibid.*

7 Clark, B.H., *Eugene O'Neill : The Man and His Plays* (Jonathan Cape, Thirty Bedford Square, London. 1933), p. 117.

8 *Ibid.*

9 *O'Neill*, p. 43,

10 *Ibid.*, p. 171.

11 *O'Neill : A Collection of Critical Essays*, p. 28.

12 *Conversations on Contemporary Drama* (Macmillan, London,1925), p. 216.

13 *Form and Idea in Modern Theatre*, p. 123.

14 *Eugene O'Neill and His Plays : A Survey of His Life and Works*, "The Hairy Ape," p, 43,

15 *O'Neill*, p. 43.

16 *Ibid.*, p. 41.

17 Sutton Graham, *Some Contemporary Dramatists* (Leonard, Parsons, London, 1924), p. 178.

18 *Eugene O'Neill: The Man and His Plays* (Jonathan Cape, London, 1933), p. 116.

19 New Herald Tribune, 16th Nov., 1924, quoted in *Eugene O'Neill : The Man and His Plays*, p. 116.

20 *Ibid.*

21 *Ibid.*, p. 118.

22 *Ibid.*, p. 119.

23 *O'Neill*, p. 2.

24 *Eugene O'Neill, and His Plays : A Survey of His Life and Works*, "Eugene O'Neill as Social Critic," p. 390.

25 *O'Neill the Man and His Plays*, "New Herald Tribune," p. 116.

26 *O'Neill*, p. 41.

27 See Egri, Lajos, *The Art of Dramatic Writing* (Simon and Schuster, New York, 1963), p. 164.

28 *Some Contemporary Dramatists* (Leonard Persons, London, 1924) p. 178.

29 *O'Neill*, p. 41.

30 *Ibid.*

31 *Eugene O'Neill and His Plays : A Survey of His Life and Works*, Woollcott, A., "The Hairy Ape," p. 161.

32 See *Eugene O'Neill and His Plays : A Survey of His Life and Works*, Woollcott, A., "The Hairy Ape," p, 161.

CHAPTER XI

T. S. Eliot's *Murder in the Cathedral*

The *Murder in the Cathedral* is a religious play dealing with the martyrdom of Archbishop Thomas of Canturbury. This story of the suffering and sacrifice of a particular preacher of Christ's gospel, however, has, in fact, a universal significance because it is essentially concerned with the meaning and significance of martyrdom in general, which, in terms of Christian belief, is an enactment of the passion and crucifixion of the Saviour Himself, with firm faith in the idea of resurrection constantly present in the background. The nature of the story, therefore, presents the initial problem in regard to the play, that is, whether it is proper to consider it a tragic theme at all either in terms of the Aristotelian theory or the concept of tragedy in general. A martyr accepts suffering deliberately and cheerfully as a trial sent down by God and a part of the final fulfilment of God's own design which may be dark and mysterious to the limited and imperfect understanding of man. It is, therefore, at once a source of sorrow and rejoicing, and the final sermon preached by the Archbishop himself clearly emphasises this point of view. He tells the audience that the Mass said on the Christmas day has a special significance and is a crucial reminder of the meaning of the Saviour's own life and death: "For whenever Mass is said, we re-enact the Passion and Death of Our Lord; and on this Christmas day we do this in celebration of His Birth. So that at the same moment we rejoice in His coming for the salvation of men, and offer again to God His Body and Blood in sacrifice, oblation and satisfaction for the sins of the whole world." From this he naturally passes on to the explanation of the real significance of martyrdom undergone by a faithful Christian: "A martyrdom is always the design of God, for His love of men, to warn them and to lead them to bring them back to His ways. It is never the design of man; for the true martyr is he who has become the instrument of God who has lost his will in the will of God, and who no longer desires anything for himself, not even the glory of being a martyr. So, thus, as on earth the church mourns and rejoices at once, in a fashion that the world cannot understand; so in Heaven the Saints are most high, having made themselves most low, and are seen, not as we see them, but in the light of Godhead from which they draw their being." (Interlude).

Richard B. Sewall says that a Christian saint cannot be a tragic hero: "The Christian in his suffering can confess *total* guilt and look to the promise of redemption through grace. The martyr seeks suffering, accepts it gladly, 'glories in tribulation'. The tragic man knows of no grace and never glories in the suffering. Although he may come to acquiesce in it partly and 'learn' from it, his characteristic mood is resentment and dogged endurance. He has not the stoic's patience, although this may be part of what he learns. Characteristically he is restless, intense, probing and questioning the universe and his own soul."[1] The difficulty, in cases as the present one, is that "the death of the martyr presents to us not the defeat, but the victory of the individual; the issue of a conflict in which the individual is ranged on the same side as the higher powers, and the sense of suffering consequently lost in that moral triumph."[2] "This is, I suppose." concludes Louis L. Martz, "what I.A. Richards also means when he declares that 'the least touch of any theology which has a compensating Heaven to offer the tragic hero is fatal'— fatal, that is, to the tragic effect."[3] Martz shows that even

"Hamlet and Oedipus are in the end on the side of the higher powers" and they are saintly in their acute sensibility to evil. There is, no doubt, a catholic theology underlying the *Murder in the Cathedral* and this may make the unchristian audience unresponsive to it. But what makes the play tragically effective is its "deepening the spiritual meaning of Becket's martyrdom as an act of heroism...(and his) spiritual progress to a state of readiness for Christian martyrdom."[4]

In spite of the above fact, however, a careful student of the play will not assert unhesitatingly that the nature of the story does not come under the purview of tragedy. As a matter of fact, the story presents a double perspective, one of which is associated with the Protagonist and the other with the Chorus, which is composed of the Women of Canterbury and the Priests under the Archbishop. They represent the common humanity and its weaknesses as spectators of the action in the play itself and form a bridge between the dramatic action of the play and the readers and spectators outside the play. It is not necessary to emphasize the fact, which has been stressed by all the critics of this drama, that the Greek device of Chorus introduced here by Eliot is in complete conformity with the statement of Aristotle that the Chorus should be an integral part of the play, even in the nature of an independent character though not directly connected with the movement of the action. Eliot has "enlarged the original function of the Chorus in the light of the Christian liturgy. It represents the common people and mediates between them and the action as in Greek drama, but also 'chorus is choir,' the articulate voice of the body of worshippers."[5] If we look at the play from the point of view of the Chorus, which partly symbolises all of us, we shall have little difficulty in concluding that the play deals with a tragic action and possesses some of the most notable characteristics of tragedy as defined and elaborated by Aristotle in the *Poetics*.

The famous definition of tragedy occurring in Chapter VI

of the *Poetics* underlines certain aspects of the story and its implications which we have repeated on several occasions in the foregoing chapters. Under this definition, it is a serious story of suffering leading to the death of the Protagonist, who is a man of exceptional nature and stature, but not unlike us, common human beings, and whose unmerited suffering, therefore, is calculated to produce the sentiments of fear and pity. Pity arises from the magnitude of the unmerited suffering and fear from the consciousness that a suffering of his type may befall us also. Viewed in this light the story of Archbishop's sacrifice is serious, painful and leads ultimately to his death. The Protagonist himself reminds the audience again and again that action is suffering and suffering is action, and this suffering has to be examined here from the viewpoint, not of the sufferer himself, but of those who are witnesses to that suffering. When Aristotle emphasised the twin emotions of fear and pity as peculiar to the tragic story, his mind was fixed solely upon the reaction in the mind of the audience rather than the feelings of the hero himself. He does not say a word about the psychological changes which the Protagonist himself may undergo in the course of his suffering. Whether he is elated or depressed, feels triumphant or defeated, whether he is aggressive under the blows of destiny or submits humbly and passively to them—are the questions which are not raised at all by the Greek law-giver. The whole emphasis falls upon the peculiar response which the suffering of this type, befalling a person of a particular nature, may evoke in the hearts of the spectators or the readers of the play. From this view-point, it is not difficult to understand that the action presented in the play is one of intense suffering, even to the men and women who are watching it at a distance, because they actively participate in the trial of the Protagonist. The point is empasized again and again in the utterances of the Chorus and the exclamations of the Priests. The mood of excitement and foreboding

which is created in the opening Chorus is not only kept up
throughout, but presented in such a way that the sentiments
mount in intensity, reaching thus the climax in the crucial
moment when the agents of worldy justice put in their appearances as the hounds of hell ready to pounce upon the noble
representative of the Church.[6] The point may be illustrated
with the help of a few quotations taken at random from tho
different stages in the development of the plot. We begin
with the first Chorus:

> Here let us stand, close by the Cathedral.
> Let us wait.
> Are we drawn by danger ? Is it the knowledge of safety,
>   that draws our feet—
> Towards the Cathedral...
>
> ...   .
>
> Some presage of an act
> Which our eyes are compelled to witness.

Then comes the speech of the Messenger:

> I fear for the Archbishop, I fear for the church,
> I know that the pride bred of sudden prosperity,
> Was but confirmed by a bitter adversity.

The fear of the Messenger is endorsed by the Chorus:

> Ill the wind, ill the time, uncertain the profit,
>   certain the danger.
> O late late late, late is the time, late too late,
>   and rotten the year;
> Evil the wind, and bitter the sea, and grey the sky,
>   grey grey grey,
> O Thomas, return, Archbishop, return, return to France,

The suspense of the spectators, as we have already suggested mounts higher and higher till the advent of the main catastrophe which ends with the murder of the Protagonist. The Priests become almost overwhelmed with the sense of fear for themselves as for their leader and entreat him insistently though lovingly to seek the shelter of the church and avoid the dark danger which is stalking towards him steadily and almost arrogantly. Their fear is echoed by the Chorus also:

> I have smelt them, the death bringers, senses are
>   quickened.
> By subtle forebodings; I have heard
> Fluting in the night-time, fluting and owls, have seen
>   at noon
> Scaly wings slanting over, huge and ridiculous.

The Priests join in a chorus, as it were, to entreat and persuade their master and head of the Church:

> My Lord, they are coming. They will break through
>   presently.
> You will be killed. Come to altar.
> Make haste, my Lord. Don't stop here talking.
> It is not right.
> What shall become of us, my Lord, if you are killed;
> What shall become of us.

Again the Chorus utters its sense of bewilderment and horror:

> Numb the hand and dry the eyelid,
> Still the horror, but more horror
> That when tearing in the belly.
> Still the horror, but more horror
> Than when twisting in the fingers,
> Than when splitting in the skull.

More than footfall in the passage,
More than shadow in the doorway,
More than fury in the hall.

The action of the play fully conforms to the Aristotelian requirement of unity in different aspects, that is the unity of atmosphere and the purity of the tragic element embedded in it, intensified by the sense of necessity or the law of cause and effect, as well as the unity of time. The outer action which deals with the external events leading to the sacrifice of the Bishop begins with a conflict, which is clearly stated at the opening of the play:

His pride always feeding upon his own virtues,
Pride drawing sustenance from generosity,
Loathing power given by temporal devolution,
Wishing subjection to God alone.
Had the King been greater, or had he been weaker
Thing had perhaps been different for Thomas.

It means that the main action arises from the clash of two towering, arrogant and unbending personalities, the King on the one hand and the Archbishop on the other. They symbolise the secular and religious authorities respectively. Thus, the action is raised to the universal level of the conflict between the worldly and unworldly forces, or in a general way, between evil and good in the world. The conflict is intensified by the determination of the Protagonist not to submit and yield, nor to fly the threat which is presented by the royal authority and the royal agents who are likely to do him to death as soon as he ventures out of France and steps upon the soil of England. The action moves steadily and through well marked stages, each bound with the other by the law of 'necessity,' and each contributing to the effect of of the whole, which is tragic according to the analysis we have given above. But apart from this outer action, there is an action which is much more significant and noteworthy for the purpose of our analysis. This may be described as the inner conflict, i.e., the conflict in the heart of the Protagonist himself between the supreme necessity of submitting his own will to the will of God and thus sacrificing all powers, privileges and the pleasures which he has already enjoyed as the most trusted Counsellor of the King, and the temptation offered by those worldly advantages, which he has not yet been able to quell completely. This conflict is presented dramatically in the shape of a situation which recalls the chief motif of the mediaeval morality plays. The human Protagonist is visited by four tempters. The first three tempters represent the external, worldly temptations and the fourth is the temptation most powerful and insidious because it is latent in the nature and personality of the hero himself. This temptation is the sense of pride which a martyr may feel in the nobility of his action which does not only distinguish him from the ordinary human beings, but offers him the uplifting hope that he will be earning a place among the saints in heaven. The Archbishop himself clearly explains the meaning of this fourth temptation. The Fourth Tempter introduces himself to the Archbishop with the mystifying remark that he is unknown and nameless to him, yet, he (Archbishop) knows him full well, though he has never seen his face at any time before. Then he throws the bait with a glorious description of the fruits of martyrdom:

> King is forgotten, when another shall come:
> Saint and Martyr rule from the tomb.
> Think Thomas, think of enemies dismayed,
> Creeping in penance, frightened of a shade;
> Think of pilgrims, standing in line
> Before the glittering jewelled shrine,
> From generation to generation

Bending the knee in supplication,
Think of the miracles, for God's grace,
And think of your enemies, in another place.

This description brings the Bishop to the shocking realization
that his greatest opponent is lurking in his own heart, and has
to be grappled with resolutely in order to complete his preparation for martyrdom:

Who are you, tempting with my own desires?
Others have come, temporal tempters,
With pleasure and power at palpable price
What do you offer?   What do you ask?

The Archbishop finally triumphs over this most potent inner
temptation and expresses his sense of relief in the most
significant and perhaps the longest address to the Chorus
which closes the first section:

Now is my way clear, now is the meaning plain;
Temptation shall not come in this kind again.
The last temptation is the greatest treason:
To do the right deed for the wrong reason.
The natural vigour in the venial sin
Is the way in which our lives begin.
          ...   .
But for every evil, every sacrilege,
Crime, wrong, oppression and the axe's edge,
Indifference, exploitation, you, and you,
And you, must all be punished.   So must you.
I shall no longer act or suffer, to the swords end.
Nor my good Angel, whom God appoints
To be my guardian, hover over the sword's points.

While discussing the tragic plot, Aristotle is at pains to

emphasize certain important elements which must be present in the action suitable to the ideal tragedy. He observes that the plot should be complex, i.e., it should involve the 'reversal of situation' and the 'recognition'. So far as the outer action of the present play is concerned, the plot movement does not conform to this requirement because the whole action starts with a sense of suspense arising from an impending catastrophe and steadily moves towards the actual coming of the disaster involving the death of the Protagonist. But these elements are present in the inner action which arises from the conflict in the heart of the Protagonist himself. The four tempters represent the four stages in the inner progress of the Archbishop from obscurity and ignorance to the clear light of spiritual illumination. The Fourth Tempter comes with the fullest confidence that he will be able to overcome the resistance of the Christian hero and lead him back to the life of worldly power and pelf which he is determined to resign. But actually his coming proves a turning point for the spiritual progress of the Protagonist and thus an apparently hopeless situation veers round to its opposite, namely, the inner victory of the hero. Aristotle rightly points out that the effectiveness of this 'reversal' is complete if it happens simultaneously with 'recognition,' which we interpret here in a sense spiritual rather than physical. The victory of the Protagonist is concommitant with the 'recognition,' that is the fullest realisation of the paramount necessity of quelling his pride and submitting his will to the will and design of God. Martyrdom is the right end which cannot be achieved by wrong means and the means will be wrong, without doubt, if the person courting it is prompted by his sense of pride or intoxicating hope of the rewards his sacrifice is sure to bring to him after death, not only in this world, but more surely in the kingdom of heaven adorned by saints and martyrs.

This brings us to the consideration of the Archbishop as the tragic hero of *Murder in the Cathedral*. Our 'attention is centred on Becket himself in his isolation, his hour of crisis when he is tempted by the four tempters, who balance the later appearance of the four knights."[7] Now if we take the external conflict into account we shall find that the character of Becket is static.[8] He seems to be an appointed martyr to suffer death for the sin of others. But if we take the inner or the spiritual conflict into account, we find that Becket's character has a definite development. Like all the genuine tragic heroes Becket also begins in the ignorance of his inner self—of the desire lurking in his heart which is made explicit to him by the Fourth Tempter and which leads to 'recognition,' i.e, Becket's realization that he was attempting to do the "right deed for the wrong reason" in his preparedness for martyrdom. As demanded by Aristotle, the Archbishop has an exalted stature, external as well as spiritual. He is virtuous but not without frailty, which, besides making his suffering tragic, at once makes him human. He has a human weakness—a desire for glory—glory in martyrdom and a sense of pride in this glorification. He invites our sympathy for him through this element of 'hamartia'.

Francis Fergusson says that "Eliot does not grasp Thomas imaginatively as a person; he rather postulates such a man, and places him, not in God's world but in a theological scheme. He then indicates both the man and his real elements which he assembles: Tempters, Priests and Chorus of Women."[9] The greatest objection to Becket's presentation as a tragic hero is that saints are immobile and suffer passively to rejoice in the glory of their end (death) The other reason for hesitating to accept Saints as tragic heroes is that they are promised a divine reward in their death and when there is a promise of divine compensation for death, the hero's death fails to produce the desired tragic effect. But Cleanth Brooks[10] has rightly observed that Becket is not Passive in the sense that this passivity detracts from the tragic effect. To use the magnificent words which Milton used for Samson, Becket can be considered as "then vigorous most, when most unactive deemed." Eliot has made it clear in the play that "suffering is action." Becket may be said to have this "acceptance of suffering" which tends to shatter the tragic effect of any tragedy. But this "acceptance" is not untragic for two reasons: This "acceptance is not a weary submission," nor is it "necessarily a joyful submission to what the hero recognises to be the just order of things," because Becket is unconsciously motivated by an ambition of the glory of martyrdom which is the "right deed for the wrong reason." This acceptance, remarks Brooks, becomes tragically effective when it "springs from a desire for knowledge of the full meanings of one's ultimate commitments."[11] Becket, after the frailty in him has been revealed to him by the Fourth Tempter, and he has attained self-knowledge, has this acceptance. A similar acceptance we discern in Oedipus also when he has attained self-knowledge. Becket needs to know, adds Brooks, "whether he is acting out of human pride or out of submission to God's will, and will not really know until he has tested his convictions to the final limit, which is death."[12]

"Goodness is apt to be immobile and uncombative. In refusing to strike back it brings the action to a standstill."[13] Becket's character, says Louis L. Martz, "is certainly immobile and in a sense, uncombative."[14] Becket himself says:

We are not here to triumph by fighting, by strategem,
Not to fight with beasts as men. We have fought the beast
And have conquered. We have only to conquer
Now, by suffering.

Butcher further remarks: "Impersonal ardour in the cause of right does not have the same dramatic fascination as the spectacle of human weakness or passion doing battle with the fate it has brought upon itself."[15] But it is clear in Becket's case that the weakness he has in him makes the cause of his fight porsonal for sometime until he comes to the realisation of the 'wrong reason':

Is there no way, in my soul's sickness,
Does not lead to damnation in pride...
...Can I neither act nor suffer
Without perdition.

Passive in a sense Becket is, no doubt. But this passivity is the result of the development of his spiritual being. This has been summed up by Grover Smith very precisely: "When Becket speaks to the Chorus he thinks of himself as the actor, the source of will, and of the Women as passive recipients of sorrows and benefits resulting from his choice of martyrdom. But when the Fourth Tempter flings the same words back in his teeth,[16] Becket seems to realize that unless the sufferer refrains from willing to suffer and thus from soiling his hands with his own blood, he cannot be a true martyr. After nearly blundering, Becket recognizes that not only the Women but he himself must be passive. He must only consent to the divine will....[17]" Thus, "by recognizing divine necessity, the central character frees himself from the horror of the world's apparent disorder, and ultimately from the human limitations of physical death."[18]

The plot of *Murder in the Cathedral* has been described as the "moral-quest" theme of the moral interludes or the tribulation theme of the Book of Job. And Becket may be taken to symbolise Christ, the Saviour of the sinning humanity. But Becket's character is sufficiently individualized by the references to his past exalted positions and also the sin of the pride of martyrdom lurking in his heart. In spite of the fact that *Murder in the Cathedral* presents a theological perspective of life, and the Archbishop is a saintly figure, we find that the central figure here is human with the element of 'hamartia' in his character. We sympathise with his spiritual tension and feel a sense of exaltation at his reconciliation which is a complete realisation of the fact that the martyr is required to resign his will to the will of God. The tragic impact of Becket's character is fully felt by us, if we look at the whole play from the view-point of the Chorus, and our sympathy for him is a sufficient testimony to this.

This takes up to the consideration of the next point in our analysis, namely, the nature of 'catharsis' involved in this play, which we have partly glanced at in the opening paragraphs of our analysis and also in the discussion of the nature of the tragic hero. Under Aristotelian definition the tragic plot must arouse fear and pity and make a 'catharsis' of these and like emotions. The pity arises from the sense of unmerited suffering of a man, who is like us in many respects and naturally reminds us of similar disasters which destiny may have in store for us also. We have already proved that if we look at the play from the view-point of the spectators in the play itself, i.e., the Canterbury Women and the Priests around the Protagonist, we shall not hesitate to conclude that the action is calculated to arouse the sentiments peculiar to the tragic story. "In *Murder in the Cathedral* Becket acts out his passion alone, but the effect of his martyrdom is felt in the lives of the Women of Canterbury"[19] and we who identify ourselves with these Women experience the same tragic impact. But as the plot is based upon a profound religious idea involving sin, expiation and suffering, the last utterances of the Chorus lay considerable emphasis upon this aspect. The sacrifice of a saintly figure at the hands of a selfish, blind secular force is a crime in the eye of God, which stains not only the active agents, but also all those persons, who have watched it passively and helplessly and thus allowed such a sin to be committed. The point is made clear in the following lines uttered by the Chorus :

I have smelt them, the death-bringers ; now is too late.

For action, too soon for contrition.
Nothing is possible but the shamed swoon
Of those consenting to the humiliation.
I have consented, Lord Archbishop, have consented.
Am torn away, subdued violated,
United to the spiritual flesh of nature,
Mastered by the animal powers of spirit,
Dominated by the lust of self-domination,
By the final utter uttermost death of spirit,
By the final ecstasy of waste and shame,
O Lord Archbishop, O Thomas Archbishop, forgive us,
    pray for us that we may pray for you, out of shame.

It is pertinent to refer here to the light-hearted and mocking tone quite apparent in the last speeches of the murderers, who try to justify the dark deed just committed by them. It introduces a note of comedy which may be interpreted by hasty critics[20] or the students of the play as a sort of anti-climax, clearly calculated to detract from the real intensity of the tragic effect. Francis Fergusson says : "The immediate effect of the Knights is farcical—but if one is following the successive illustrations of the idea of the play, their rationalization (of the murder) immediately fits as another instance of wrong reason. If it is farce, it is like the farce of the Porter in *Macbeth*"[21] or the conversation of the grave diggers in *Hamlet*. The sin committed by a man becomes a crime of deepest dye if the perpetrator is quite oblivious of its real nature and the consequences which are likely to flow from it not only to the world at large but to their own soul. The mockery is symptomatic of the spiritual degradation and corruption in man which illuminates the meaning of the self-sacrifice of the Saviour and its enactment by His saints and martyrs on this earth. It sets a sharper edge on the poignant contrition which inspires the moving lines of the Chorus we have quoted above. Aristotle does not elaborate the real nature of the pecliar effect produced by the tragic story, and the nature of 'catharsis,' therefore, has given rise to an un-ending controversy among critics and scholars. But there is more or less a general consensus of opinion that tragic 'catharsis' may best be described in the words of Milton as "calm of mind, all passion spent." We have now to see how far such a mood can be attributed to the persons witnessing this play whether inside the play itself or outside. We have already shown that the chorus and Priests are humbled by a sense of sin and repentance born out of the realization that they have allowed themselves to participate in a deed which is sinful in the eye of God. If we identify ourselves with them (and the play cannot be fully appreciated without such an identification), we can fully share their feelings and the sense of sin which overwhelms them. Now contrition or repentance is said to be the genuine sacrifice to God and the real beginning of a spiritual life which is based upon the faith that the whole world moves according to the design of God or as Hamlet says "there is a Providence in the fall of a sparrow." This mood may not be described as "calm of mind, all passion spent," yet it is the best prelude to and preparation for it.

The last point in our analysis of the play is its style, Aris-totle has said that the style of tragedy should be simple and clear without being mean. It should be lofty without being rhetorical and should vary with the change in situations and emotions. It should be dramatic and should help the move-ment of the plot. When we apply these criteria to the *Murder in the Cathedral*, we find that they are all well illustrated here. The style of the present play is simple and clear. Take for example, such lines as ths following :

Servants of God, and watchers of the temple,
I am here to inform you, without circumlocution:
The Archbishop is in England, and is close outside the city.
          ...   .

What, is the exile ended, is our Lord Archbishop
Reunited with the King, what reconciliation
Of two proud men.

These lines, besides being simple and clear, help the movement of the plot. The conversations of the Priests with the
Messenger, for example, make the external conflict of the
play between the King and the Archbishop clear to us. The
First Priest voices the danger to the Archbishop's life and the
security of the church :

I fear for the Archbishop, I fear for the Church,
I know that the pride bred of sudden prosperity
Was but confirmed by a bitter adversity.
I saw him as chancellor, flattered by the King...., etc.

Then the Chorus voices in the same strain :

Evil the wind, and bitter the sea, and grey the sky,
grey grey grey.
O Thomas return, Archbishop, return, return to France.

Again, the past positions held by Thomas have been made
clear through his conversations with the Tempters, and the
Fourth Tempter exposes to Becket his 'wrong reason' by
flinging the same words to him which he uttered to the
chorus. This device of repetition, which is frequently used by
Eliot in the present play, enhances the effectiveness of the
situation. This starts Becket's spiritual conflict. Thus, says
A.M. Rillie, "the success of *Murder in the Cathedral* is
achieved at the verbal level, for there is neither action nor
character."[22]

The perspicuity of style is perceptible at many places. Take
the instance of the Interlude which has an obvious Biblical
simplicity and clarity : "A martyrdom is always the design of

God, for His love of men, to warn them and to lead them, to bring back to His ways. It is never the design of man; for the true martyr is he who has become the instrument of God, who has lost his will in the will of God, and who no longer desires anything for himself, not even the glory of being a martyr....," etc.

The style besides being dramatic is strikingly lofty and poetical when the emotional intensity demands this. This is most clearly perceptible in the Choruses of the Women of Canterbury and the dialogues of the Archbishop. Raymond Williams says, "The verse of the Choruses is an obvious success. Its movement is an exciting realization of a kind of dramatic experience which the theatre had entirely lost."[23] Note, for example, the following lines :

Here is no continuing city, here is no abiding stay.
Ill the wind, ill the time, uncertain the profit, certain the
  danger,
O late late late, late is the time, late too late, and rotten
  the year;
Evil the wind, and bitter the sea, and grey the sky,
  grey grey grey.
O Thomas, return, Archbishop return, return to France.
Return. Quickly. Quickly. Leave us to perish in quiet.
You come with applause, you come with rejoicing, but
  you come bringing death into Canterbury:
A doom on the house, a doom on yourself, a doom on the
  world.
We do not wish anything to happen.
Seven years we have lived quietly,
Living and partly living.

"The most important advance of verse of this kind," says Raymond Williams, "is that language reasserts control in performance. The problem of performance is the application of these rhythms, within which all the visual elements of performance are contained and prescribed. This is perhaps Eliot's most important general achievement."[24] Francis Fergusson says, "the histrionic basis of Eliot's verse...is the source of its unique and surprising vitality...he imitates action by the music and imagery of his verse."[25] Thus, the style in the present play, besides being clear and elevated, is highly dramatic.

Then the style of *Murder in the Cathedral* is capable of great variations in keeping with the variations in situations and emotions. For this, Eliot employed a variety of metres as well as two stretches of prose. This point has been summed up by E. Martin Browne:[26] "The most superficial level, that of the quarrels between Becket and the Knights, is rhymed doggerel.... More subtle, and sometimes rather crabbed, is a four-stress rhyming verse for dialogue for the Tempters who dramatize the tortuous progress of Becket's inner struggle.... There is an easy, near-blank-verse for dialogue with the Priest and Women.... And for the Chorus, a very varied series of forms, from the three-stress lines of the Women's domestic talk...to the long complexes of pleading or of praise...."

Thus, we see that the style of *Murder in the Cathedral* has simplicity of diction and is elevated above the ordinary speech as it can convey the deepest meanings through the devices of the symbolic use of words and repetition. It is capable of great variation whenever the change of situation or emotion demands it and is highly dramatic. Besides conforming to the Aristotelian canons of tragic style, *Murder in the Cathedral* has a subject-matter which is universalised. B.H. Clark says that "the simple faith of the Archbishop triumphing over himself as well as over his external enemies came at a time of world-wide financial depression and so, perhaps took on new meanings.... Only in *Murder in the Cathedral* has Eliot made the broad contact with humanity which is essential to success in the popular theatre."[27] The hero is exalted and has the element of 'hamartia' which brings about his inner conflict and leads him to spiritual tension and suffering and makes him human. The plot is a complete whole and has the unity of action. It has the element of 'anagnorisis' and 'peripeity'. The tragic effect of reconciliation, of 'catharsis,' is produced through Becket's realization of the supreme necessity of resigning his will to the Will of God. The Chorus has been employed here in a much larger sense and a greater effective manner that what we find in the ancient Greek plays. But we have to look at the play from the viewpoint of the Chorus who are the representatives of the audience and the humanity at large in order to realize its tragic significance.

FOOTNOTES

1 *Essays in Criticism*, Vol. IV, 1954, "The Tragic Form," p. 354.

2 *Aristotle's Theory of Poetry and Fine Art*, p. 311.

3 *Tragic Themes in Western Literature*, p. 150.

4 *The Anatomy of Drama*, p. 117.

5 Jones, D.E., *The Plays of T.S. Eliot* (Routledge and Kagan Paul, London, 1961), p. 58.

See Maxwell, D.E.S., *The Poetry of T.S. Eliot* (London, 1960), p. 188.

6 See Fergusson, Francis, *The Idea of a Theatre* (Princeton University Press, Princeton, N.J., 1949), p. 212.

7 Lumley, Fredrick, *Trends in Twentieth-Century Drama* (Barrie and Rockliff, London, 1960), p. 84.

8 See Smith, Grover, *T.S. Eliot's Poetry and Plays : A Study in Sources and Meaning* (Phoenix Books, University of Chicago Press, Illinois, U.S.A., 1961), p. 185.

9 *The Idea of a Theatre* (Princeton University Press, Princeton, New Jersey, 1949), p. 214.

10 *Tragic Themes in Western Literature*, p. 4.

11 *Ibid.*, p. 5.

12 *Ibid.*

13 *Aristotle's Theory of Poetry and Fine Art*, p. 310.

14 *Tragic Themes in Western Literature,* "The Saint as Tragic Hero, p. 150.

15 *Aristotle's Theory of Poetry and Fine Art,* p. 311.

16 "You know and do not know....," etc.

17 *T.S. Eliot's Poetry and Play : A Study in Sources and Meaning,"* p, 188.

18 Smith, Carol, H,, *T.S. Eliot's Dramatic Theory and Practice* (Princeton University Press, New Jersey, 1963), p. 80.

19 *T.S. Eliot's Dramatic Theory and Practice,* p, 26.

20 Smith, Grover, *T.S. Eliot's Poetry and Play : A Study in Sources and Meaning,* p. 184.

21 *The Idea of a Theatre,* p. 213.

See also *The Elements of Drama,* p. 126.

22 *The Review of English Studies,* Vol. XIII, 1962, "Melodramatic Device in T.S. Eliot," p. 275.

23 *Drama from Ibsen to Eliot,* p. 229.

24 *Ibid.*

25 *The Idea of a Theatre,* p. 218.

26 *The Dramatic Verse of T.S. Eliot: A Symposium,* compiled by Richard March and Tambimuttu (London, 1948), pp. 199-200, quoted in *The Plays of Eliot,* p. 36.

27 *A History of Modern Drama,* pp. 214-15.

See also *The Masters of Drama,* p. 729.

Conclusion

Literature is indubitably a dynamic thing and literary principles enunciated in a particular age have their direct bearing primarily on the creative works of that age. At the same time it cannot be gainsaid that great literary works deal with universal problems of humanity which are demonstrably relevant to all countries in all ages. So, generalisations made from such works are bound to have relevance to the writings of later ages also. Thus, there are some guiding principles of art which have universal validity. Just as there are certain principles of morality, recognized, if not universally, at least very generally, by all civilized men, by reference to which we govern our conduct, so are there certain principles of wide, if not universal, validity by reference to which we guide our decisions in matters of literary taste. The *Poetics* of Aristotle is a repository of principles, most of which have permanent validity, while a few are pertinent to the plays of his own age and language. They have been variously interpreted and modified through the ages and have even been misunderstood and bitterly opposed, yet their validity has survived all the vagaries and vicissitudes of literary taste. We shall elaborate this point by a brief examination of Aristotle's theory of tragedy in the changing contexts of social and critical canons.

For most of the Ranaissance and neo-classical critics, the tragic hero meant a person of high and eminent position in society. His fall from the high position of prosperity into a low and miserable state constituted the essence of tragedy. The principle of 'propriety' and 'consistency' in character was taken to mean 'decorum' and wooden 'types'. The subject-matter of tragedy was the affairs of kings, princes and eminent leaders or some state concern. The unities of time and place were enjoined upon the playwrights without any strict reference to the *Poetics*, and the principle of 'catharsis' was interpreted as the evacuation of the emotions of pity and fear, which, if unpurged, may prove detrimental to the moral and spiritual health of man. Sometimes it was taken to mean a process of hardening through the repeated effect of tragic performance which made the inevitable misery of man quite familiar and blunted its edge in life. Tragedy was to aim at moral instruction first and pleasure later on. The style of tragedy was to be poetical in the medium of verse to keep it on a high plane of emotional and moral intensity. Till the end of the eighteenth century, discussions of tragedy centred round the *Poetics* of Aristotle and all interpretations and modifications were simply variations on this norm.

Later on, some philosophical and psychological theories were advanced to explain the nature of tragic 'catharsis' without strict adherence to the essential artistic nature of tragedy which is the main plank in Aristotelian discussion. These theories are conditioned by the large philosophical or psychological systems propounded by the critics concerned. Tragedy, for example, became, with Schopenhauer, a means of bringing about in man a sense of resignation by presenting before him the miseries and futility of human existence. It was again interpreted by Nietzche as a device to produce the sense of the affirmation of life through emphasis on its essentially tragic and miserable nature. It was again with Hegel a conflict between two moral forces, each justified in itself when considered in isolation, but each alone, in fact, incomplete and exclusive of the other which it denied. The tragic effect, thus, arose from the vindication of the moral justice and a sense of reconciliation in the end. Then again the ancient medical implication was revived, and psychoanalysis averred that as obsessions are removed by re-producing the same situation and emotion which had caused obsessions in the patient, similarly, by presenting a tragic spectacle of life and exciting the emotions of pity and fear, tragedy brings about a state of emotional balance. It is in this excitation and purgation of the emotions of pity and fear, which otherwise tend to induce morbidity in man, that the pleasurable calm of tragedy lies.

Then certain principles which Aristotle did not make mention of, were, for a long time, accredited to him. The principles of the unities of time and place and that of poetic justice are familiar cases in point. From the Renaissance to the neo-classical age, as we have noted, the modifications and interpretations of Aristotle's *Poetics* constituted a process of codification and increasing rigidity. But towards the close of the eighteenth century, as we have seen, the neo-classical rigidity was shattered, and critics like Diderot and Beaumarchais raised their voice in favour of the common man and his ordinary affairs as appropriate subjects for tragedy and the cult of classical unities gradually went over board in this current of opposition.

With the changed political and social contexts in the nineteenth and twentieth centuries, the principles of Aristotle have been sought to be interpreted in wider terms. There are some principles in the *Poetics* which are applicable to a large bulk of tragedies written in different ages and they require little modification. The principles of 'mimesis,' plot-construction and style, for example, may be cited as such elements. It is generally accepted, for example, that serious literature is an imaginative re-creation of life. So, 'imitation' of life in tragedy means that the playwright, who is the 'maker,' selects materials from human life and represents them through the prism of imaginative art. The Aristotelian concept of plot as complete and whole, with a beginning, a middle and an end governed by the low of 'probability' or 'necessity' should not be taken to apply to tragedy alone. It is equally applicable to all works which aim at the representation of life. This simply means that a work of art picks out a segment of life from the chaotic materials of human existence and its function as a work of art is to give a shape to this material so that this segment of life can stand by Itself. "No story," says John W. Asthon, "in its entirety has, strictly speaking, either beginning or end. Always there are antecedent events that explain what is now happening; always what is now happening results in some later development[1]." But what Aristotle actually means is that the playwright should draw out of the chain of events in the life of a man only a particular, limited sequence which for one reason or another may be considered significant and relatively complete in itself. In other words, the sequence should be comprehended without too great a reference to what has gone before, and without leaving too many threads of the story incomplete. Then so far as the style of tragedy is concerned, the first requisite of it, says Aristotle, is clarity. But exclusive simplicity and clarity may degenerate into banality and monotony. Hence the tragic style is required to be perspicuous and elevated.

There are, however, some principles in the *Poetics* which have been topics of much controversy and varied interpretations through the ages. The conception of the tragic hero and the tragic effect of 'catharsis' are such principles. As we have shown, the tragic hero should not mean exclusively a person belonging to a high social position. All that is required is that he should be over life-size. In the course of the action the hero grapples with some great force, in such a way that he shakes off all individual concerns and particulars and assumes a universal stature. It is not necessary that the play should open with a character who is larger than life. He may rise to a higher level of existence during the development of the action. Then the hero should be human and like us so that we may sympathise with him and thus experience the emotional pleasure of tragedy. It is for this tragic effect that the element of 'hamartia' is necessary, because purely innocent suffering is not conducive to the production of genuine tragic effect. This conception of the tragic hero is obviously based, as Aristotle has demanded, on a serious action—a subject-matter which is universal or is universalized during the development of the plot to underline the eternal note of sadness in human life. But Aristotle rightly insists upon the production of the aesthetic pleasure which is peculiar to this form of art. As Butcher has suggested, we all experience, when we witness a tragic performance or read the play, a sense of identification with the hero, because he is human and like us and is struggling with some problem which becomes the concern of every one of us. Through empathy, we forget our sublunary, petty concerns of routine life and imaginatively experience a life which is higher. We feel pity, fear and admiration in the struggle of the hero in which he is physically vanquished, but his dignity—and through him the dignity of man—is established even in his death and physical defeat. When we see or read a tragedy we feel an emotional stir in us which is allayed by the end of the play and a feeling of the "calm of mind, all passion spent" settles upon us. Aristotle has rightly demanded that a tragedy should be effective on the stage as well as in the closet, and this emotional effect of the play should be felt even when it is read.

Some of Aristotle's principles of tragedy are obviously narrower in their bearing. The necessity of Chorus and Song in tragedy are such instances, though the former has been most effectively used even in the twentieth century, in plays like *Murder in the Cathedral*. Aristotle's approach to tragedy underscores its essentially artistic nature. Tragedy is an organic whole in which all the elements work harmoniously to bring about the desired tragic effect. This is why Aristotle has discouraged the employment of any extraneous device to produce this aesthetic pleasure of tragedy. No importance has been given to spectacular and histrionic elements in a tragic play for this very reason.

In the modern age also the principles of the *Poetics* are applicable to numerous plays written in entirely changed social contexts. The only thing one needs to keep in mind is that these principles are to be interpreted more liberally without violating their spirit. We have dealt with various types of tragic plays selected for detailed analysis only to demonstrate the potential validity and wide applicability of the principles of the *Poetics*. The analysis has served to enlarge the scope of these principles with acceptable modifications necessitated by the changed social, political and economic atmosphere in which the plays have been produced, but these modifications do no violence to the spirit of those principles.

We may briefly explain the nature and extent of these modifications. The action of tragedy, said Aristotle, is 'serious' and related to a man of eminent position. This remained the concern of kings and princes until the eighteenth century. But by the end of the eighteenth century a growing democratic ideal shifted the interest to the common man and his problem in tragedy. Mrs. Alving, Maurya, Nan, Mrs. Jones, Stanhope and Yank are all common people with their own problems which are apparently average and ordinary. But these characters become over life-size as demanded by Aristotle. This largeness of their stature comes from within as they grapple with great problems, and, consequently, their conflicts take on a universal significance. Mrs. Alving comes in conflict with heredity because of the strong individuality of her character; Maurya's stature is raised to the tragic height when she comes out defiant against the great natural force, i.e., the sea; Nan comes in conflict with environment and heredity combined and undergoes exaltation; Yank rises to the tragic height through the spiritual tension resulting from his search for a place where he can 'belong;' and Stanhope triumphs humanly over the terrors of war and transforms death itself into an agency necessary for the restoration of the broken bonds.

Aristotle says that a tragic hero should be human and have the element of 'hamartia'. This 'hamartia' in the Greek tragedies was the hero's pride or 'hubris' which used to bring him in collision with fate or gods, but Aristotle identifies it with an error of judgement or a wrong step blindly taken. This element is necessary for tragic effect because an entirely innocent hero does not produce the desired tragic effect. But the element of 'hamartia,' as our analysis has shown, is not always necessary to bring about the catastrophe and Aristotle himself, insisted upon 'unmerited suffering' as the cause of pity. This is best exemplified by *Riders to the Sea* and also *The Tragedy of Nan* to some extent. Nan's 'hamartia' may be said to be her gullible nature and frankness which prove dangerous in the wicked, materialistic world in which her lot is cast but her tragedy is not strictly due to her weakness. Maurya collides with the unconquerable force symbolized by the sea which directly affects her life by devouring her sons one after another, without any fault of her own. 'Hamartia' in Mrs. Alving is the wrong step she took in deciding to stay with her depraved husband only to bear him a syphilitic son, while in Yank it consists in his pride and lack of adjustability or refusal to accept anything less than what he desires. But in *The Silver Box* and *Journey's End* the 'hamartia' is general and collective rather than individual and particular.

The subject-matter of tragedy, as implied in Aristotle, should be universal. If the subject of tragedy is a parochial problem or a problem for which a temporal solution can be found out and "where the causes of disaster are temporal, where the conflict can be resolved through technical or social means, we may have serious drama, but not tragedy." Maurya is confronted with an unconquerable and incomprehensible force against which there can be no easy antidote. No ready solution is possible to Mrs. Alving's problem either. She struggles against heredity which is the modern counterpart of the ancient Greek fate, god or the supernatural agencies, and is, thus, inscrutable, incomprehensible and unconquerable to human beings. In *The Tragedy of Nan* the conflict is between the heroine and her environment which together with heredity makes the solution of her problem impossible, bound as it is with the nature of wicked materialists like Dick Gurvil and of mean, selfish creatures like Mrs. Pargetter, who are naturally and unaccountably hostile to simple and innocent creatures. The problem in *The Silver Box* is apparently temporal and social, yet the tragic effect is enhanced by the utter helplessness even of the strong-willed individual before the laws of society which are pitiless like the decree of fate so far as the poor are concerned. Yet it has to be admitted that the problem posed by *The Silver Box* is not so universal as to produce the genuine 'cathartic' effect of tragedy. The problem of Yank, however, admits of no easy solution. Yank represents the eternal search of human soul for a place where it may 'belong'. He experiences the tension of a soul struggling to find a place where it may 'belong'—it is a conflict of man with his own self—his 'unconscious' in the Jungian sense which, O'Neill says, is the modern counterpart of the Greek idea of fate. *The Hairy Ape* begins with the contemporary problem of conflict between the people in the lowest stratum of society and the rich privileged ruling class. But the major issue here is the problem of man's conflict with his own self. It is this issue which makes the subject-matter of universal significance. In *Murder in the Cathedral,* the problem is universal by the same token. Besides representing a conflict between the secular power and the

Church, the play depicts the spiritual struggle of a saint to get over the weakness which is lurking like a thief in his own heart.

All the plays, which we have analysed, conform to a great extent to the principles of plot construction as stated by Aristotle. The basic thing in plot is 'conflict' upon which the whole structure is built up. In all these plays, as we have shown above, there is some conflict or the other which is the mainspring of the plot. In fact, without conflicts,—inner or outer—action will not move forward. Then the plot should be a complete whole, and we have shown that all the plots of the plays that we have analysed are generally of this type. *Ghosts* and *The Tragedy of Nan* have employed the device of *Oedipus Rex*, where the causes of conflicts have already occurred, and lie outside the main body of the action, but are mentioned during the course of the action where they are required. All the plots have a clear-cut development. They are governed by the principle of 'probability' or 'necessity'. In no play, *deus ex machina*, frowned upon by Aristotle, is employed to resolve any tangle. Most of the actions, as we have shown in our analyses, can be divided into two parts—'complication' or the rising action and 'unravelling' or the falling action. Aristotle regarded 'anagnorisis' and 'peripeity' as necessary for the tragic plot. It is because these two elements, if they occur simultaneously, can give a powerful impetus to the plot movement. 'Recognition' in the *Poetics* is primarily related to the plot and is apparently physical, though pregnant with emotional possibilities. A slight modification, however, will extend its implication to cover the psychological change in the protagonist himself. In *Ghosts* these elements occur when Mrs. Alving discovers the continuing presence of her husband's depravity through its transmission to her son as he behaves with Regina in the same way as his father had behaved with Regina's mother. In *The Tragedy of Nan* these elements occur when Nan is forsaken by all and even by Dick Gurvil and discovers that the hearts of these people are mean, selfish, and rotten. She realizes now that the life she had desired to live was impossible in this wicked world. In *Riders to the Sea* these elements are absent. It is because the play is very short and the plot does not admit of character development for lack of 'magnitude' in the Aristotelian sense. Here the effect or the play is brought out by other means, such as the creation of tragic atmosphere, dialogue and the character of Maurya. In *The Hairy Ape* these elements come in the last scene where Yank goes to seek fraternity with the gorilla. In *Murder in the Cathedral* they are present in the inner conflict of Becket who ultimately realizes the truth that he was doing the 'right deed for the wrong reason'. *The Silver Box* and *Journey's End* represent the types of tragedy which Aristotle has described as 'simple,' 'pathetic.'

The effect of tragedy is the primary thing and all the elements combined together aim at producing this effect. Aristotle's conception of 'catharsis' has been the most talked of and most variously interpreted and in some cases the most throughly misinterpreted thing. But we have shown that if rightly interpreted, the concept applies to all genuine tragedies written in all ages. A tragedy produces the emotions of pity and fear. We feel pity at the undeserved sufferings of the hero, and fear because the hero is human and like us and grapples with a problem which is everybody's problem. We admire the hero for the courageous and unrelenting, though unequal, fight he puts up against the force with which he collides because of some frailty in his character or some error of judgement or because he is forced by circumstances to do so. These emotions are not only excited but allayed by the play because of the inevitability of the end and orderliness of the artistic representation. We rise above our own concerns and are absorbed in the impersonal world of the work of art, and are gradually brought to a state of submissions to the inevitable, which is enlivened by our approval of or admiration for the courage of the person facing it all.

Now in *Ghosts* we pity Mrs. Alvings because she suffers undeservedly, though her suffering arises from the wrong step taken by her in her deciding to live with her dissolute husband. We feel the emotion of fear because Mrs. Alving is fighting with heredity, a force by which any of us in her situations might be crushed. The whole action develops in such a way that in the end we all realise that Mrs. Alving would have met with no other end in her struggle than this. We admire her courage but pity her helplessness in the face of the hell which has been let loose on her by a single slip. In *The Tragedy of Nan*, the heroine suffers undeservedly or rather innocently. Hence we feel pity for her. This pity, however, is redeemed from sentimentalism by her utter contempt of the life around her and exhilarating eagerness to embrace the quiet of her inevitable death. She is reconciled with her tragic lot and starts on her mystic journey to meet the harvest tides of the Severn. Here also we feel the inevitability of her end. Everybody has left her, even the one who, she thought, would bring happiness to her. The only way out for her, when she has been forsaken by all and has attained an insight into the deep reality of life, is death. Yank in *The Hairy Ape* also meets with the inevitable end after he has failed in his attempt to find a place where he could 'belong'. The tragic effect here results from the spiritual tension that Yank feels after his happy illusion of 'belonging' has been shattered. In *Riders to the Sea* Maurya's coming out defiant in the end and her reconciliation with her lot bring about this effect on us. We admire her stoic calm in the moment of her unspeakable grief. We sympathize with her because she is human like us and is the very symbol of eternal motherhood, and we pity her for her innocent suffering. But this pity does not degenerate into sentimental pity because of the strong sense of admiration we feel at her silent but heroic struggle with fate symbolized by the sea. Here the effect is greatly increased by the creation of a most suitable atmosphere and the use of a style which has great power of creating tragic effect on the audience or the reader. In most of these plays we feel the tragic effect because the characters are human and like us but are raised to a higher level of existence by suffering. But when we come to a problem-play like *The Silver Box* we find that neither the hero is elevated by suffering nor is the subject-matter universalized to the extent required by great tragedy. The result is the dominance of pity over the emotions of fear and admiration. Even the sense of 'catharsis' and reconciliation is subdued considerably because we leave the auditorium with a bitter indignation in us for the rich and their society. The action, no doubt, develops towards its inevitable close but the problem remains temporal and the hero defeated, though defiant. In *Murder in the Cathedral*, the tragic effect comes from the spiritual tension which the Archbishop experiences. Here death is not material for our purpose nor did Aristotle insist on it. In this play manifestly the emotion of fear dominates over pity. The women of Canterbury, through whose eyes we look at the whole action, are horrified. But there is a clear note of reconciliation in the Archbishop's realization of the supreme necessity of resigning his will to the Will of God and consequently the women are also reconciled. We realize that even a man of the Archbishop's position has to undergo spiritual torture within himself because of some inordinate desire in him. It is this weakness, in fact, in Becket which makes his character human and an object of our sympathy. Thus, we see that various tragedies produce this effect variously. In some, one emotion dominates and in others, another. But Aristotle never insists that these emotions are to be produced in such and such proportions.

The last element to be discussed is style. Aristotle has

specified certain points of style which have not been disputed seriously. It is speech through which everything in the play is expressed. The first requisite of style, therefore, is clarity, without meanness, which requires the use of current words, words used in everyday life. But if only such words were used, the style will become trite. The style of tragedy, besides being clear, should be lofty and dignified. Loftiness in style may be achieved by using unusual words—words which are high sounding, complex and capable of conveying deeper feelings. Hence the use of metaphors is recommended. The important point to keep in mind, says Aristotle, is 'moderation' in the use of such words. The style should neither be too commonplace and hence dull nor too lofty to become rhetorical and hence artificial. A certain loftiness in style, as we have seen in the analyses of the plays, comes from the intensity of emotions, even though the words might be commonplace. Mrs. Alving's description of her past life with her husband, her expression of the desire for a life of happiness, Nan's conversation with Jenney expressive of her desire to be loved by a man, Gaffer's half-intelligible mutterings about his dead wife and the Severn tides, Yank's expression of his conviction of 'belonging', Paddy's description of the sort of life the sailors in the past have had and Yank's address to the gorilla in the last scene' the two syllables uttered by Mrs. Jones "Oh, Sir, "—are some of the instances where the plain style becomes lofty. The whole of *Riders to the Sea* is written in a style which is clear, poetic, emotional and at the same time lofty. Maurya's description of the "fearfulest thing" she saw, the expression of her sense of reconciliation with her fate and her challenge to the sea are the finest pieces of poetic composition in prose. The style of *Murder in the Cathedral* becomes ritualistic and Biblical in its simplicity but at the same time it is elevated without losing the effect of immediacy. The colloquial and realistic prose of *Journey's End* becomes a powerful instrument of tragic effect through the strong suggestive force inherent in the situation itself. Here the intensity of emotion lends fire and wings to common words. Much has been said and written about dramatic style but one would agree that the fundamentals of it were long ago stated by Aristotle in his own brief and pregnant manner.

Aristotle constructed the outline of the ideal tragedy through a careful examination of the creative literature extant in his own country. He must have adopted the process of selection and elimination before formulating his general principles. His idea of tragedy, therefore, is exclusive to a certain extent and he never claimed that it is applicable to all specimens of tragic drama which have already been produced or which may be produced in times to come. The later expansion and proliferation of the tragic drama under the changing contexts of social, moral and artistic values have naturally proved the exclusiveness of the Aristotelian concept, without, however, contradicting the conviction, which has inspired the present study, that even in an age of confusion and complexity like our own, apparently so different from the Aristotelian era in ancient Greece, great tragedies have been and are still being written on the lines laid down, clearly or by implication, in the *Poetics* more than twenty-two centuries ago.

FOOTNOTE

1 *Types of English Drama*, p. 3.

BIBLIOGRAPHY

Critical References

Abercrombie, L., *Principles of Literary Criticism*, India, Vora and Co., 1962.

Adams, Henry Hitch, and Hathaway, Baxter (ed.), *Dramatic Essays of the Neo-classical Age*, New York, Columbia University Press, 1950.

Anderson, Maxwell, *The Essence of Tragedy and Other Footnotes and Papers*, Anderson House, 1939.

Arthur and Gelb, Barbara, *O'Neill*, New York, Harper and Bros., 1960.

Archer, W., *Playmaking : A Manual of Craftsmanship*, London, Dodd, 1929.

Asthon, John, W., *Types of English Drama*, London, Macmillan, 1940.

Atkins, A.W.H., *English Literary Criticism : The Medieval Phase*, London, Methuen, 1943.

————, *English Criticism, 17th and 18th Centuries*, London, Methuen, 1954.

Baker, George P., *Dramatic Technique*, Boston, 1919.

Baldwin, Charles Sears, *Renaissance Literary Theory and Practice*, Columbia University Press, 1939.

Bentley, Eric (ed.), *The Play : A Critical Anthology*, New York, 1951.

————, *The Playwright as Thinker*, London, Robert Hale, 1948.

Bentley, E.R., *The Modern Theatre*, Doubleday, 1960.

Bowley, A.H. (ed.), *Psychology : The Study of Man's Mind*, London, 1949.

Bourgeois, Maurice, *John Millington Synge and the Irish Dramatic Theatre*, London, Constable and Co., 1913.

Bradley, A.C., *Oxford Lectures on Poetry*, London, Macmillan, 1955.

Bradbrook, M.C., *Ibsen the Norwegian*, London, Chatto and Windus, 1948.

Brown, J.A.C., *Freud and the Post-Freudian*, Penguin, 1962.

Brooks, Cleanth (ed.), *Tragic Themes in Western Literature* : *Seven Essays by B. Knox and Others*, New Haven, Yale University Press, 1960.

Butcher, S.H., *Aristotle's Theory of Poetry and Fine Art*, Dover Publications, Inc., 1951.

Bywater, Ingran, *Aristotle on the Art of Poetry*, Oxford, Clarendon Press, 1920.

Carry, M., and Haarhoff, T.J., *Life and Thought in the Greek and Roman World*, London, Methuen, 1940.

Charlton, H.B., *Castelvetro's Theory of Poetry*, Manchester University Press, 1913.

Clark, Barrett H., *A Study of Modern Drama*, New York, 1928.

—————, *Eugene O'Neill* : *The Man and His Plays*, London, Jonathan Cape, Thirty Bedford Square, 1933.

—————, (ed.), *European Theories of Drama*, London, D. Appleton and Co., 1929.

—————, *A Study of Modern Drama*, London, D. Appleton and Company, 1928.

Clark, B.H., and Freedley, George (ed.), *A History of Modern Drama*, New York, D. Appleton Company, Inc., 1954.

Clein, Ellehauge, *Striking Figures Among Modern Dramatists*, Copenhegen, Levin and Munksgaard, 1917.

Clifford Allen, *Modern Discoveries in Medical Psychology*, London, Macmillan, 1937.

Coleman, Elliott (ed.), *Lectures in Criticism*, New York, Harper and Bros., 1961.

Collins, J. Churton (ed.), *Apologie for Poesie*, Oxford, 1924.

Cooper, Lane, *Aristotle on the Art of Poetry*, New York, Ithaca, 1942.

——————, *Poetics of Aristotle, Its Meaning and Influence*, Cornell, 1923.

Copleston, F., *Arthur Schopenhauer : Philosopher of Pessimism*, Burns Oates and Wasbourne, 1946.

Corkery. Daniel, *Synge and Anglo-Irish Literature*, Ireland, Cork University Press, Oxford, B.H. Blackwell Ltd., 1947.

Cunliffe, John W., *Modern English Dramatists*, London, Harper and Bros., 1927.

Daiches, David, *Critical Approaches to Literature*, London, Longmans, Green and Co., 1956.

Dickinson, Thomas H., *The Contemporary Drama of England*, London, John Murray, Albemarie Street, 1920.

Eaton, W.P., *The Drama in England*, New York, 1930.

Egri, Lajos, *The Art of Dramatic Writing*, New York, Simon and Schuster, 1960.

Elizabeth, Drew, *Discovering Drama*, New York, 1894.

Ellis-Fermor, Una, *The Frontiers of Drama*, London, Methuen, 1946.

——————, *The Irish Dramatic Movement*, London, Methuen, 1954.

Else, Gerald F., *Aristotle's Poetics: The Argument*, Cambridge, Massachussetts, Harvard University Press, 1957.

Falk, Doris V., *Eugene O'Neill and the Tragic Tension*, New Jersey, 1958.

Fergusson, Francis, *The Idea of a Theatre*, Princeton, New Jersey, Princeton University Press, 1949.

Flickinger. Roy C., *The Greek Theatre and Its Drama*, Chicago, University Press, 1932.

Flugel, J.C., Man, *Morals and Society: A Psychoanalytic Study*, London, 1945.

Forster, E.M., *Aspects of Novel*, Pelican, 1963.

Fretag, Gustav, *The Technique of Drama*, New York, 1894.

Gassner, John, *Form and Idea in Modern Theatre*, New York,

The Dryden Press, 1956.

Gassner, John (ed.), *O'Neill : A Collection of Critical Essays*, New Jersey, Prentice-Hall, Inc., Englewood Cliffs, 1964.

Granville-Barker, H., *The Use of Drama,* London, Sidgwick and Jackson, 1947.

—————, *On Poetry in Drama*, London, Sidgwick and Jackson, 1937.

Hamilton, Clayton, *Conversations on Drama,* London, Macmillan, 1925.

Hamilton, Edith, *The Greek Way to Western Civilization*, New York, The New American Library, Norton and Company, Inc., 1952.

Haweis, H. R., *Chaucer for Schools*, London, Chatto and Windus, 1916.

Henn, Thomas Rice, *The Harvest of Tragedy*, London, Methuen, 1956.

House, Humphry, *Aristotle's Poetics,* London, Rupert Hart-Davis, 1956.

Hull, Helen (ed.), *The Writer's Notebook*, Barnes and Noble, 1960.

Jaeger, Werner, *Aristotle*, London, Oxford University Press, 1948.

Johnston, George Burke, *Ben Jonson*, New York, Columbia University Press, 1945.

Jones, D.E., *The Plays of T.S. Eliot*, London, Routledge and Kegan Paul, 1961.

Jourdian, E.F., *The Drama in Europe in Theory and Practice*, London, Methuen, 1924.

Jung, C.G., *Two Essays on Analytical Psychology*, tr., Hull, R.F.C., London, 1953.

—————, *The Practice of Psychotherapy,* tr., Hull, R.F.C., London, 1954.

—————, *Freud and Psychoanalysis,* tr., Hull, R.F.C., London, 1961.

—————, *Psychology of the Unconscious,* tr., Hull, R.F.C.,

London, 1961.

Jung, C. G., *Modern Man in Search of a Soul*, tr., Dell, W.S., W.S., and Baynes, Cary F., London, 1936.

Ker, W.P., *Collected Essays*, Vol. I, London, Macmillan, 1925.

Kitto, H.D.F., *Greek Tragedy : A Literary Study*, London, Methuen, 1950.

————, *Form and Meaning in Drama*, London, Methuen, 1960.

————, *The Greeks*, Penguin, 1957.

Klein, David, *Elizabethan Dramatists as Critics*, New York, Philosophical Library, 1963.

Knight, G. Wilson, *Ibsen*. Edinburgh and London, Oliver and Boyd. 1962.

————, *A Study of British Drama*, London, Phoenix House Ltd., 1962.

Langbaum, Robert, *Poetry of Experience*, London, Chatto and Windus, 1957.

Leavis, F.R., *The Common Pursuit*, London, Chatto and Windus, 1958.

Leech, Clifford, *O'Neill*, London, Oliver and Boyd, 1963.

Lucas, F.L., *Tragedy : Serious Drama in Relation to Aristotle's Poetics*, London, The Hogarth Press, 1957.

————, *The Drama of Chekhov, Synge, Yeats and Pirandello*, Cassell, 1964.

————, *Literature and Psychology*, London, Cassell, 1951.

Lumley, Fredrick, *Trends in Twentieth-Century Drama*, London, Barrie and Rockliff, 1960.

Matthew, Brander, *A Study of Drama*, Boston, 1910.

Matthiessen, F.O., *The Achievement of T.S. Eliot*, London, Oxford University Press, 1947.

Maxwell, D.E.S., *The Poetry of T.S. Eliot*, London, 1960.

Miller, Herbert, J., *Spirit of Tragedy*, New York, Alfred A. Knopf, 1956.

Millett, Fred B., *Reading Drama: A Method of Analysis with Selections for Study*, New York, Harper and Bros., 1950.

Morgan, A.E., *Tendencies of Modern English Drama*, New York, 1924.

Nicoll, Allardyce, *Introduction to the Theory of Drama*, London, George G. Harrap and Company Ltd., 1937.

—————, *World Drama*, London, George G. Harrap and Company Ltd., 1952.

—————, *British Drama*, London, George G. Harrap and Company Ltd., 1947.

—————, *The Theatre and Dramatic Theory*, London, George G. Harrap and Company Ltd., 1962.

Nietzche, *Birth*, tr., Housman, W.M.A., London, 1923.

O'Cargill, N.B., Fagin, W.J., and Fisher, *Eugene O'Neill and His Plays*, London, 1962.

O'Connor, William Van, *Climates of Tragedy*, Baton, Rouge La, 1943.

Parker, D.H. (ed.), *Schopenhauer : Selections,* London, 1928.

Peacock, Ronald, *The Poet in the Theatre*, London, Routledge and Kegan Paul, 1946.

Powe, P.P., *J.M. Synge : A Critical Study,* London, Martin Secker, 1912.

PREFACE TO :

Dryden, John, *Troilus and Cressida*.

Masefield, John, *The Tragedy of Nan*.

Milton John, *Samson Agonistes*.

Synge, J.M., *The Playboy of the Western World*.

—————, *The Tinker's Wedding*.

Progoff, Ira, *Jung's Psychology and Its Social Meaning,* New York, 1955.

Prince, A., *Synge and Anglo-Irish Drama*, London, Methuen, 1961.

Raphael, D.D., *The Paradox of Tragedy,* London, George Allen and Unwin Ltd., 1959.

Richards, I.A., *Principles of Literary Criticism,* London, Routledge and Kegan Paul, Ltd., 1961.

Richards, T.W., *Modern Clinical Psychology,* London, 1946.

248

Riviere, Joan, tr., *Sigmund Freud, Collected Papers,* Vol. II, London, 1953.

Ross, W.D., *Aristotle,* London, 1949.

Roberts, R. Ellis, *Henrik Ibsen : A Critical Study,* London, Martin Secker, 1912.

Robertson, J.G., *Lessing's Dramatic Theory,* London,Cambridge University Press, 1939.

Robertson, Lennox (ed.), *Irish Theatre : Lectures Delivered during the Abhey Theatre Festival held in Dublin, August, 1938,* London, Macmillan, 1939.

Russell, Trusten Wheeler, *Voltaire, Dryden and Heroic Tragedy,* New York, Columbia University Press, 1946.

Scholes, Rober (ed.), *Approaches to the Novel : Material for a Poetics,* San Francisco, 1961.

Shaw, G.B., *Dramatic Opinion and Essays with an Apologie,* Vol. II, New York, Brenteno's, 1907.

—————, *The Quintessence of Ibsenism,* London, Constable and Jackson, 1941.

Smith, Grover, *T.S. Eliot's Poetry and Plays : A Study in Sources and Meaning,* Illinois, University of Chicago Press, 1961.

Steiner, George, *The Death of Tragedy,* London, Faber and Faber, 1961.

Spingarn, J.E., *A History of Literary Criticism in the Renaissance,* New York, Columbia University Press, 1925.

—————(ed), *Critical Essays of the Seventeenth Century,* London, Oxford University Press, 1909.

Stoll, E.E., *Shakespeare and Other Masters,* Cambridge, 1940.

Styan, J.L., *The Elements of Drama,* London, Cambridge University Press, 1960.

Stuart, Donald Clive, *The Development of Dramatic Art,* New York, Dover Publications, Inc., 1960.

Sutton, Graham, *Some Contemporary Dramatists,* London, Leonard Parsons, 1924.

Symonds, Percival M., *Dynamics of Psychotherapy,* Vol. II.

New York, 1957.

Thomson, Alan Reynolds, *The Anatomy of Drama*, University of California Press, 1946.

Thorndike, A.H., *Tragedy,* Boston, 1908.

Thouless, Priscilla, *Modern Poetic Drama,* London, Oxford University Press, 1934.

Vanghan, C.E., *Types of Tragic Drama*, London. Macmillan, 1908.

Verrall, A.W., *Lectures on Dryden,* London, Cambridge University Press, 1914.

Ward, A.C. (ed.), *Specimens of English Dramatic Criticism XVII-XX Centuries,* London, O.U.P., 1946.

Weisinger, H., *Tragedy and the Paradox of the Fortunate Fall,* London, Routledge and Kegan Paul, 1953.

Wellek, Rene, *A History of Modern Criticism,* New Haven, Yale University Press, 1955.

Williams, Raymonds, *Drama from Ibsen to Eliot,* London, Chatto and Windus, 1954.

─────, *Drama in Performance,* Muller, 1954.

Weygandt, Cornelius, *Irish Plays and Playwrights,* New York, Cambridge, Boston, 1913.

Wimsatt, William K., and Brooks, Cleanth, *Literary Criticism : A Short History,* New York, Alfred A. Knopf, 1957.

Journals

Comparative Literature, Vol. V, No. 2, 1953, Weinburg, Bernard, "From Aristotle to Pseudo-Aristotle."

─────, Vol. VI, 1954, Auden, John M., "Dryden and Saint-Evremond."

─────, Vol. VII, 1955, Gassner John, "Forms of Modern Drama."

─────, Vol. IX, 1959, Schier, Donald, "Voltaire's Criticism of Calderon."

English, The Magazine of the English Association, Vol. VI, No. 34, Spring, 1947, Malcolm, J.E., "Maeterlinck and the Static Drama."

English Studies, 1949, Potts, L.J., "Ben Jonson and the Seventeenth Century."

Essays in Criticism, Vol. IV, 1954, Sewall, Richard B., "The Tragic Form."

————, Vol. V, 1955, Lawrence, Michael, "The Political Tragedies of Chapman and Ben Jonson."

————, Vol. VI, 1956, Morrell, Roy, "The Psychology of the Tragic Pleasure."

————, Vol. VI, 1956, Lawrence, Michael, "Miss Burton's Argument for 'Political Tragedy'."

————, Vol. XII, 1962, Gaskell, Ronald, "The Family Reunion."

Essays and Studies by Members of the English Association, Vol. VIII, 1922, Smith, G.C. Moore, "Tragedy."

Essays by Divers Hands, Vol. XII, Morgan, Charles, "The Nature of Dramatic Illusion."

———— Vol. XXXI, 1962, Kitto, H.D.F., "Tragic Drama and Intellectualism."

Fortnightly Review, Dec., 1911, "The Art of J.M. Synge."

Harvard Studies and Notes in Philology and Literature, Vol. XIX, 1937, Nolte, Fred. O., "Lessing's Emilia Galotti in the Light of Hamburgische Dramaturgie."

Horizon, Vol. XVI, 1947, Trilling, Lionel, "Freud and Literature."

International Journal of Psychoanalysis, Vol. XV, 1934, Strachey, James, "The Nature of the Therapeutic Action of Psychoanalysis."

Modern Philology, Vol. XXXIV, 1936, Keon, Richard, "Literary Criticism and the Concept of 'Imitation' in Antiquity."

Modern Language Notes, Vol. XXXV, 1940, Roulston, Robert Bruce, Review, Robertson, J.G., *Lessing's Dramatic Theory.*

————, Vol. LXIII, 1948, Verron, Hall Jr., Review Herrick, Marvin T., *The Fusion of Horatian and Aristotelian Literary Criticism.*

Modern Language Notes, Vol. LXV, 1950, Heitner, Robert, "Concerning Lessing's Indebtedness to Diderot."

PMLA, Vol. XLIII, 1928, Thomson, "Melodrama and Tragedy."

—————, Vol. XLIV, 1929, McIntyre, Clara F., "The Word 'universality' as applied to Drama."

—————, Vol. LXVIII, Dec., 1953, Alexander, Doris M., "Psychological Fate in Mourning Becomes Electra."

—————, June, 1959, Arestad, Sverre, "Ibsen's Concept of Tragedy."

Philological Quarterly, Vol. IX, No. 2, 1930, Herrick, Marvin T., "Aristotle's Pity and Fear."

—————, Vol. XIV, Oct., 1935, Duncan, Thomas Shearer, "The Deus ex Machina in Greek Tragedy."

—————, Vol. XXXII, 1953, Giovannini, "Historical Realism and the Tragic Emotions in Renaissance Criticism."

—————, Vol. XIX, 1940, Zucker, A.E., "Southern Critics of 1903 on Ibsen's Ghosts."

—————, Vol. XXIV, Jan., 1945, Pitcher, Seymour M., "Aristotle's Good and Just Heroes."

Sewanee Review, Vol. L, 1942, Coffman, George R., "Tragedy and a Sense of the Tragic."

—————, Vol. L, 1942, Smith, Winifred, "Mystics in the Modern Theatre."

Scrutiny, Vol. IV, 1936, Santayan, George, "Tragic Philosophy."

Studies in Philology, Vol. LIV, 1957, Tyre, Richard H., "Versions of Poetic Justice in the Early Eighteenth Century."

The London Mercury. Vol. XXVIII, 1933, Sparrow, John, "John Galsworthy."

—————, Vol. XXXI, 1936, Clarks, Austin, "The Problem of Verse Drama To-day,"

The Modern Language Review, Vol. XII, 1917, Robertson, J.F., "Lessing's Interpretation of Aristotle."

The Magazine of the English Association, Vol. VI, No. 4,

252

Spring, 1947, Leech, Clifford, "The Implications of Tragedy."

The New York Times, October 18, 1953, Harbage, Alfred, Review, *Ben Jonson of Westminster.*

The Review of English Studies, Vol. XVII, 1941, Dowlin, Cornell March, "Plot as an Essential in Poetry."

————, Vol. XX, 1944, Dowlin, Cornell March, "Sidney and Other Men's Thought."

————, XXXVIII, 1962, Rillie, John A.M., "Melodramatic Device in T.S. Eliot."

The Times Literary Supplement, May 8, 1937, "Mr. Eugene O'Neill : An Iconoclast in the Theatre."

————, Aug. 7, 1937, "Modern Poetic Drama : Conventions and Private Practice."

————, Aug. 14, 1953, Review, Weisinger, H., *Tragedy and the Paradox of the Fortunate Fail.*

————, May 25, 1956, "The Essence of Ibsen."

————, Dec. 14, 1956, "The Tragic Vision."

————, Dec. 14, 1956, "Crisis in the Theatre."

————, Aug., 1959, "A Hope for Tragedy."

————, Jan. 7, 1965, Review, Lattimore, Richmond, *Story Pattern in Greek Tragedy,* Athlone Press, 1964.